D1431310

PREMISES FOR PROPAGANDA

PREMISES FOR PROPAGANDA

The United States Information Agency's
Operating Assumptions in the Cold War

Leo Bogart

Abridged by Agnes Bogart

THE FREE PRESS
A Division of Macmillan Publishing Co., Inc.
NEW YORK

Collier Macmillan Publishers
LONDON

The Free Press
A Division of Macmillan Publishing Co., Inc.
866 Third Avenue, New York, N.Y. 10022

Collier Macmillan Canada, Ltd.

Library of Congress Catalog Card Number: 75–18007

Printed in the United States of America

printing number
1   2   3   4   5   6   7   8   9   10

Library of Congress Cataloging in Publication Data

Bogart, Leo.
    Premises for propaganda.

    Bibliography: p.
    Includes index.
    1. United States. Information Agency--Case studies.
2. Propaganda, American--Case studies. 3. Propaganda--
Case studies.   I. Bogart, Agnes. II. Title.
E744.5.B57   353.008'1   75-18007
ISBN 0-02-904390-5

Contents

Preface

The study reported in this book was commissioned in June, 1953, by the U. S. Information Agency to help plan its own program of research. The purpose was to identify and articulate the "operating assumptions," explicit and implicit, that guided or underlay the daily work decisions of the Agency's propaganda personnel and thus to describe the areas of ignorance, confusion, or internal contradiction that merited further investigation.

As an essay in policy research, the study sought to identify beliefs and practices that did not jibe with the best available knowledge. The revelation of these inconsistencies was expected to lead to research that could resolve the questions; or it was expected to lead directly to actions.

The report was completed in 1954 and submitted to USIA Director Theodore Streibert, although the study had been launched under the previous administration of Robert Johnson.[1] The report was never acted upon. Instead, it was immediately classified "Confidential," and remained in the locked files of the Agency, in spite of persistent efforts, under successive administrations, to release it for publication. The argument against release for many years was that the study revealed too much that was still relevant and politically sensitive. These contentions lost their authority after passage of the Federal Freedom of Information Act, and the report was finally declassified.

Why should this twenty-year-old report still be of contemporary interest? It may be looked upon from a number of different perspectives: as history, as policy research, and as an intimate picture of how a propaganda organization operates.

A number of books and monographs have described the operations of USIA. They provide a comprehensive picture of the Agency's history, struc-

---

[1] Streibert was a former president of the Mutual Broadcasting System; Johnson, a former associate of Henry Luce, had been president of Temple University.

ture, and scope of activity, yet they do not approach their subject from the perspective of international mass communications. By contrast, this report attempts to convey the flavor of how propaganda is actually produced, and of the dilemmas that daily confront those who produce it. It also says something about the practitioners of propaganda, by revealing their heterogeneity, brilliance, and naiveté, in their own words.

This research may therefore be considered as a case history in the sociological study of bureaucracy. Government agencies are notoriously resistant to external examination and study, whether by sociologists or by journalists, and the U. S. Information Agency is no exception. In the original research plan, there was never any intention to study either the official formal structure of the USIA as an organization or the informal working arrangements of its administration and staff, in Washington and in the field. However, to understand the Agency's operating assumptions required an examination of its operational procedures, personnel, and budget. Since my assignment was to define problems, I tried not to avoid the very real organizational problems of the Agency, which were more compelling than many of the theoretical propaganda questions, and which apparently continue to exist.

Thus, a more recent study of the Agency, by Ronald I. Rubin,[2] notes that:

> The USIA has been prevented from implementing the various goals established for it by the Executive Branch and Congress due to internal as well as external factors . . .
>
>   1. The inability of the Agency to clarify its basic operating assumptions. These include a determination as to whether it is to function as an information or propaganda instrument . . . In addition, USIA has failed to develop a systematic policy as concerns the population groups whose favor should be most pursued in promoting American objectives . . .
>
>   2. The failure to clearly define the role of USIA in the Executive Branch in reaching foreign policy decisions.

At the time of the study, USIA was still a new and marginal institution without a clearly established home base. Its constituent elements had been pulled together from a number of different places, and its personnel represented an improbable mixture of foreign service officers, media specialists, and linguists who were difficult to squeeze into the conventional civil service hierarchy.

The subject matter and the conclusions of the study in no sense lend themselves to generalizations about government agencies. But there is a constant evocation of themes that are surely inherent in the federal bureaucratic syndrome: conflicts of interest among presumably cooperating divisions within the same organization; a periodic subordination of substantive programmatic concerns to a preoccupation with the budget; susceptibility to external political

---

[2] Ronald I. Rubin. *The Objectives of the U. S. Information Agency, Controversies and Analysis.* New York: Frederick C. Praeger, 1966, p. 10.

pressures, and a special concern with the good will of Congress; jockeying for position in relation to other government agencies.

There would be no point in publishing this report today if it were merely a historical document or case history. The questions it poses continue to perplex not only a new generation of propagandists, but also those who are interested in the theory of mass persuasion.

This study, although its historical setting is vastly different from the political conditions of the present day, illuminates the essential dilemma of democracy in conflict with dictatorship. It is in the very nature of an adversary relationship to create a qualitative change in the character of the antagonists. The aggressive role they are enacting requires them to repress those sentiments that do not serve the purpose of gaining a victory. Tolerance of contrary or contradictory opinions, acknowledgment and open disclosure of the demerits as well as the advantages of one's own position—all are to be taken for granted in the normal, everyday life of a democracy. However, they represent great weaknesses in the face of a single-minded adversary who will use any means to achieve his ends. The same dilemma plagued American propagandists throughout the Vietnam War. Here the American cause was linked to the defense of an unsavory regime, and the American military engaged at times in its own deliberate policy of distorting the truth to serve political self-interest rather than military objectives.

As history, the report documents a significant period in American foreign policy, one in which the Western and Communist powers were engaged in active tests of strength around the world. The Cold War has lately been a subject of substantial historical revision and review. New interpretations have been offered of Stalin's break with his Western allies immediately after the end of World War II, his decision to occupy areas of Eastern Europe in defiance of agreements, his acceleration of a massive program of internal repression within the Soviet Union, his policy of massive rearmament (including the development of a nuclear arsenal) while the United States disarmed, and the assault by the Communist parties of Western Europe on the American Marshall Plan. A new light has been cast on the North Koreans' attempt to take over the South, which led the United States into its first grim war in mainland Asia. All these developments have now been reinterpreted by some scholars as reluctant and inevitable self-defensive responses to the provocative schemes of Harry Truman and Dean Acheson!

A generation of intellectuals—including historians—were conditioned during the period of the Vietnam War to question and oppose American foreign policy and to assume that its Communist opponents were the protagonists of oppressed people longing for redress of long-standing grievances.

It is hard to reconcile this revisionist perspective with the mendacity and viciousness of Communist attacks upon the United States during the Cold War. A "no-holds-barred" approach characterized Soviet propaganda in this, its most blatant and perhaps most successful phase. American soldiers were depicted routinely as monsters who flung newborn infants into fires and cut off women's breasts.[3] Charges of germ warfare were leveled at U. S. forces in Korea, and their "atrocities" were documented with doctored photographs showing the Japanese Army in China in World War II. (After My Lai and its coverup by the U. S. Army command, charges of germ warfare no longer seem quite as preposterous as they once did, but they have nonetheless never been supported by the slightest shred of evidence.)

The corruption and immorality of American society were shown with the aid of imaginary and faked quotations (for example, "Christ on the Cross would not have suffered if he could have drunk a Coca-Cola").

Goebbels shrewdly observed that outrageous charges may evoke more belief than milder statements that merely twist the truth slightly, and since his time, totalitarian regimes have made heavy use of this proposition. At the time of this study, U. S. estimates of propaganda efforts by the Soviet Union and its allies ranged between $1.5 and $2 billion a year, or about 2 percent of the Soviet gross national product, and at least twenty times as much as the American propaganda budget.

The propaganda activities of the American government are of comparatively recent origin. Half a year before American entry into World War I, President Woodrow Wilson set up the Committee on Public Information under George Creel; it was disbanded half a year after the war ended. The Committee's efforts were directed far more at domestic morale than at foreign opinion.

A resumption of propaganda activities took place in 1938, when a Division of Cultural Cooperation was established in the State Department to implement President Franklin D. Roosevelt's "Good Neighbor" program with Latin America. This operation underwent several transformations to become the Office of the Coordinator of Inter-American Affairs some four months before Pearl Harbor.

The Office of War Information was set up under radio newsman Elmer Davis half a year after America entered World War II. Like its predecessor Creel Committee, OWI had both domestic and overseas responsibilities. "Psychological warfare" directed against the enemy was conducted by the Office of Strategic Services. (Within the State Department, an Office of Public Information was set up at the beginning of 1944, and at the end of that year, the poet Archibald MacLeish was appointed the first Assistant Secretary of State for Public and Cultural Affairs.)

According to a postwar Brookings Institution study by Charles Thomson, the wartime division of labor between OWI and OSS produced a division of philosophies that continued in USIA at the time the present study was undertaken and that undoubtedly continues to the present day: "This struggle abounded in personalities, but was not fundamentally personal. It rested on differences between those who believed that propaganda should form part of the

---

[3] Edward W. Barrett, *Truth Is Our Weapon,* New York: Funk and Wagnall's, 1953, p. 177.

program for subversive operations, and should consist of any action, true or false, responsible or irresponsible, which would effectively hamper the enemy at any point; and those who believed that propaganda should be a public, responsible government operation to tell the truth about the war, about the United States and its allies, as a means of describing democracy and freedom, our war aims, and our determination to win both the war and the peace.'' [4]

Only a few weeks after Japan's surrender, on August 31, 1945, President Truman dissolved OWI and the information activities of the Coordinator of Inter-American Affairs and set up an Interim International Information Service within the State Department under Assistant Secretary William Benton, a former advertising man and future Senator. In 1946, an Office of International Information and Cultural Affairs was set up in the State Department; it was renamed the Office of International Information and Educational Exchange in the fall of 1947.

These ad hoc arrangements were supplanted early in 1948 with the passage of the Smith-Mundt Act (Public Law 402), which authorized the first peacetime propaganda program in American history, to present a ''full and fair picture'' of the United States to the world at large. The Office of International Information under career diplomat George Allen was split off from the Office of Educational Exchange, both remaining within the State Department.

The objectives of the Smith-Mundt Act were ''to promote a better understanding of the United States in other countries, and to increase mutual understanding between the people of the United States and the people of other countries.''

Under both the second Truman and first Eisenhower administrations, OII (subsequently renamed the International Information Agency) underwent a succession of management changes, and it was periodically scrutinized by Congressional and presidential inquiries. President Eisenhower's Committee on Foreign Information Activities, headed by investment banker William H. Jackson, recommended coordination of all the government agencies engaged in propaganda-related activities through an Operations Coordinating Board (OCB), which was duly set up. The Jackson Committee report was also critical of the Voice of America, and urged that it reduce the stridency of its anti-Communist tone.

In 1974–75, a committee headed by former CBS President Frank Stanton, under the auspices of Georgetown University, reviewed the operations of both the USIA and the State Department's cultural exchange program and recommended a radical reorganization. The panel was made up largely of members of the U. S. Advisory Commissions on Information and on International Educational and Cultural Affairs.

The Stanton Panel's report contrasted the government's information tasks in

---

[4] Charles A. H. Thomson, *Overseas Information Service of the United States Government*, Washinton, D. C.: The Brookings Institution, 1948, p. 19.

the era of detente with those of the Cold War period described in this book. "In its early years, most of USIA's operations were of necessity on the foreign policy side, waging ideological warfare and heavily dependent on the fastest available media. Today, in an era that actively seeks a relaxation of tensions and where issues are seen to be complex rather than clear-cut, USIA has moved heavily into the cultural field with long-range media."

For the anti-Communist clichés of another day the panel substituted a new set of phrases. It suggested that the mounting array of world problems called for "a new style of leadership" and "a new kind of cultural diplomacy" and that "detente both requires and makes possible the fuller international expression of American ideas." "The new program must also be genuinely reciprocal" in order to find "cooperative solutions to our common problems."

The panel recommended that the State Department's Bureau of Educational and Cultural Affairs, which handles the Exchange of Persons Program, be rejoined to the Information Agency, to overcome "the organizational separation between people and media." The resulting Informational and Cultural Affairs Agency would be returned to the State Department, with the director reporting to the Secretary of State. A new Office of Policy Information would be headed by a Deputy Undersecretary of State.

The panel proposed that the Voice of America be separated from the rest of the information program as an autonomous federal agency, since placing it within the State Department "would severely compromise its independence as a source of news." At the same time, it proposed that State "should be directly responsible for explaining and articulating U. S. foreign policy over the Voice." Thus, the inherent dilemmas of American propaganda, articulated in this volume, continue to find new expression.

In 1953–54, the Voice of America was broadcasting daily some 210,000 words and twenty-eight program hours in thirty-four different languages. There were 160 USIS libraries or information centers around the world. A daily press service or "wireless file" of about 6,000 words was distributed to 10,000 newspapers. Twenty-five periodicals were being regularly published, and a vast program of special publications ranged from high-level theoretical texts on communism to comic books. Four hundred sixty-six reels of film footage were being produced, and movies in twenty-two languages were being shown worldwide on 6,000 sound projectors.

Examples of current activities can be found in the Agency's official reports, which abound in "success stories" like these: In one unidentified country, "A Communist, maneuvered into talking with a local USIS employee over a glass of wine, said: 'The influence of USIS publications among the workers is very great. In fact, it's incredible . . . The workers take them home and pass them on to their friends after they have read them.' As a direct result of this propaganda, the effective circulation of the Communist press has fallen off considerably." In Peru, "Fourteen schools, including the Peruvian 'West Point,' requested English teachers from the Bi-national Center in Lima.'' In Brazil, ''Otherwise inaccessible people in the interior were reached by a mobile unit.'' In British East Africa: ''At Nairobi, between February and June, the number of regular library users increased more than 100 percent.'' In Thailand: ''In acknowledging receipt of a book packet (sent to 19,000 Buddhist temples), one priest wrote that the books 'contain virtually everything, from practical suggestions . . . to stirring themes which remind us that there are enemies within and without threatening our nation and our religion.' '' In France: ''Sixteen percent of all radio sets are tuned in to VOA.''

The flavor of operations during this period is also conveyed by the captions of photographs in the Agency's monthly newsletter for its own personnel: ''Dr. Robert L. Johnson (Director) enjoys a friendly chat with Dr. Emmett J. Murphy, Director of Public Relations, National Chiropractic Association, and Senator Karl Mundt, at the All American Conference to Combat Communism . . . The administrator addressed the representatives of some sixty top-flight national organizations on the subject of anti-Communist books . . . showing the activities of USIS libraries abroad.''

''USIS Cairo: President Mohamed Naguib visited the USIS booth at the Cairo Electronics Exhibition last month, and was presented with copies of the USIS film catalog and other information material, by Mohamed Whaba Bayoumi, staff projectionist.''

At two decades' distance, and with an entirely new cast of international characters in continuous performance, both the objectives and the practices of American foreign policy present a far different picture than is described in this report. In the era of Henry Kissinger, secret personal diplomacy has largely replaced the public rhetoric that has seemed so important a part of international relations since the rise of fascism. Proclamations of detente with both the Soviet Union and China have lowered the level of publicly expressed antagonism between the United States and the Communist powers. Correspondingly, they have diminished the importance of propaganda as an instrument of the national purpose.

Twenty years ago, two great political blocs confronted each other. What a contrast to the present crazy-quilt division of the world into a complex multiplicity of factions, with incongruous antagonisms and accommodations and only the most precarious ideological alliances! The ''Third World'' has been more of a politician's phrase than a political reality, but it symbolizes the rise of important forces that present propagandists as well as diplomats with a set of targets, objectives, and strategic problems vastly different from those discussed in this book. The concept of ''world public opinion'' as a meaningful, independent political force has lost credibility as a result of the expansion of the United Nations membership to include dozens of statelets and principalities of dubious political permanence. African and Arab nationalisms have demonstrated a capacity for independent action that exploits the rivalry and anxiety of the Great Powers.

The emergence of a nuclear arms stalemate between the Soviet Union and the United States has invalidated the earlier assumption that their disputes could be indefinitely escalated. Thus, the tone of their propaganda has been mollified. The unopposed success of Soviet arms in crushing Eastern Europe resistance during the 1950s and 1960s has demonstrated the unwillingness of the United States to come to the military defense of those who take its propaganda to heart. The Cuban missile crisis showed that the Soviet Union, like the United States, would back off from a nuclear confrontation. But the development of nuclear arms and missile delivery systems by other countries and the growing and successful use of political blackmail combine to suggest that the old bipolar balance is being replaced by new multilateral exercises of force.

Twenty years ago, when this study was made, memories of World War II and of its horrors were still vivid, and the political emotions of Europe were direct continuations of those that prevailed in wartime. These bitter feelings have faded in intensity. A generation of Eastern Europeans, reared under Socialism, has come to accept many of its institutions as permanent and desirable. In the Soviet Union, the opposition, restrained rather than crushed, has found new voices, and foreign broadcasts are no longer obliterated by jamming.

The development of the great schism in the Communist camp has been followed by an unprecedented Soviet tolerance of minor deviationism in the policies of individual national parties. The economic recovery of Western Europe and Japan has created strong independent forces within the American system of alliances. A capacity for autonomous political action has been manifested in the succession of wars in the Middle East, the display of economic power by the oil-producing nations, the emergence of independent African states, the growth of guerilla movements in Southeast Asia, and the long agony of Indochina. All these familiar strands of recent history have made the tasks of propaganda, like those of diplomacy, incredibly more complex than they were at the height of the Cold War, when the world was politically polarized.

The political rhetoric of that period was still, at least to a substantial degree, an outgrowth of the ideological self-righteousness of World War II, when terms like "freedom," "democracy," and "the Free World" could be used without a trace of cynicism or self-consciousness and with the expectation that they would strike a responsive chord. Sophisticated political observers could speak unblushingly of the war to win men's minds and souls. There was strong belief in the power of words and ideas to influence events.

As President Eisenhower said in an address to the staff of the Agency in November, 1953, "We are now conducting a cold war. That cold war must have some objective, otherwise it would be senseless. It is conducted in the belief that if there is no war, if two systems of government are allowed to live side by side, that ours, because of its greater appeal to men everywhere, to mankind, in the long run will win out. That it will defeat all forms of dictatorial government because of its greater appeal to the human soul, the human heart, the human mind."

"In the contest for men's minds," wrote former Assistant Secretary of State Edward W. Barrett, "truth can be peculiarly the American weapon." [5] Senator Homer Capehart put it more bluntly a few years later when he said the job of the Agency "is to sell the United States to the world, just as a sales manager's job is to sell a Buick or a Cadillac or a radio or television set."

It was generally assumed that throughout the world, public opinion could be influenced, could be shaped, and that ultimately it would have to be heeded by those who ruled, no matter how evil and ruthless they might be. Who today still maintains this faith? Instead, there has come about, on the part of America's government, its intellectuals, and its general public, a reawakened appreciation of the uses and importance of power, divorced from ideals or ideology. In part, this change in outlook reflects the realities of the nuclear standoff and uneasy awareness of the possibilities of disaster. In part, it reflects the processes of fractionation in international politics to which I have just referred. This very fractionation has reduced the level of dependable and unquestioning support enjoyed by the United States among a variety of former client countries around the world. The illusion of being on the side of the angels becomes more difficult to sustain when few others share it. A succession of regional wars and civil wars in Asia and Africa has further weakened the proposition that international conflicts are essentially expressions of the great division of the world into its Communist and "anti-Communist" components. The "Good Guys" often have turned out to be suspicious or hostile toward the United States, and, in any case, the "Good Guys" don't always win.

In a world in which the triumph of justice and truth is as often as not impeded by naked force, the power of public opinion fades, and the very concept of public opinion may be disregarded as a force in international politics.

In January, 1974, the U. S. House of Representatives voted to discontinue support of the International Development Association, and although it seems unlikely that this vote really marks the end of U. S. foreign aid, it may well mark the end of an era.

From the beginnings of the Marshall Plan, it was assumed that in its extensive programs of economic aid throughout the world the United States was not merely serving humanitarian purposes, but positively influencing the public opinion and the policies of the host countries. Today, economic aid is no longer the unique province of the United States, and it is rendered not merely for the overt political purposes of Israel, Japan, the Soviet Union, and China, but for the more elusive and perhaps largely humanitarian motives of Sweden and West Germany. As a percentage of the U. S. federal budget, aid has been greatly reduced in scope; it is limited to the underdeveloped countries, and (except in cases of famine or other emergencies), it is extended with little pretense that it serves any purpose other than the support of foreign policy. John Foster Dulles's refusal to support construction of the Aswan High Dam is perhaps the

[5] Op. cit., p. ix.

most notable and also notably disastrous illustration of an attempt to use (or deny) aid as a political weapon.

After the debacle of the second Nixon Administration, large elements of the American public have become disillusioned with the political process. Out of the prevailing malaise has come a new tendency toward isolationism. Among this country's postwar allies in Western Europe, Latin America, and Japan, a variety of counterpart tendencies have similarly evolved to produce a loss of faith in ideology in general and feelings of cynicism, distrust, and distaste for the United States.

Vietnam, Watergate, and the faltering of America's economic growth have eroded the enormous prestige with which this country emerged from the war against fascism. America is no longer perceived abroad as the principal and most vigilant guardian of human dignity; perhaps more significantly, a declining number of its own citizens see their country in this role.

And, in America itself, it is hard to find vestiges of the sense of messianic mission with which the country concluded its crusade in World War II and that led it directly to the series of tests of power with communism, the cold war, that heated up to become the real and disagreeable wars in Korea and Vietnam. That same sense of mission fueled the machinery of propaganda that had been assembled in the early 1940s, as much to sustain domestic morale in wartime as to win the allegiance of the uncommitted, encourage our allies, and weaken the spirit of our enemies. Only the sense of mission attracted people of talent into government service, and kept many of them in it after the war ended, as the United States faced new adversaries and as national leadership underwent a series of changes. The most significant such change occurred with the advent of the first Eisenhower Administration and the ascendency of Senator Joseph McCarthy. As Vice President Richard M. Nixon put it, "Joe wasn't a bad guy. You simply had to understand him."

In the sordid history of the McCarthy phenomenon, the crippling of America's propaganda apparatus is perhaps no more than an incidental misdemeanor. In his efforts to demonstrate that foreign policy under the Democrats had been directed by Communist agents and their dupes, McCarthy quickly came to grips with the International Information Agency. In March, 1953, hearings before his Sub-Committee on Investigations of the Senate Committee on Government Operations, McCarthy relentlessly badgered Reed Harris, the Agency's distinguished deputy director, who had been a student rebel at Columbia University during the politically stormy days of the Great Depression many years earlier.[6]

On the pretext of discovering "evidence" of Communist infiltration into the Agency's libraries and film services, McCarthy dispatched his assistants, Roy

[6] Harris subsequently rejoined the Agency under the administration of Edward R. Murrow.

Cohn and the real estate heir, G. David Schine, on a tour of U.S. information centers in Europe. Their utterances and nocturnal antics in hotel corridors fascinated and horrified the foreign press.

McCarthy's staff reported finding "more than 30,000 books by Communist authors or those who have aided the Communist cause," including many that were "blatantly pro-Communist, pro-Soviet, and anti-American," such as books by Ilya Ehrenburg and "the notoriously pro-Soviet apologist, the 'Red Dean of Canterbury.' " The committee recommended that "the personnel department of this important program should be placed under men with sound anti-Communist experience."

Both Cohn and Schine proposed candidates for IIA policy positions. Under pressure from the team, a directive (subsequently amended) to American libraries around the world banned books by "any controversial persons, Communists, fellow travellers, etc." Books were burned.

The McCarthy raids hastened the reorganization of the USIA as an independent agency outside the State Department, a move that Secretary John Foster Dulles had favored in any case. At the same time, the budget was slashed from the Korean War peak, falling from a pre-McCarthy level of $96 million to $75 million. This, however, included $5 million required as termination pay for employees who were fired, $4 million to move the Voice of America from New York to Washington, and $15 million for the Exchange of Persons program, which was separated from IIA and remained (and remains) in the State Department. By October, 1953, the roster of employees (about half of them U. S. nationals) had been cut from 13,500 to 9,281. (This cut turned out to be excessive, and a new recruiting effort had to be launched the following year.) [7]

Reductions in force caused by the budget cuts were, however, less significant than the voluntary departure of many dozens of dedicated and principled professional propagandists whose motivation to serve the government could not withstand the indignities of McCarthyism. A further impetus to such resignations was given by the announcement of the Voice of America's move to Washington. Voice operations had been located in the nation's broadcasting hub since their inception in 1942, and many senior staff members, including the politically sophisticated European émigré intellectuals, were strongly rooted there.

In retrospect, it appears that the USIA study to be reported here was made close to a watershed dividing point at which the Information Agency was transformed from its earlier crusading spirit into just another manifestation of bureaucracy. (Curiously enough, this transformation coincided with the separation of the Agency from its parent State Department, but this is no way a matter of cause and effect.) The research reflects something of both these phases: the

[7] Thomas C. Sorensen, *The Word War: The Story of American Propaganda*, New York: Harper & Row, 1968.

genuine preoccupation with ideas and ideals on the part of professional persuaders for a cause, as well as the self-serving rivalries and struggles for advantage.

Throughout this book, the use of the word "propaganda" is devoid of any pejorative connotation, although in the twenties and thirties it was customarily used in a disparaging sense, equating, in the eyes of the cynics, the methods and merits of the Allied and German sides in World War I. It was in that war that propaganda lost its former religious meaning and acquired a sudden new importance as "psychological warfare." The "propaganda analysis" initiated by Harold Lasswell, Goodwin Watson, and others in the mid-1930s was prompted by the assumption that the statements of totalitarian governments represented cunning and deliberate distortions of the truth to serve deeper strategic objectives.

It remained for the British, who long ago managed to reconcile the institutions of imperialism with those of democracy, to set a propaganda standard in World War II that the United States wisely copied. The BBC's reputation for integrity, its flat, objective tone at times of both adversity and triumph, gave rise to the American propaganda doctrine that "Truth is Our Weapon," a doctrine that acquired the credence of its own practitioners. It maintained that credence until it was torn apart at the Saigon and Pentagon press briefings during the Johnson Administration.

The age of propaganda is by no means over, but it no longer has active importance as an instrument of foreign policy. In part, this evolution may be traced to the political developments to which I have alluded, which make the relations of power and ideology among nations more complex and multipartite than in the past. Another factor in the decline of propaganda is the tremendous expansion of exposure to all the mass media throughout the world, of which the emergence of television is only one manifestation. Although the Chinese still seem to do so, it is increasingly difficult to maintain a country in isolation from ideas and information that are common in the rest of the world, as could be done in a period when shortwave radios were relatively few. The rising standard of living in the Soviet Union and Eastern Europe has largely invalidated the World War II concept of the clandestine audience for radio broadcasts from the West. In a world where it is easier to obtain access to a variety of viewpoints through normal channels, the role of the propagandist is diminished.

Finally, the decline of propaganda reflects perhaps nothing more than the incapacity of individuals and of nations to sustain a high pitch of attention to the same persuasive messages repeated through time. Exhortations, claims, and arguments that were fresh and novel in the early 1950s no longer arouse public indignation or fervor today. It is hard to arouse high feelings over the evils of the Soviet dictatorship (or, for that matter, "capitalist imperialism") when the evils are perpetuated decade after decade. For analogous reasons, operating propagandists can no longer command the same prestige and (comparatively speaking) the same budgets from their governments as in the Cold War era. (To illustrate this point, USIA's budget rose 86 percent in its first decade as an independent agency, while in the same period, 1953–1963, the entire federal budget grew at a much slower rate, 48 percent. In the decade since then, the federal budget grew by another 134 percent, but the USIA budget by only 34 percent, barely parallel with inflation.)

In yet another respect, the developments of the past twenty years cast this study in a different light. There has been a shift in the prevailing sentiment regarding the action possibilities of social science. During World War II, the specialized skills of psychologists, sociologists, political scientists, and even anthropologists, were mobilized and used effectively by the military and by such war-related agencies as OWI. Since social scientists themselves were strongly motivated to support the war effort, the practice of applied research gained popularity. It was expected that government funding would be available, and that government policies would be responsive to research conclusions. These expectations continued in the immediate postwar period, and received perhaps their most impressive corroboration in the Supreme Court's school desegregation decision of May 17, 1954, with its massive citation of social science references.

In this same period, four other facilitating forces came into play: (1) The expansion of higher education, with a corresponding growth of university research centers and staffs; (2) the establishment of the Ford Foundation and the growth of other foundations that placed strong new emphasis on the support of applied social research projects; (3) the boom in consumer marketing, which stimulated survey research and made its utility accepted by the nation's business elite; (4) the expansion of national health and welfare programs, with an emphasis on experimental (and therefore researchable) projects, and a tremendous increase in the research budgets of the National Institute of Mental Health.

Spurred by the great social and political changes of the postwar period, as well as by the greater availability of research funding and of career opportunities, the number of psychologists grew from 4,427 in 1946 to 34,070 in 1973, while the number of sociologists grew from 2,998 to 8,088 in the same period.

Yet, in spite of the spectacular increases in the number of social scientists and in the amount of government support for their projects, it would be hard to argue that the prestige and authority of social research among government officials is any higher today than it was when the USIA study was made. In fact, it may be plausibly argued that it is less. There has been heavy reliance on social research by such presidential commissions as the Otto Kerner Commission on Civil Disorder, the Milton Eisenhower Commission on the Causes and Prevention of Violence, and the Commission on Obscenity and Pornography. In every instance, their conclusions and recommendations have been largely ignored.

The debacle of Project Camelot caused a sharp restriction of officially sponsored social research projects overseas. The Vietnam War turned large numbers of social scientists away from any applied research designed to assist the U. S. government in the conduct of foreign policy and military operations. A new radical school of social scientists, emerging from the campus turmoil of the late sixties, preached a return to revealed doctrine and disdain for empirical investigation. Even the study of such problems as poverty and race relations was bedevilled by charges that it was merely a racist ploy by middle class white academicians and bureaucrats to exploit the downtrodden minorities.

The study of communication and persuasion has undergone particularly great changes, in respect to what both its practitioners and its users expect from it. Josef Goebbels launched the myth of a "scientific propaganda" with an irresistible power to influence beliefs and to induce desired actions. The U. S. Army Information and Education Program's wartime research, under Carl Hovland, set an extraordinary model for applied research to perfect the persuasiveness of troop indoctrination messages and materials. In the same tradition, research on advertising copy appeals and on "consumer motivation" was regarded by a few of its more naive or cynical spokesmen, and by equally cynical outside observers, as a miraculous form of "hidden persuasion" that placed the public at the mercy of the sinister social scientists of Madison Avenue. While such illusions still occasionally surface, both the public and Madison Avenue have somehow become inured to the fact that competition continues in the marketplace in spite of the most guileful research. And social psychologists, seeking the philosopher's stone of persuasiveness, have introduced a steadily pyramiding number of ifs, ands, and buts into all the generalizations that once seemed very simple and clear.

The objective of the present study, to define high-priority areas for research, necessarily presumed not only that such research was feasible, but that it could come up with definitive answers. The voluminous outpouring of social science literature in the past two decades would not provide much sustenance for this belief. The great questions that have confronted the art of rhetoric since Aristotle continue to confound us. But many lesser and more specific questions are being answered. And many questions of this kind, posed in this study, could already have been answered at the time by knowledgeable people, including some in the Agency itself. In propaganda organizations, as in any other organizations, there is apt to be a division of opinion between those who know what is true and those who with equal conviction know what is false.

The notion that social science findings can be directly translated into government policy no longer has much currency. But at the time of the USIA study there was a widespread belief that social scientists could provide guidelines for the practice of propaganda. The USIA made extensive use of academic consultants. With the advice of Paul Lazarsfeld and his associates at Columbia University, the Voice of America in New York had built up an impressive social research staff of 150, headed by the sociologist Leo Lowenthal and including Ralph White, Marjorie Fiske, Joseph T. Klapper, and Harold Mendelsohn. Extensive surveys of communications habits and attitudes were conducted all over the world. Much later, another and smaller research operation was set up within USIA in Washington. Its first director, Ben Gedalecia, was a former OWI writer who had done a stint of several years as research director of the American Broadcasting Company. Gedalecia struggled to centralize the Agency's research activities; this necessarily brought him into conflict with the larger, more sophisticated, and well-entrenched research establishment headed by Lowenthal in New York. The work of the Schramm Committee (which is described in the Introduction) was coordinated by Gedalecia's Washington office, which commissioned the study.

The research contract was awarded to McCann-Erickson, Inc., whose president, that extraordinary advertising impresario, Marion Harper, Jr., was a member of the Schramm Committee. I handled this assignment while manager of market research at McCann-Erickson.

The report was transmitted to USIA in November, 1954. By that time, the research and intelligence functions of the Agency had been reorganized under Henry P. Loomis, a Republican appointee who served USIA with distinction under several administrations and who is now president of the Corporation for Public Broadcasting. Gedalecia returned to New York to become research director of the Batten, Barton, Durstine & Osborn advertising agency. The Office was cut back to a professional staff of five. The research units of the Voice of America and the other media were abolished. The Agency's worldwide program of survey research was sharply reduced and never resumed even a semblance of its former scope. The Schramm Committee was disbanded.

To my knowledge, neither USIA Director Theodore Streibert nor Associate Director Abbott Washburn (now a Nixon appointee to the Federal Communications Commission), ever read this report. Its validity was discounted on the grounds that (1) the quotations were not attributed to specific, identified individuals, and (2) there was no indication as to what percentage of the Agency's personnel agreed or disagreed with the various assumptions that were laid out. (In short, the study had to be redefined either as legal "testimony" or as an "employee attitude survey," when in fact its original proponents saw it as an agenda statement for research.)

The steep reduction in the Agency's research program, along with the discontinuities in both its research and general managements, doomed any prospect that the Schramm Committee's original concept would be implemented. Nonetheless, successive managements of the Agency resisted the efforts I initiated early in 1955, and continued for a dozen years thereafter to have the study declassified and released for publication.

This report, originally prepared in five volumes, has been abridged to about two-fifths of its full length. The original format and sequence have been retained, but I have added brief introductory comments to each section. The report begins with a broad look at the objectives of America's propaganda program and the formation and implementation of policy. It goes on to discuss the selection of propaganda targets and the problems of adapting output to meet the needs and expectations of a wide variety of audiences. Propaganda techniques are described and debated with respect to the attribution, credibility, and tone of output. Content is discussed both under the heading of how to project the American story and how to wage "the fight against communism." There are chapters on the use of the individual media and on the relations between Washington and field activities. Finally, the report deals with the qualifications of working propagandists and the problems of evaluating the effects of the program.

Although this point is made in the original Introduction, which follows, it is essential for the reader to remember that all of the statements made in the report paraphrase or summarize the words of USIA's working propagandists. None of them are intended to echo my own interpretations or opinions, which are offered only in the Conclusions.

In the coding and classification of the assumptions I was assisted by Charles M. Kinsolving, Jr. The original manuscript was typed by Joan Walters Lent; the abridgment by Marie Thornton. Both have my thanks and my sympathy.

Leo Bogart
New York

I

Introduction

THIS STUDY WAS INTENDED to implement a program of research recommended to the Director of USIA in June, 1953, by a special committee drawn from universities and industry.[1]

The committee began by observing that, "we cannot afford to play blind man's buff with this country's international information program." It proceeded to consider both the existing research projects undertaken by the Information Agency and a number of the problems confronting the Agency that required research. Its reasoning was as follows:

> The committee assumes that the success of IIA's [2] program can be measured by the extent to which it helps to affect information levels, influence opinions and attitudes, and bring about action in directions specified by our foreign policy and IIA objectives. The committee further assumes that to work at maximum effectiveness toward these goals, an international information program must
>
> - Operate with a set of valid assumptions regarding the process of international communications;
> - Operate with a clear and adequate knowledge of the groups to which the program is directed;
> - Operate with an objective and continuing audit of its own performance.

[1] The committee had as its chairman Wilbur Schramm, Dean, Division of Communications, University of Illinois, and, as members, C. B. Carpenter, Chairman, Department of Psychology, and Director of the Instructional Film Program, Pennsylvania State College; Robert B. Downs, President of the American Library Association, and Director of Libraries and Library School, University of Illinois; Marion Harper, Jr., President, McCann-Erickson, Inc.; Oscar Katz, Director of Television Research, Columbia Broadcasting System; Herbert C. Ludeke, Manager, Development Section, Research Division, Curtis Publishing Co.; John W. Riley, Jr., Chairman, Department of Sociology, Rutgers University; Ralph W. Tyler, Dean, Division of the Social Sciences, University of Chicago, and Director-elect, Center for Advanced Study of the Behavioral Sciences.

[2] As a Division of the Department of State, the Agency was known as the International Information Agency.

1

On that basis, the committee wishes to make a number of recommendations concerning the kind of research and evaluation IIA needs.

Recommendation 1. That you pull together the wealth of existing research results on the communication process, evaluate them, formulate them in terms applicable to IIA's problems, and use them—so far as they go—as a foundation of theory and principle behind your operation.

Recommendation 2. That you identify the working assumptions under which IIA operates, evaluate them, and make clear to planners and operators the nature of the assumptions on which their decisions are based.

Recommendation 3. That as working assumptions are identified and evaluated, you build a program of research to test assumptions which, though promising, have inadequate factual basis at present for evaluation.

Recommendation 4. That you interpret the results of the research program suggested in (3), together with the usable results of (1) and (2), to the planners and producers of IIA, as a continually expanding base for better informed planning and production.

This report of USIA's operating assumptions was designed to carry out the first part of Recommendation 2. Its principal task was set as one of making explicit, and placing in a semblance of systematic order, the principal premises, policies, opinions, and beliefs, as well as the items of knowledge, experience, and lore, which guide the organization's operating practices and decisions.

The expectation was that problems for research would be indicated by the study in three ways:

1. It would show the existence of controversy. Where different parts of the organization appeared to be working in the light of contradictory or inconsistent assumptions, research might be needed to clarify the question.
2. It would call attention to the subjects on which operating personnel were themselves doubtful, and state unsolved questions for research.
3. It might reveal instances in which the Agency's assumptions did not jibe with existing social science theory or research findings. The discovery of such incompatibility between the viewpoint of the working operator and that of the social scientist would at least suggest the need for a look into the causes of difference.

It was *not* the purpose of the study to evaluate the assumptions uncovered, or to take the next step of submitting detailed suggestions for further research. The intention was rather to cast light on relevant assumptions, to reveal the reasoning behind them, to indicate differences in opinion and practice, and to point to problems wherever they occurred.

At the outset it was decided that attention should be focused on the decisions made by operators in running the information program. There was no intention of examining the workings of the organization in a management sense. As the study progressed, it became apparent that some of the most significant findings lay precisely in this latter sphere. They arose inevitably whenever purely operational assumptions were examined.

The assumptions stated in official memoranda and directives are not necessarily those that guide working operations. The operator's thinking may be at variance with his practice. A gap may exist between theoretical and working assumptions because of limitations of resources and personnel, because of the opportunities presented by events, or because of tradition or inertia.

It is perhaps inevitable that a study of this kind should focus attention on USIA's weaknesses more than on its strengths. The weaknesses are, after all, the proper subjects for research—as well as for corrective action. As an outsider's view, the study unquestionably has failings, both in its comprehensiveness and in its nuances. The problem is well described in the following two comments made by Agency executives at the outset of the investigation:

> People will try to explain things in the terms you want rather than because they have usually thought in those terms. Probably they have never thought it was important to explain it before.

> I would say that the essential error of the picture you are getting of this Agency is about the same as the relationship of the description of a primitive society by an anthropologist and the true activity of that society as the natives themselves experience it. The native will always feel that the anthropologist's picture is very illuminating, but that it is somewhat distorted. It may be full of insights but it has almost the same value for us as satire might, satire being a distortion designed to make you see things with the recognition of oddities in it that you might take for granted. You will have some of that value for us. A really grown-up, mature agency ought not to get an outside consultant to come in and hold its hand any more than a really grown-up person needs to go to a psychoanalyst. Assumption number one is that we're not grown up.

If there is any single premise governing this research, it is that many of the essential problems confronting the information program have not changed very much throughout its history. The big questions arise again and again and are not easily answered.

II

How the Study Was Made

A STUDY OF USIA'S OPERATING PREMISES AND ASSUMPTIONS might proceed from analysis of a number of different types of data:

1. The output of the program itself: the endless quantity of material published, broadcast, and filmed.
2. Official documentation: directives, guidances, policy papers, field reports, and great masses of memoranda accumulated in the files of all parts of the Agency.
3. The public record: legislation and the transcripts of hearings of Congressional committees.
4. Observation of the program at work: attendance at meetings, participation in day-by-day activities.
5. Interviewing of program personnel.

The last of these five sources of data appeared to offer the best possibility for amassing and analyzing a substantial volume of useful information with maximum validity and in a realistic setting. Of course, the other four sources were also used. There was informal observation of program activity and study of USIA output and of documentary material, but these were useful chiefly to provide the necessary background against which intelligent and efficient interviews could be conducted.

Two alternatives presented themselves in the decision to use the interview method:

1. *The Questionnaire Approach.* There was the intriguing possibility of beginning with a formal questionnaire that might be administered to a wide sampling of Agency personnel, both in the United States and in the field. This would have had the advantage of providing a large and reliable (or indeed perhaps complete) sampling. It would have resulted in quantitative findings that could be stated clearly and firmly for the Agency as a whole. It would also

4

have permitted a statistical analysis that might have provided revealing indications of differences among the assumptions held by personnel in different status grades, media services, area operations, and other relevant subdivisions of the Agency. It would have had the further advantage of providing adequate coverage of USIA's farflung field activities and their personnel.

However, there would have been great disadvantages to using a mass-administered questionnaire, whether this took the form of a written document or of direct interviewing. Such a questionnaire would necessarily have been limited in length. It probably would have had to confine itself to those assumptions that were Agency-wide in scope, thus ignoring or minimizing the specialized problems of particular media and areas. Most important, it would have had to begin with the researchers' preconceptions as to which assumptions were actually held and which were important. A questionnaire or interview schedule of this type would have presented a list of selected assumptions and invited respondents to check the degree of their agreement or disagreement. This approach would have permitted little or no exploration of the reasoning behind the assumptions held, or of how they were related (in a philosophical rather than statistical sense).

2. *The Informal Interview Method.* The form of interview selected was the "informal" or "intensive" type familiar in social and psychological research, a "discussion" between the interviewer and his respondent, as opposed to a formal interrogation. The "discussion" must, however, be wholly one-sided if the interview is to be successful and valid. The interviewer's purpose is to draw out the respondent's views by indicating his interest and enthusiasm for the subject rather than by expressing (or even hinting at) his own opinions. This form of interviewing adapts itself in manner, style, and subject to the individual who is being interviewed. Thus, it is possible to focus directly on his job experiences, interests, and current activities.

This is not to say that the interviews lack structure. They were preceded by considerable informal contact with Agency personnel, and examination of output and Congressional Committee testimony. The first draft outline of the Categories for Coding Assumptions was prepared before interviewing began, and provided a series of reference points from the start. In general, the interviewer was aware in advance of areas likely to be fertile sources of assumptions in a discussion with each respondent. However, the interview structure was sufficiently flexible to permit and encourage additional subjects to arise.

The interviews had three phases. After the interviewer had introduced himself, assured the respondent of complete anonymity, and presented a brief description of the study, the respondent was asked to explain the nature of his job, the responsibilities it covered, and something of his previous work experience with the Agency. This served the purpose of orienting the interviewer, suggesting topics for discussion, and, more important, breaking the ice by getting the respondent to talk about what he knew best and what was least threatening and controversial.

The description of the job and the interviewer's questions about the job led naturally to the second phase. Now the interviewer attempted to get the respondent to articulate the premises on which specific decisions vital to his job were based and the reasons, not always apparent, why things were done as they were. In most instances such questioning led directly to discussion by the respondent of the problem areas in his work: divergences of judgment between him and his associates, and points of indecision, doubt, or confusion in his own mind. If the respondent did not voluntarily refer to such "problem areas," a deliberate attempt was made to guide him into talking about them. It was usually pointed out that significant assumptions could be most readily uncovered in the context of these areas of debate.

In the final section of the interview, emphasis was placed on introducing subjects that the interviewer knew to represent key problems or issues in the particular respondent's work or in his part of the Agency (if these had not been brought up voluntarily). The primary effort, however, was to have the respondent himself introduce the topics for discussion.

The typical interview was about two hours long. Many ran into repeat sessions totaling up to eight hours of interview time. It was decided at the outset that any gain in objectivity that might come about by having several persons conduct the interviews, or by having different people do the interviews, interpret them, and write the report, would be far more than offset by the advantages of continuity and of accumulated and transferable experience in a single researcher.

Interviews were conducted in private, or in near-privacy. (On some occasions, it was not feasible to ask a man interviewed in his own office to dismiss his secretary from the room.) In three or four instances, respondents insisted on having an associate join them, in spite of every possible discouragement.

I took shorthand notes, which resulted in virtually verbatim transcripts. There was no indication that this diminished rapport or reduced the frankness of response in any measurable degr e. In my subjective judgment, only three respondents of the 142 exhibited signs of serious resistance.[1]

It is evident from this description that no two interviews were alike either in format or in the nature of the subjects discussed. From a research standpoint, this represents both a disadvantage and an advantage.

The disadvantage arises from the fact that no real statistical analysis of the interview data is possible. The same questions were not asked in every interview and the subjects were not covered in a uniform manner. Even when they were raised in many interviews, they were obtained in different contexts.

The advantage of this method is that it permitted a high degree of adaptation to the great variety of specialized job assignments and area interests repre-

---

[1] One was a former Soviet general, and one a highly placed Foreign Service Officer who later moved on to a top position in the State Department.

sented in USIA. It gave coverage of a far wider range of subject matter than could have been gathered by any uniform questioning method, and made for far greater rapport with the respondents (and a consequently much higher proportion of useful and frank comment) than might have been obtained through a more formal interviewing approach.

A formal questionnaire designed for a statistical analysis would have demanded a sample carefully designed to be fully and accurately representative of *all* categories of Agency personnel. An intensive interview prompts a need for articulate and well-informed respondents rather than a random selection. This need gave rise to the following decisions at the outset:

1. It was expected that the status hierarchy of the Agency would at least roughly approximate levels of experience, ability, and general informedness. Therefore, it was decided to concentrate as heavily as possible among the top civil service grades and key positions, and to sample more diffusely down the scale.

2. It was assumed that persons dealing with the "intellectual" and theoretical problems of the Agency, primarily policy people, would be most directly concerned with the Agency's basic assumptions, and as many as possible were interviewed.

3. It was further assumed that technicians, clerks, and administrative personnel were less apt to be good prospects for ideas about propaganda than operators engaged in planning, producing, or disseminating output. This decision necessarily limited the possible scope of the study. (It would be wrong to discount the importance to the collective thinking of the Agency of the assumptions held by the "nonpropagandists" in its ranks.)

Domestic personnel were selected for interviewing as follows: The interviewer began with the organization chart and worked his way down through the line of key personnel in each major division, seeking to interview *all* individuals at the top levels.[2] Below the branch or unit chief level, selection of respondents was influenced by the persons already interviewed. They were usually persons already named by several previous respondents,[3] or those whose job responsibilities appeared most significant. Throughout, a deliberate effort was made to cover all types of activity, and all geographical area interests.

Interviews were also held with six persons who had recently resigned from responsible positions with the Agency.[4] Field personnel freshly returned for home leave or reassignment were interviewed when available.

Interviewing took place between October, 1953, and May, 1954. By the

---

[2] A certain percentage were invariably in the field or otherwise unavailable. In a few instances, officials had recently joined the program, and were not interviewed, although available.

[3] An individual was rarely interviewed at the sole suggestion of his supervisor.

[4] They were included in the sample either because they had had exceptionally long or significant experience in the information program or because their successors had been with the Agency briefly or had not yet been appointed.

end of 1954, an additional thirteen of the persons interviewed had resigned from the program.[5]

Distribution of the Respondents, and of All Agency Operating Personnel [6]

	SAMPLE	USIA
Staff [7]	19%	3%
IPS (Press and Publications)	18	10
IMS (Motion Pictures)	11	2
IBS (Broadcasting)	25	29
ICS (Libraries)	12	3
Field	15	53
	100%	100%
Total	(142)	(1,718)

The distribution of persons interviewed differed from the distribution of persons in the program as a whole in the following respects:

1. Field personnel were greatly underrepresented. About half of the Agency's operating personnel were in the field, but only 15 percent of the interviews were with persons freshly returned from field service. However, this imbalance was in large part offset by the high proportion of domestic operators with field experience. In all, 37 percent of those interviewed had worked for the Agency in the field.
2. As planned, the sample concentrated heavily on top-echelon personnel. Seventy-nine percent of those interviewed were GS-13 (or equivalent foreign service grades) [8] or above, compared with only 28 percent of the Agency's total.

[5] There is no indication that the views of these individuals, or of the six who had left the Agency before the study began, differed in any substantial respect from those represented in the remainder of the sample; they were drawn from all parts of the Agency, and represented a variety of political and program philosophies.

[6] There were no complete statistics readily available for all Agency operating personnel as defined for this study. The figures presented here are approximations based on data obtained from the Personnel Office at two different times and on two different bases. The data for Washington were obtained by checking through the Agency's occupational titles list and eliminating personnel with clerical, administrative, and technical job titles. The data on field personnel were obtained by taking all U.S. citizens in the field program and eliminating all with a civil service (or equivalent FSS) grade of GS-6 or lower. A similar procedure was adopted for IBS, except that personnel of the facilities and engineering branch were eliminated. This means that the percentage figures for IBS and the field are inflated by inclusion of administrative personnel.

[7] Includes area directors and assistants, Offices of Policy and Research (and one personnel officer).

[8] In 1953, the salary range for a GS-13 was $8,360 to $8,760, and the civil service grades ran from GS-1 up to GS-18.

3. There was proportionately heavier representation from staff personnel (policy, area directors' offices and research) than from the media services.
4. The smaller media services were overrepresented in terms of the total number of interviews, whereas the International Broadcasting Service was underrepresented. If respondents had been chosen on a strictly proportionate basis, only seven or eight persons would have been interviewed in the (ICS) Library and (IMS) Motion Picture Services, and it was felt desirable to conduct at least a minimum number of interviews in each media service. As a result, there were relatively more interviews with low-echelon personnel in the smaller services.

A report based on the writer's intuitions or impressions might have been written after a reading of the 2,100 pages [9] of interview transcripts. In this instance the complexity of the data suggested the need for a more detailed analysis. Accordingly, a systematic coding procedure was set up.

Each interview was carefully read and reread. Every statement which in any sense appeared to represent an assumption or premise was marked. These included not only opinions but also descriptive statements bearing on the techniques and problems of international communication. These assumptions were paraphrased, summarized, or copied directly on three- by five-inch cards.

Often, a single phrase or sentence was a source for a number of different assumptions, all interlaced. About 10,000 assumptions were recorded on cards and classified, and the report written from them.

The original coding categories in general followed Harold Lasswell's classic description of propaganda research: who says what to whom through what means and with what effect? The categories were continuously revised and expanded as the study progressed. (An outline of the major categories is appended.) Because they cover so much ground, the data provide only a crude indication of the degree to which a given assumption is held throughout the Agency. Some subjects occurred only in occasional interviews, and comments upon them might appear to be idiosyncratic (from a count of the cards), although there is actually widespread agreement on them. Certain assumptions are so widely held that it is possible to refer to them as subjects of consensus; others clearly represent the thinking of mavericks. For analytical purposes, the popularity of an assumption bears little relation to its importance as a subject of controversy and of possible research.

The study was not intended to be in any sense a "public opinion survey" of the Agency. It was *not* its purpose to measure or break down attitudes on any key questions in statistical terms. Such opinions might be altogether irrelevant from the standpoint of a disciplined organization working under guidances and directives. Moreover, opinions would be subject to sharp fluctuations with

---

[9] The interview transcripts average fifteen double-spaced pages apiece.

shifts in Agency administration or rank-and-file staffing, or with changes in foreign policy.

The great bulk of assumptions are *not* subjects of controversy and reflect official guidance, shared articles of faith, and accumulated wisdom. The main task of the study was to define the areas in which there was a lack either of clarity or of consensus, since these were the areas that demanded fresh thought, action, or research.

III

Objectives

ALTHOUGH THE OBJECTIVES OF USIA are spelled out in its official documents and policy statements, they are variously interpreted by operators at different levels and with different work assignments. This chapter discusses the interpretation of propaganda objectives in relation to national objectives. It raises questions about the relationship between long-term strategic goals and short-term tactical goals. The need for worldwide consistency and uniformity is set off against the practical requirements of adapting objectives to a variety of situations in different countries. Does the Agency always aim at specific political goals (as in opposing communism), or is the modification of public opinion an acceptable objective in itself? The latter course presumes that an important part of the Agency's task is to cultivate friendship for the United States by demonstrating the common interests it shares with other peoples. In practice, propaganda operators with specific and limited assignments are apt to reinterpret the Agency's overall goals to fit their own needs or professional interests.

The distribution of USIA's efforts among its various objectives is controlled by Congressional appropriations committees. Operators are often frustrated in reconciling the continuing pressures from Congress with their own professional standards of performance.

THE OBJECTIVES OF THE U.S. INFORMATION PROGRAM are intimately bound to national and foreign policy. Information Agency personnel, even when most critical of the program, are intensely loyal to the fundamental U.S. aims that it expresses and universally believe that although American public opinion and policy may deviate from a wise course at times, both will ultimately swing back into the right direction.

NATIONAL AIMS AND INFORMATION AIMS

Undeniably, some Agency personnel are confused about national aims, especially about the limits of resistance to Soviet aggression. A fundamental point on which many questions are raised concerns the alleged tendency of American policy to divide the world into two opposing camps, "each hugging its own hydrogen bomb close to its chest."

> There is a refusal on the part of the U. S. to recognize that there are not just two great camps in the world, but a great many middle positions, including socialism—a word to which Americans react antipathetically.

On the whole, the sense of confusion is rarely felt in connection with national policy itself. Rather, it involves the expression—or lack of expression— of policy. U. S. foreign policy is felt to be phrased in such broad terms that it "promises people things that they had usually been led to expect from only God and luck."

There is a high degree of consensus within USIA on the major purposes of the information program. Operators spontaneously espouse objectives that are consistent with those enunciated in official statements of policy. However, because the various media services and their subunits are concerned with specific tasks, their members frequently see program objectives in narrower terms than those set forth in the official "Statement of Strategic Principles." Moreover, every medium at one time or another carries on activities that do not directly bear on program objectives but support such long-range objectives as attracting an audience.[1]

Another complication is that objectives have shifted as the international political picture and national and Agency administrations change.

> The objective in Germany used to be reorientation. Then it shifted to the full and fair picture, and now it's defined, first, as Western orientation of Germany and, second, the European Defense Community.

As each new administration of the Agency, in its turn, has released to Congress or the press statements of its grand new schemes and intentions, the old pros in the organization tend to greet them with an air of bemused cynicism. In their view, the main objectives and essential problems remain the same through all political vicissitudes.

> I can dig out for you a glowing set of objectives dished out here. "This is it, boys, we are now in the factual business; we are now going to expose Soviet imperialism; we are going to support American foreign policy; we are going to expose the big lie." That was greeted around here with a big laugh, because that's what we have been trying to do for a long time.

[1] This issue is discussed in Chapter XII, "Using the Media."

OBJECTIVES: CLARITY AND SCOPE

Major objectives should be clear, and priorities among them should also be clear.

From the official viewpoint, USIA's objectives are very clear. They are set forth in policy directives that carry out the intentions of Congress (embodied in Public Law 402), of the President, and of the National Security Council.

However, in the judgment of many operators, USIA objectives are far from clear. Diffusion of objectives is a result not only of their number but also of the way they are enunciated. To succeed at propaganda requires leaving a broad residual effect, which means that the propagandist must first decide what residual effect he wants to leave. Accordingly, neither Congress nor the USIA administration has ever clearly set down what the function of American propaganda is supposed to be. Thus, the true mission of the Agency has never been evaluated or spelled out.

> What are we trying to do as a program? I'm convinced that we really don't know what is the basic assumption of the job that the Information Agency has to do.

Too often, in this view, USIA hopelessly outreaches itself by taking as its aims the full range of U. S. foreign policy objectives. There appears to be no fundamental agreement as to whether the character of the program is basically negative or positive. "Nobody will say whether the Agency's fundamental objective is opposition to communism or the Soviet Union, or defense of the positive role of the U. S. abroad."

National objectives are defined in political or military terms rather than in terms of an information or propaganda program.

> I don't think our objectives are set up as propaganda objectives. I think we work with the same objectives as a political officer does, and I think it's a mistake.

Related to this is the complaint that the Agency's actions are governed by "feel" rather than by scientific discipline. "There is no reasoned body of doctrine as to why we are doing what we are doing." Because there does not exist a "valid communications theory" applicable to the information program, decisions are made on an ad hoc personal basis.

It sometimes appears to its personnel, absorbed in projects that develop their own autonomous momentum, that USIA has not made up its mind whether or not its activities are conducted for their own sake.

> This Agency is the victim collectively of a kind of schizophrenia. We like to think of an information program as a kind of a do-good project, a humanitarian thing, in its ideal form. And there's a group that says this is a means to an end.

Another sharp criticism is that objectives are "too vague," "too general to be usable," "not sufficiently well thought out." To say that USIA's objective is "to create a climate of peace and friendship," or "to forward the interests of the U. S. abroad," or "to have people in favor of the U. S." is not to define objectives.

A similar objection is that USIA has too many objectives and that, as a result, its efforts have been too diffuse.

> I have advocated that periodically on given posts you bring your program to a halt, except for basic things, and take a look at it from the standpoint of reviewing your objectives and tasks in the order of priority and then reviewing your assets and personnel as of that moment and come to a decision as to which of your objectives can actually be attained with what you have on hand. If, in doing that, you find that the first five of your priorities are simply out of your grasp at the present time, have the courage to face up to it and put them on the shelf. If you can accomplish tasks 5, 7, and 9, you may find that you have the resources to do the others. The normal tendency is to spread yourself thin and try to cover the whole field. And sometimes you cannot do it.

(For example, in Indonesia it may be advisable to forget the economically important Chinese and concentrate attention on the government; then the desired objective with the Chinese may be attained through the mediation of a complacent or favorably inclined regime.)

One explanation for the proliferation of USIA's objectives is inertia, the continuation of a great many projects that had some past success.

> It's been talked around here for years, but no one has gotten the cogs meshed in this damn thing. We have media services rushing off in nine or ten different directions with very little topside coordination to mesh these four or five outfits into one team moving toward the same goal. The Eisenhower speech (on "Atoms for Peace") was supposed to be an example of all media getting together. From our standpoint, it's a very routine operation, something we do day-in, day-out all year round. On that one, there was an attempt to sit down with all the media and say we are all going to pump this for the next ten years. Unfortunately, these instances are far too rare and remote to make them worthwhile. Basically, we are all supposed to be in the same business, spreading the same ideals, aspirations, and policies. There seems to be a reluctance on the part of the people who call the turn to permit the boys who are going to carry the water back to get in on the act.

Another problem that crops up is that tactical objectives have not been clearly defined for the individual media. In the eyes of at least one Agency observer, it has not been established whether USIA is trying to achieve immediate or long-run results, or even what the immediate and long-range objectives are.

Emphasis on long-run objectives stems from a feeling that the Agency's task is gigantic; USIA can attain its aims only by a slow, steady effort that eventually will begin to show results, perhaps in a generation or more. "Beating communism may take two generations." USIA activity is only a fraction of the total U. S. influence on foreign countries, and cannot be very effective in achieving short-run objectives, particularly in peacetime. This makes it all the more imperative to concentrate on long-range strategic aims.

Objectives are easy to confuse with specific themes or tasks: to secure peace; to show that atomic energy can be used for world good and that the United Nations succeeded in Korea; to make the people of an occupied area (Trieste) understand U. S. military authority and adopt a friendly attitude.

There are few arguments for concentrating on short-term objectives as such, although it is recognized that these often tend to dominate the program because of practical considerations. Setting specific short-run objectives makes it easier to measure progress.

> Whether we would state our purpose as an information program in very general broad long-range terms or whether we would try to achieve the much more down-to-earth immediate objectives that we can perhaps see some progress toward in a reasonable length of time. Obviously, the more concrete we can make our statements the more we can change them as situations change.

A common observation is that many operators emphasize tactical rather than strategic considerations "because of the feeling that everything must pay off right away." Appropriations must be justified before Congress:

> I don't think we get our money or justify our program on the basis of long-range stuff. I think we are trying to sell ourselves in terms of potentials rather than in terms of what we are actually doing. This program was originally sold on the basis of the fact that it could have some immediate effect on the Cold War struggle.

The semantic nicety of the distinction between objectives and tasks sometimes leads to disagreement within USIA on the question of how flexible objectives ought to be.

According to one point of view, the program should be flexible. Its aims should be subject to reevaluation in a changing world situation. It may be necessary to change objectives for a given country by the time the Public Affairs Officer in the field has achieved those originally stipulated.

The opposing viewpoint holds that objectives should be stated in Washington and be "monolithically ordered" worldwide. They should therefore not vary from one country to another, although they should be narrowed down for each country and the priorities somewhat shifted. These should be stated in a standardized form, even though each country mission may have its own ideas of what its objectives are. Public Affairs Officers (PAO's) [2] in the field should determine only the means and forms of accomplishing the mission set for them by Washington.

> Unless somebody is providing them stuff on the basis of what we are trying to do there, a hell of a lot of our output is going to be expended on unrelated activity, so it

[2] The PAO in each country heads the U. S. Information Service activities there, and reports to the Chief of Mission, although he represents the Agency.

can't be solely a mission-by-mission, country-by-country program based on a lot of generalities, glittering or otherwise.

It would follow from this position that the country missions must drop their own ideas as to what they should be doing.

Everybody had their own ideas of what their objectives were. When you started to tabulate these things and the priority placed on different factors, you found a terrific scattering of shots. They just range over the widest possible scope. All NATO countries should have shown up in the country papers at a pretty narrow scatter, but it doesn't work out that way. Too much has been left to the country PAO to decide what their objectives are. That should be left to Washington. They should be left to decide the form of accomplishing objectives and the techniques they use. Some countries would put implementation of U. S. foreign policy first, others would put NATO first, others would put support of the democratic process first. There was no unanimity in the standardization of the terms that they used. You found that the same ideas were expressed in four or five different ways, and it made you wonder, "Is this the same for Germany as it is for Italy?" I think there's a need for reducing these ideas to a more standard way of expressing them.

OBJECTIVES: PERSUASIVE OR POLITICAL

The ultimate purpose of the information program is to affect the political actions of the countries in which it operates. Within USIA little debate would take place over this thesis. However, two main schools of thought develop on how the ultimate political goals are to be attained. The first school of thought believes that political action is the only legitimate objective of USIA, while the second holds that USIA is essentially concerned with the process of persuasion itself; with creating changes in people's thinking, and that ultimately changes of opinion may lead to political action. But such action is not in itself a working objective.

When the objective is considered to be persuasion, it follows that USIA's activities are seen as individual and subjective in their effects, the Agency seeking to change the inner workings of people's minds, to achieve a "climate of opinion," favorable to the U. S., "into which day-to-day events can fall." "We are waging a battle for men's minds in which we can clash with the Communists on their own grounds."

"The primary object of the whole thing is to force people to take sides," or to keep them on the side of the U. S. USIA's purpose with any audience is filled if it can "start them thinking."

"USIA must create a climate of peace and freedom," "a favorable predisposition, so that when things come along that are unfavorable to us, there's less desire to believe them." It must offer "ideas that will compete with Communist ideas."

Those who see political action as the end result of the Agency's efforts begin with the premise that goodwill is not sufficient. "If you can't use this goodwill for some purpose, you might as well have bad will."

USIA is not "selling one kind of soap to match Soviet soap." The only objective of propaganda is action on the part of the target audience, action paralleling American interests, regardless of what the audience thinks of the U. S. Without a call to action, it is difficult to rouse people from their apathy.

> Since our actual ultimate objective is to produce actions rather than mere beliefs or attitudes, the actionable aspects of our message should not be lost sight of. Where action by the listener is possible, either now or in the possible future, the nature of that action should be—at least occasionally—clearly stated.

> The basic objective is to move people in some direction, and to get those who are passively on our side to act.

Those who take this tack acknowledge that Americans want to be liked by other people but argue that this has nothing to do with USIA objectives, which are to get people to take effective action on concrete problems in which both they and the U. S. have a stake.

Building understanding and liking is a longer task than achieving immediate political goals. USIA goals may be stated in specific terms, such as getting friendly individuals into power, gaining the support of a country in the UN, or holding a foreign government in firm alliance with the West.

Yet, even those who feel most strongly that USIA must be geared to action have faith that ideas will lead to action, that governments are affected by the thinking of their constituents and by their conceptions of what the constituents are thinking. Thus, USIA is a "political instrument." In free countries it can bring pressure to bear through public opinion to cause a government to modify its actions.

> One of the assumptions or premises is this: If we didn't have any Cold War there would not be a need for such an organization as ours. The job of all of this organization, through the pressure which it can muster in the minds of people, is to keep the enemy off balance so that we can deal more effectively with him in the political sphere.

Supporting U. S. foreign policy is clearly stated and accepted as the major general objective of USIA. This means that one of USIA's major tasks is "to keep the U. S. position clear in the world," to explain "why America does what it does politically," and "to keep before the foreign public the U. S. position on any of the day's current problems or events."

> What we want to do, regardless of how we do it, is to make the peoples and the governments of these countries understand our policies on world affairs so that they will support us at any given moment if the chips are down, which may not be for 15 or 25 years.

If the information program is seen as an arm of U. S. foreign policy, it follows logically that such a program is needed "to explain U. S. actions and to hold together people friendly to the U. S. point of view," under any political circumstances. "USIA should be in business, even if there were no Cold War."

OBJECTIVE: FIGHTING COMMUNISM [3]

USIA is in business to fight communism. Its prime and only objective is a strong, dynamic anti-Communist program. This firmly held view within USIA ranks is supported by the contention that Congress, especially appropriations committees, believe this to be USIA's most important mission—even its sole one.

> All the top people at one time or another were forced into the position of agreeing with the contention of some Congressman that the sole purpose of USIA is to fight communism, not to support the aims of the United States in general or foreign policy. This led to difficulties in policy because you always had to justify any major act in terms of fighting communism. With some of our Congressmen it had to be a direct thing. It had to be "How many Communists did you kill today?"

The original objectives of the information program were not explicitly anti-Communist, however. The official USIA "Statement of Strategic Principles" recognizes the struggle with world communism as an important aspect of USIA objectives, but does not make it the most important one: "To unite the Free World in order to reduce the Communist threat without war."

Is the enemy Soviet imperialism or communism? According to the paper on "Strategic Principles," the Communist rulers possess two weapons: (1) the Communist ideology and the worldwide Communist movement; and (2) the military and political strength of the Soviet Union and the satellite countries. However, there does not appear to be any clear-cut definition or agreement among program personnel as to whether the main point of attack should be the Communist philosophy and system or Soviet expansionism. While Congress is said to believe that the fundamental objective is to attack communism, many operators believe Soviet imperialism rather than communism is most vulnerable.

> To what extent are we going to fight Soviet communism? It's an unresolved element in national policy. Our whole program is blurred by the ambiguity over the nature of communism. We oscillate. There's a period in which we believe our propaganda is most effective if it presents what is called something positive, and then when it's negative—anti-Communist, the concept of being against Soviet imperialism. People are espousing either of the two doctrines. Whenever it comes down to cases—"Are we against the Soviet Union because of its communism?" people tend to say, "No." When we come down to asking, "Are we against the Soviet Union because of its essential dynamics?", people say, "No." It's the old question of

[3] The tactics of opposing communism are discussed in Chapter VI.

evil. It's made more difficult to establish a rational and consistent working agreement by the need to safeguard ourselves against the charge of being insufficiently anti-Communist.

USIA must combat Soviet communism because it is associated with expansionism. If the Soviet Union were not Communist it would not be a problem. America is not against the Soviet Union as such.

Dissent: Russia would be expansionist in any case:

I would say the Soviet Union in being Communist has a special attitude toward expansionism but I would say it would be expansionist now regardless of what kind of government it had.

The arguments for emphasizing anti-communism are stated in such terms as these:

Our primary emphasis should be attack rather than defense—attack on the Kremlin rather than approval of America. This is true, at least, if our primary objective is defined as promoting collective security rather than advertising America. History has shown that nations can unite against a common danger, even when they do not like each other.

We discarded the positive approach because there didn't seem to be any. We didn't have a new economic or social program going in Italy. We didn't have deeds on the part of the United States that we could exploit, so from there we turned to a search for a negative or counter-propaganda activity that might be helpful.

Another argument is that attacks on communism fit any occasion, no matter what the state of U. S. negotiations with the Soviet Union. Revealing the inherent immorality of communism need have nothing to do with refuting Communist charges against the U. S. This point is contrary to another opinion, that communism should be attacked directly only if the attack can be related to some news event.

Communism is evil. There is strong feeling within the Agency that communism is not merely the adversary of U. S. interests but that it is inherently and unqualifiedly false and wicked.

I have never seen any facet of communism that will hold up and that cannot be shown up. There isn't one single point of their doctrine that they're not vulnerable on. They're vulnerable on their success, on their philosophy, on their protests of belief in human liberty and human rights.

OBJECTIVE: SHOWING MUTUALITY OF INTEREST

One of the important stated goals of USIA is to foster among people overseas a sense of mutual interest with the United States.[4] This serves the direct

[4] The "Mission of USIA," according to a presidential directive, is "to submit evidence to peoples of other nations by means of communication techniques that the objectives and policies of the

foreign policy aim of creating a united front against communism, and also the less direct propaganda aim of building support for the U. S. in foreign public opinion. Underlying all of the Agency's thinking on this point is a recognition that the Free World can survive only by solidarity. This requires understanding of the U. S. by its allies and identification of the U. S. with the aspirations of other people.

As one program spokesman states, the objective is to "submit evidence to other people that their hopes and aspirations are advanced by our policies and objectives; to bring out the mutuality of interest between ourselves and other people of the world and to relate their wants to ours, to get them to join with us in achieving these goals." (In fact, there are those in the information program who believe that it is just as important to acquaint resident or visiting Americans with the achievements of a target country as to inform the local population about the U. S.)

As a guiding principle, identification with other peoples' aspirations and interests is considered incompatible with "trying to ram America down their throats." The idea is to show the target audiences that Americans are basically like them in aims, desires, and interests; that they share a common heritage with the U. S., either through kinship, as "part of Western civilization," or in some other way, and to show that the U. S. has successfully dealt with problems similar to those they face.

It is therefore considered helpful to show people overseas that Americans understand them and their problems. The U. S. appreciates its allies and means well toward them. One version of this doctrine is a kind of "big brother" attitude, as in the notion that people overseas look for guidance to the U. S. and recognize the advantages of "tying their kite to the American string."

Fostering a sense of mutuality of interest is not merely a matter of building their identification with the United States, but of creating a sense of solidarity for the non-Communist world in the face of common danger. This implies that a task of the information program is to support any movement toward international cooperation and cohesion, even when the United States is not itself a party to it.

"FRIENDSHIP" AS AN OBJECTIVE

USIA's task of persuasion is often visualized as one of creating a favorable "climate of opinion." In this view, information activity is directed to making people more friendly to the U. S., to American institutions, and to Americans as individuals, with the expectation that this will make them more likely to act in concert with the U. S. on political matters.

United States are in harmony with and will advance their legitimate aspirations for freedom, progress, and peace."

Confidence in U. S. foreign policy will be built abroad if the U. S. is admired and approved. If individual Americans are respected and liked, this leads to more respect and liking for the U. S. as a whole. In such a friendly atmosphere, "propaganda has a better climate of receptivity." (There is a more skeptical way of stating the same point: It cannot be demonstrated that friendliness causes support for U. S. foreign policy, but it certainly does not hinder it; therefore, any effect it has must be to the good.)

Underlying this argument is a psychological premise that friendliness toward the source of a message makes the audience more susceptible to it; that people will not listen to a message unless they respect the source. This thesis is not universally accepted; it is also argued that initial friendliness toward the propagandist makes no difference in creating susceptibility to the message, provided an audience can be attracted to it.[5]

"Winning friends and influencing people" is the objective which operators often state as a summary of what the information program is trying to accomplish. Winning friends for the U. S. may be defined as a counterpart to alienating people from the Soviets. However, it is seen by some zealous operators as part of the overall job of promoting American over European cultural influences in backward areas.

In this interpretation, attempts to modify foreign institutions along U. S. lines go hand in hand with attempts to heighten the prestige of the U. S. vis à vis European countries, which have been taken as models in the past. The idea behind the Agency's English teaching program, for example, may be considered not only to make English a common language, but also to sponsor the use of American rather than British texts and to make the American pronunciation (rather than the British one) standard. Overcoming French or German cultural preeminence in an area like the Middle East can appear to be an important aim for field personnel.

> If we encourage the development of English as a second language in the Arabic world, we set the stage for a transition from the French to the American system of education, we facilitate the exchange of people and ideas, we make possible the spread of American periodicals in the area.

But is friendship really an objective? There is vigorous questioning within the Agency of the premise that "if people come to know us, they will become our friends, in the real hard-headed notion of foreign policy friends."

> One of the assumptions on which we operate overseas is that there is not only a relationship but often a pretty positive correlation between (1) the success that we have in overcoming stereotypes that foreigners hold of Americans or aspects of American life such as those on race relations, capitalism, war-mongering, and imperialism and

---

[5] Actually, the experimental evidence indicates that a message forced on an unfriendly audience will make them less friendly, but there are innumerable opportunities to convey ideas or information to audiences which are neither distinctly friendly nor unfriendly, and here the results are likely to be positive.

(2) the degree of alteration in receptivity that these same foreigners have for our overall foreign policy objectives. In other words: To the extent that a foreigner becomes convinced that the Negro situation in the United States is far better than he thought it was, do we bring him over to accepting one or more of our foreign policy objectives? This is a hornet's nest, and some people get mad at you for asking the question. They say "obviously." I would like to know what the relationship is.

The critics of "friendship" as an objective point out that in most countries making friends for the U. S. is irrelevant to the purposes of a propaganda campaign.

> Our objectives are not particularly to win friends and influence people except to further the security of the United States. Not just having friends and hoping they love America, but having friends and not worrying about them while we develop our major concern, which is Russia.

> I don't think it makes a hell of a lot of difference in Europe whether people like us or not. If it did we shouldn't have put $50 billion into the Marshall Plan, because that probably created a reliance that boomeranged on us.

The problem, say the critics, is not trying to make people like America but getting them to understand American motives. They argue that the attitudes of a European public toward a political arrangement like NATO would be based on a realistic appraisal, not upon how much they like Americans. "People can still act with and for the United States and U. S. objectives without liking us particularly." For example, a West European left-wing intellectual can like the U. S. and work closely with Americans and still follow the Communist line.

> In one country you might want to make friends, make the people think all Americans are good. In most countries you really ought to be saying, "We don't give a damn whether they are our friends or not." No matter what they think of us as people we want them to take actions of their own that parallel the interests of the United States. What you want to do with a Frenchman is not to make him an admirer of the United States. We want to make him feel that if the Russians cross the Elbe he ought to take up his rifle and fight. God knows I'm not proposing that we offend people, but friendship is not our ultimate objective. A lot of Frenchmen like Americans instinctively on a personal basis, but then they'll go out and vote against us.

If their friendship is to be won, foreign audiences must first be made familiar with the U. S. This is usually interpreted to mean that "presenting a picture of America belongs as a foundation in every one of USIA's country programs." Thus, building familiarity may be seen as an "objective in itself."

> I think it's very important to make as many friends for this country as we possibly can in the sense that they're informed people who are not ready to believe lies about us. If you don't operate on the principle that making them knowledgeable about the United States has a value of its own, then you can't really appreciate the program.

According to one opinion, USIA need not be concerned about instilling a favorable understanding of American traditions; audiences must be persuaded not in terms of American history, but in terms of their own strivings and aspirations.

USIA should describe how the American free-enterprise economy operates. This may be carried further: USIA should promote capitalism in a form acceptable to the rest of the world. The concept that USIA's purpose is to "advertise America" may be expressed literally. If foreign peoples recognize that there is a high level of culture in America, it will change their notion that they must go to Europe for home furnishings and equipment, and this will result in more sales of American goods.

USIA must not merely project a positive image of America, but counteract unfavorable impressions and stereotypes. Such impressions may arise from Soviet propaganda, from the tradition of anti-U.S. feelings in certain areas (like Latin America), and from those actual features of American life that other people find unattractive or unsavory.

The major stereotypes to be counteracted are that (1) the U. S. is undemocratic or abusive of racial minorities or is a nation of rigid social classes, (2) Americans are "barbarians without any culture," (3) America is oriented toward war, and (4) America is imperialistic.

This line of thought has yet another implication. To maintain its position of world leadership, the United States must have an active information program. As a great power, involved in momentous and controversial decisions, and constantly misrepresented by its Soviet adversary, America has many reasons for wanting to disseminate an accurate (or even flattering) explanation of its actions, motives, and character.

Another oft-cited objective of the information program is the support of democracy abroad. U. S. foreign policy aims to strengthen not only the unity of the free world but also its institutions. Thus, it becomes an aim of the information program to support and strengthen the internal political structures of America's allies.

For example, operators point out that the main objective in a country threatened by communism (like Iran or Thailand) may be to increase the stability of the government and reduce unrest; this may be more important than the attack on communism itself. In Taiwan, the aim is to support the morale of the Chinese Nationalist forces.

Throughout the Far East, an objective is to get the overseas Chinese to cut their ties with China and to reassign their loyalty to the country in which they live. (Or it may be "to get them thinking of Nationalist rather than Communist China when they think of China.") Strengthening democracy in an undeveloped country closely identified with the U. S. (like Korea) may serve the end of building U. S. prestige.

Strengthening America's allies may be interpreted broadly to include all efforts to foster economic growth by getting target audiences to help themselves. The argument runs like this: Communism thrives on insecurity. U. S. national policy, through our foreign aid programs, works to raise the level of economic security throughout the non-Communist world. USIA therefore has the job (especially in underdeveloped areas) of showing people how to improve their standard of living, since this reduces the appeal of communism.

> It depends on what impression you want to create and your basic aspirations. Your aspirations in Southern Italy might be to help them cultivate their land more effectively, because then they can eat more and sell more. A good film on soil erosion would be a useful thing. It all comes back to reducing the influence of communism, because if they can make more money out of their day's work it will reduce their susceptibility to communism. It might be that the only problem in Southern Italy is to get them to produce bigger crops.

Aiding economic progress abroad may be done by reference to successful American experience. (For instance, it is useful to inform people in France or Italy of how Americans pay their income taxes, since it will strengthen their governments if the lesson sinks home.)

Apart from the immediate political value of supporting friendly democratic governments, it is sometimes argued that strengthening democratic institutions has long-range value in and of itself. As one operator puts it: "Our main objective is to spread democratic institutions so they will be peace-loving." This reasoning may be carried further. In backward countries without a democratic tradition, USIA should stimulate the development of trade unions, promote women's rights, and encourage two-party systems: "One of our objectives is or should be to interest them in the democratic way of life as exemplified by the 'Town Meeting of the Air' and forums on television."

In nondemocratic countries outside the Soviet bloc (like Spain or Yugoslavia), USIA must try to get across an understanding of the workings of democracy. Similarly, USIA must encourage democracy in the former Axis states. In fact, it must be recalled that democratization was the major purpose of the information program immediately after the war in Japan and Germany. It remains as a major theme in USIA efforts in these countries.

While the aim of supporting democracy is one which no one in the Agency can reject in principle, there is general recognition that its pursuit may interfere with U. S. foreign policy. This is particularly true in colonial areas, where support of democratic aspirations would lead to direct conflicts with the ruling power (as in French North Africa). On a less serious level, it is pointed out that excessive emphasis on democracy may change national character undesirably. As one operator remarks, somewhat cynically, "The policy in Germany is now to make them into soldiers again and has switched from preaching democracy." Here is another comment, along similar lines:

> I remember going through every item of output in Turkey and I found a rather elaborate program with the Ministry of Education for reprinting in Turkish a number of textbooks on American educational methodology and I said, "Why?" They said it was a good thing. I said, "What in your country papers said that your job was to try to influence the methodology of Turkish education?" "Well, it was based on Nazi

authoritarian systems." As I understood it, the strength of Turkey today is that it's pretty authoritarian in its government. I don't know whether we have an immediate task of destroying that.

From the thesis that USIA must strengthen democratic institutions abroad follows a whole line of program emphasis, sometimes criticized as the "do good" approach.

Program content and activity often reflect operators' convictions that they are responsible for bringing institutions and customs closer to the American model.

We have a number of people here who will engage in certain activities—and this is particularly true of the Exchange of Persons Program, the Libraries, and possibly films—who would believe that that was a good thing to do even if there were not one Communist in the world and there were no international problems.

In this category would fall, no doubt, those who believe that the purpose of the libraries is to expound the "values of American civilization," to show the foreign public "how things are done in the U. S.," and how American ideas may be adapted to their own circumstances.

We should do a film on nursing, because throughout Latin America it is looked upon as a servant profession and the most desirable girls don't go into it.

One of our problems is to develop the communications system throughout the Arab world, or the rudiments of one, based on the book.

In our hearts we would like to change their (institutions) but we are not going to do it overnight.

Service-type activity often corresponds to positive audience interests, and may be extremely popular. Maintaining this popularity may become all-important to those whose professional self-interests are directly involved. Thus, this kind of activity may be criticized to the extent that it is taken as its own excuse for being.

For example, no operator would argue that USIA's objective is to disseminate the news. Yet, criticism of the fast media (broadcasting and publications) frequently starts by pointing out that the news-reporting mission becomes an end in itself. This is described as the effect of the professional newsman's orientation, which leads the program beyond its true job of reporting news developments in the light of U. S. foreign policy, to the point where its main mission becomes that of purveying information to the peoples of the world: "Some people think USIA is running a free newspaper or radio service for the entire world when, in fact, it is not."

As a matter of fact, there are people in the program who do think in terms of service goals of an informational character and who admit these goals frankly, for example, in saying that the function of a USIS (U. S. Information Service) library overseas is primarily as a documentation center, or that libraries are good "because they do not try to do anything to anybody."

Similarly, the professional newsman may present a plausible case to the effect that good, accurate news-reporting builds confidence in the U. S. The aim of giving information is not only to explain and clarify U. S. policy, but also to get people abroad to put faith in American newscasters as calm, objective observers on whom they can rely for true facts.

PRESSURES FROM CONGRESS

USIA's objectives are determined by Congressional appropriations committees that control the size and distribution of its budget: "These nervous breakdowns come about as we get our appropriations cut off. The amputation trauma." [6] In many operators' eyes, domestic political realities upset intelligent long-range planning and interfere with the Agency's ability to accomplish its task. The program has become attenuated and has lost vitality: "This organization, purely for domestic political reasons, is trying to fight communism inefficiently." Any effective programming is bound to produce stresses in USIA's relations with Congress and the public. Rank-and-file employees, as well as Agency managers, feel responsible to the taxpayers for maintaining high standards and return on public investment. While domestic public relations are highly important to them, they generally recognize that these links have been weak.

Therefore, one of USIA's big jobs is to sensitize the American people at large, who do not appreciate how complex a job it is to influence other people about a way of life different from their own. USIA also has to show that it is hard-hitting and profitable. At the same time, the public must understand that this organization sometimes has to be subtle and at other times direct—occasionally devious as well as open. USIA cannot publicize what it is doing. Congress is particularly insistent that it not advertise itself or report to the American public, "except through a dull document presented to Congress at periodic intervals." Furthermore, it is dangerous in a democracy to permit a large propaganda apparatus to try to influence domestic opinion. The support of Congress is necessary for the program. On this there is unanimity. But, according to one interpretation, USIA operators have an undifferentiated and immature stereotype of Congressmen.

Conversely, Congress does not have confidence in USIA. Congressional appropriations committees do not understand why the Agency is needed. The government merely pays lip service to a civilian information program. If there were no Cold War, USIA would not be in business.

The information program can be run to keep Congress happy and run economically, without fanfare or controversy, in a very routine way; but whether it will be a highly

---

[6] The "amputation trauma" had its counterparts twenty years later in the near-elimination of funding for Radio Free Europe and Radio Liberty.

imaginative, hard-selling, effective Agency, realizing its maximum potential, bringing its maximum benefits to the United States and to the Free World, when it's that kind of a placid agency, I don't know. I think inevitably anything that is effective, that is doing a job for the country, is going to produce stresses and strains. The information program is bound to be a target. If you broadcast essentially anti-Communist output, somebody is not going to like it. If you broadcast something else, somebody else is not going to like it.

An explanation of why Congressional committees essentially do not understand USIA's problems is that many Congressmen start with legal training. This gives them an "either-or" approach to problems rather than the more subtle psychological sensitivity required for a propagandist:

> He had been reading some of the leaflets and said, as an attorney, he had never won a case by the soft approach, by conceding that the other side had any case at all; and that's a cogent argument if you're operating within the limitations of judicial procedures and convincing a jury; but you very seldom use the same approach in a person-to-person argument. I don't see how a man as intelligent and informed on the information program could assert that you pull a fence-sitter over on your side by saying that he's a fool to believe whatever he happens to be believing—instead of letting him feel that you have an argument that he ought to consider.

Pressures from Congress set the program off in directions that are at variance with what Agency management itself knows is right. Program decisions are not based on objective research or professional judgments but on political pressures. The operator cannot do his job well and make Congressmen happy simultaneously.

> So much of our program is geared to gaining Congressional favor that we aim more than 50 percent of it on what effect it is going to have on Congress and less than 50 percent on what effect it is going to have on people overseas. The program has its tongue in its cheek. The Administration is in that dilemma today. They know that to sell the program and get more money you have to be anti-Communist but that that is not the way to accomplish our mission. Everybody agrees that this sort of thing is unfortunate, but the prevailing mood of the country calls for accepting this premise that the most important thing is fighting communism.

If there is a policy conflict between administrative people, who are under political pressures, and operators, who are sensitive to the program's effects on target audiences, the views of the first group prevail. Thus, the least effective parts of the program may come off best because they are least vulnerable to attack.

> People around here are so relieved when there's a part of the program that Congress either actively approves or refrains from criticizing that they think there is one sleeping dog we better let lie. "If even Congress likes it, it must be good."

Congressional committee investigations, notably that of the Investigations Subcommittee headed by Senator Joseph McCarthy, produced "an atmosphere of insecurity" and

. . . the kind of morale that dogs chased by wolves would presumably have. We have had the kind of nervous breakdown that comes from rejection by the Congress and by the public. It produces fearful people, cautious people, time-servers, and people who want quick results.

One Voice of America operator described the investigations:

That period was one of pure hysteria. Each policy meeting was a major battle, and for one reason—because at each meeting there was one person engaged in taking notes to be telephoned to the investigating committee. It was then a completely closed circuit. You could not say anything at a briefing where classified information was being handled without its being passed on. Nothing subversive was being said, mind you, but if one of us felt that it was unwise to conduct a certain type of campaign, although we were conducting many others which were more violently against the Communists, then two hours later we had a phone call from the Department in Washington saying, "We understand from Senator McCarthy's staff that at this morning's meeting you advised against doing a certain job in the field of anti-Communist operation. Will you please explain."

Congressional discussion of USIA activities exposes to public view strategy and activity that should remain secret.

We are not like the CIA. We don't function in the dark enough. Maybe these boys are right in the feeling that our first task is to recapture the confidence of Congress, but it's hell on earth to try to evolve propaganda that's going to be eavesdropped on by Congressmen.

Adverse publicity and Congressional pressures cause constant shifts of policy and operations that set the program off balance. Top officials must spend too much time preparing for hearings and protecting the Agency from Congressional pressures. Administrative confusion and diminished interest in program output are the results.

Nonetheless, some operators feel that the Agency has been too responsive to Congressional wishes and demands.

We seem to blow with every wind that comes from the Hill.[7] We realize that we are beholden to the American people through their representatives—but it's been carried to extremes. Every Tom, Dick, and Harry with an axe to grind on the Hill can swashbuckle through the thing and pull things out of context and set that part of the program, or maybe the whole program, off in an entirely new direction that may be partly at variance with what the upper echelons of the Agency have decided is right and proper and may also cause us to lose considerable credibility overseas.

USIA's attitude is wholly "colored by a sense of guilt."

The Congressional investigations create a sneaking feeling that maybe we were not getting anywhere in the world after all. A great deal of our activity is designed to show our effectiveness, particularly in terms that can be explained before a Congressman.

[7] Capitol Hill, i.e. Congress.

The executive branch, including USIA, is not free to run its job independently. "Pressure leaks through every pore." All activity, at least domestically, is dominated by Congressional surveillance: "Any propaganda agency that has to wage its battle with one eye on its rear has a hard job."

CONGRESSIONAL INFLUENCE ON PROGRAM CONTENT

Operators frequently cite Congressional opinions to explain Agency activities of which they themselves are critical. "John Taber [8] doesn't want us to reach the masses." Or, "Congress considers that all money spent on Australia, New Zealand, and the United Kingdom is wasted." They make a number of charges:

1. The Agency has been put on guard against "original thinking." It has never worked out an information policy on the Negro in American society because of "the continual pressure of politics." It is impossible to criticize the United States.

   When you get on the domestic side, trying not to tread on Congressional toes, that's not easy. We have to be damn circumspect in the way we do it, so we don't incur any wrath on the Hill.

2. Events reflecting unfavorably on the U. S. are often not reported. For a time, VOA avoided broadcasting excerpts from domestic radio commentators because members of Congress might be offended. In the Library program, the problem became especially critical as the new (McCarthy-pressured) directives on book selection came into conflict with the standards of professional librarians. [9]

3. Necessary entertainment and service functions are discouraged. Congress has prevented VOA from putting enough listener "bait" into broadcasts to make people want to tune in. Congressmen want output "with guts and impact, not mere entertainment."

4. USIA overstresses anti-communism, "to prove to the boys on the Hill that we are good Americans." The program is too openly anti-Communist precisely because of the suspicion directed against it. The need to safeguard USIA against the charge of being insufficiently anti-Communist has made it difficult to establish a rational, consistent working agreement on the Agency's basic objective.

   USIA policy becomes warped by having to justify everything in terms of fighting communism.

---

[8] The extremely conservative chairman of the House Appropriations Committee.

[9] This appears to be a recurring problem, regardless of where the pressures come from. Frank Shakespeare, a C.B.S. television executive whom President Nixon appointed to head USIA in 1969, ordered the libraries to stock up on books by "conservative" authors to balance the "liberal" works ordered on purely professional criteria.

The only way to effectively present our story to the average group [of Americans] is to show them what we were doing to fight communism and bring up examples of how we had duped the Communists. I was to some extent carried into this type of orientation in carrying on briefings. Knowing what my audience was, I knew how I could best impress them.

5. Congress demands [excessive] publicity for U. S. foreign aid.

   Congress has repeatedly wanted us to wrap all our wheat bundles in red, white, and blue packages.

6. Agency personnel are inhibited from contacting or using Communists, even where they may serve a Program purpose. It is difficult to bring defectors from communism into the United States. It is not possible to give visas to influential leftists abroad. Yet, these are precisely the people who should be sent to America under the Exchange of Persons Program.

7. Congress is leary of cultural output generally. Congressmen oppose USIS sponsorship of art exhibits, because it is not the government's function "to get into the art business." Abstract art may be actually banned. "The average Congressman is convinced that nonrepresentational art is Communistic."

   I had to avoid using the word "art." I had to avoid using language that would give any indication that the State Department was interested in helping anybody who was interested in graphic arts. That was because several years earlier the program was nearly knocked out of existence because an official was not able to identify the subject of a painting stuck under his nose by a Congressman.

   The American Congress hates to think that we are sending Cubist art to the Hottentots.

IV

Forming and Implementing Policy

ESTABLISHED PROCEDURES regulate the translation of the Agency's official objectives and changing foreign policy requirements into actual propaganda. Propagandists naturally prefer to participate in forming policy rather than merely implementing it. They are handicapped in their options, compared to their adversaries, by the basic nature of American democracy. In their relationships with the State Department, and with USIA's own policymakers, propaganda operators often experience a conflict between official requirements and the instinctive demands of their roles as media or area specialists. Among policymakers themselves, there is no unanimous approval of firm policy directives; the personality and professional authority of the individual are essential in translating guidance into effective practice. Especially in dealing with the press and radio services, policymakers are caught between the need to react quickly to the developing news and the need to think things through.

USIA's OFFICIAL FUNCTION is to further the aims of U. S. national security and foreign policy. The lines of authority are clearly understood, and broad national policy is set at the top executive level of the government. Strategy is directed by the National Security Council (NSC), which sets general objectives for the Agency. The Operations Coordinating Board (OCB) defines national goals in the field of "psychological strategy." The State Department supplies USIA with foreign policy guidance, which can then be worked out as information policy guidance by the Agency's policy office (IOP).[1]

[1] This description is still valid in 1975.

Thus, the Agency is a mechanism for furthering security and political objectives. It does not make national or foreign policy decisions. Rather, its task is to support policy already made. This may lead to the position that USIA exists to express and disseminate official opinion.

PROPAGANDA CONSIDERATIONS IN NATIONAL POLICY

Countering the view that USIA's mission is a secondary one merely supportive of national policy is another concept popular among Agency personnel. Propaganda considerations must actually enter into formulating security and foreign policy.

Just as the political implications are weighed for every psychological or propaganda action, the psychological implications of every political action must be taken into account. It is USIA's responsibility to call attention to instances where public policy does not consider the psychological impact upon people elsewhere.

The propaganda aspects should be considered at the time policy is made, not afterwards or when adverse effects have become apparent. This means that military and political decisions should be made with their propaganda implications fully in mind. Information experts must be brought in at top national policymaking levels.

Information policy must modify or change foreign policy. USIA should estimate the probable effect of foreign policy on particular geographic regions, and press for modification if it can be improved, that is, "a more forceful line on disarmament"; "a more positive line on Morocco."

National policy must often override information policy considerations, such as audience attitudes, since the Agency's problems are only part of the overall picture. (USIA predicted unfavorable Indian reactions to the U. S. military assistance treaty with Pakistan, but the treaty's importance necessarily outweighed propaganda considerations.)

Policy should make events; events should not make policy.

> As soon as policy is clearly and unequivocally defined, effective propaganda can be made; as soon as events define policy, and not vice versa, effective propaganda cannot be made.

The propagandist should be a man of action.

> You should be in the position of creating statements, events, programs that will bolster your position in terms of an end you want to achieve. There will always come along ends you cannot do anything about. The Communists are in a better position than we because they can control events. When they put their effort into something, they do so in terms of, "What is it going to achieve for us?" When we put effort into something, we do so in terms of, "Here's the situation; what do we do about it?"

PROPAGANDA AS A REFLECTION OF THE UNITED STATES

American propaganda, both in content and organization, reflects the basic characteristics of American society, thereby presenting paradoxical handicaps to its effectiveness:

1. As a democracy, the U. S. cannot change its policies as rapidly as a totalitarian government can. This is a drawback for both propaganda and foreign policy action that the Soviets do not have. The operator cannot react swiftly while policy is still being defined.
2. A society based on ethical principles is restricted to espousing sound proposals. This hampers the American position in international negotiations.
3. A democracy must embrace a multiplicity of theories, unlike Communist society with one "Bible" of working philosophical, social, and political theories. It is impossible to achieve an anti-Communist or non-Communist "gospel" because the Free World encompasses too many different cultures and philosophies.
4. Americans are less sophisticated about politics than Europeans or the Soviets. They are "too schoolboyishly eager to tell the world what we stand for and vaguely and naively confuse principles with practice."
5. The national preoccupation with the mass media inhibits thinking in terms of targets and objectives. Impatience causes unjustified speed in producing USIA's work. This results in open exposure of strategy that should be kept secret.

For several years the whole program was apparently expressed in terms of the means and techniques of mechanical media. What's our main problem here? What's to be our policy? Then, how much of the media should we use? Something tangible and mechanical. This has had a two-way, reversible effect. Experience in the field filtered in over a period of years. The people in Washington began to realize something was wrong. Showing a film to 2,000 people may look good in the records, but what good does it do? There was a time when we couldn't answer that question. "What do you mean? It's bound to have some effect." Another thing was the influence of the Voice of America. They so long stood in the American mind as the major, if not sole, activity of what we chose to call the information program that that reinforced the idea that we were an American media operation and also got the planners and policy people in Washington to stress the mechanical, media aspects of it.

Everything is ad hoc, and the hoc is pretty strong on any particular occasion. We are constantly lifting ourselves by our own bootstraps without bothering to put our boots on. We have to show results.

I don't think you should advertise your strategy of propaganda. I'm old-fashioned.

To make an article out of anything that so nakedly explains our effort to manipulate things, to create the semblance of self-interest between us and other peoples! It's like describing your technique of seduction and how you make it look like wooing, in the presence of the girl you've seduced.

6. Democratic information activities tend to be decentralized. This may adversely affect coordination in contrast with the totalitarian model:

> In a country where there's this gap between a corrupt government and the highly organized Communists who are able to take over at a moment's notice, the loneliness of USIS is most vividly apparent. We learn in a country like that how profoundly small the impact of USIS can be. That, in turn, I think, dramatizes, for those who are willing to listen and observe, the crying need—far more so than in the case of other governments—for closer coordination and integration of U. S. activities and policies by all the agencies involved.

7. Finally, a democratic propaganda organization suffers from a basic conflict over ends and means:

> This goes back to the American people's expectations. They want a propaganda agency to be a real propaganda agency, a con man outsmarting people and moving the shell faster than the foreigner can see the hand, a Goebbels approach. On the other hand, we have a distaste and distrust for poisoning the wells of thought, and we want it to be a clean, upright "American-boy" kind of agency. We want a Machiavellian, beady-eyed, glassy-eyed approach and we also want the Pollyanna type. . . . In attempting to avoid the aura of a Ministry of Enlightenment, there's no public understanding of just what it is, really, and therefore our private purposes get mixed up suddenly with our public professions. It has led to the need to show that we are hard-hitting and profitable. . . . There is no discipline for psychological warfare. . . . Psychological warfare as conducted by a democracy is not what it is in a dictatorship. . . . All of this is colored by the sense of guilt. One, that we were being the good boy, and two, that we weren't doing anything, pretending to be a news agency. . . . What it comes down to is that a democratic government within a civilization that had a vast faith in the techniques of education and advertising and a secret admiration for the degenerate, manipulative approaches of the Old World, found itself running an operation in contradiction to its own tradition and never was able to discipline its own employees or develop a sense of what its ambition was.

PUBLIC ACTIONS AND INFORMATION POLICY

It is axiomatic in USIA, as elsewhere, that actions speak louder than words. Propaganda has no effect unless it implements specific, announced policies and actions.

> An assumption that some people have, although, to the credit of this administration, it is at least aware of its fallaciousness, is that somehow information or propaganda activities can exist by themselves and for themselves without much relation to specific, announced policies and actions to implement. A lot of people would argue, and this is a fallacy, that the Russians were able to convince a lot of people that Moscow is a paradise. If they can do it, why shouldn't we? The pragmatic answer is that they haven't been able to do it. The way we are constituted, being a democracy, we couldn't possibly beat the Russians at their own game; so there's no sense building up a big story that is not true or didn't exist, because we would be found out anyway. Yet we have a real tendency to construct with words what we have not fully constructed with actions.

I think it's foolish to say we can influence people through words. We can emphasize a movement that happens to coincide with what we want; but actually events and appearances will influence the decision. We can't save the world through words.

Propaganda can never be better than policy. "You cannot have a good information program if you don't have a policy that is good." "If policy is good, they will love us; if policy is bad, nothing that we write is going to change their opinion, but it might mitigate it."

> We depend on policy to make our points and tell our story. If the policy is lousy, nonexistent, or pat, no amount of sugarcoating will make it palatable. But if the policy is on the whole acceptable—even though we raise the tariff on something that may be very important for one particular small country or area—if the overall policy is good, we can take advantage of that to take the sting out of any specific, undesirable element from the local point of view.

Actions should not contradict words. Operators refer bitterly to cases where American policy has appeared to contradict its propaganda line. Words must be backed up by actions. If a statement cannot be implemented, it should not be made in the first place.

Yet, in a sense, all USIA activity proceeds from the assumption that words have some importance and meaning apart from action and that people can be influenced by ideas and arguments. "Just as words alone will never carry a case, neither will acts alone." Successful propaganda requires a complete identity of political and propagandistic goals and acts. It helps create a favorable climate in the context of which American acts, if they are good, can be effective in changing opinions.

USIA'S RELATION TO NATIONAL POLICY

What is USIA's actual role in formulating national policy? There is an "optimistic" and a "pessimistic" view.

The optimists say that USIA can and does indicate to the State Department the psychological implications of foreign policy and does not hesitate to suggest that certain policies be adopted.[2] These recommendations carry influence.

The pessimists believe that USIA's role in formulating national policy is not as important as it should be and that the Agency's importance is not fully accepted at the highest administrative levels. It is "on the outside." It gets insufficient cooperation from the executive branch, and has inadequate access to it. It lives on "a sort of hand-to-mouth basis," with no real knowledge of what is going on "upstairs."[3]

---

[2] USIA's director had only recently become a member of the OCB. President Kennedy made Edward R. Murrow an unofficial member of his cabinet.

[3] An excellent illustration of this point is provided by an incident that occurred a few years after this study was made. The *New York Times* of February 17, 1957, reported that, "last Monday night . . . Secretary of State Dulles called in the press to reveal the biggest story of the week—

Psychological propaganda considerations enter into major decisions, but only in special, extraordinary cases—if a top Agency official personally takes a matter to a very high State Department level. Information policy has not been closely coordinated with diplomatic or economic policy, since the war's end. "The relation between USIA policy and national policy is not enough of a two-way street."

Several explanations are offered for this state of affairs:

1. There is no real belief in the importance of ideological or psychological factors in the cold war.

   The government pays only lip service to the need for a civilian information program. In my opinion, it's not really considered essential. Government and its satellites are convinced that America's strength in international relations consists of its material strength, industrial apparatus, wealth of raw materials, and technical know-how. Therefore, only such parts of the information program have found almost universal acceptance that are pretty close to the more material aspects of thinking, particularly the library and exchange programs.

2. Propaganda can't solve a serious political crisis. It should therefore not be assigned a role in creating national policy.

3. USIA personnel do not speak with sufficient authority on foreign policy. Although knowledgeable, they are inarticulate at meetings with policymakers from other agencies; their memoranda are never read.

4. There is confusion about USIA's role "in the spectrum of national policy." The scope of its activity has not been clarified. It is not clear to what extent the Agency defines its own mission or accepts authoritative definitions from the National Security Council.

USIA operators raise other grievances about national policy:

1. There is no clear-cut statement of mission. Official administrative statements on functions and objectives can be interpreted in many ways.

2. USIA has too many bosses: the State Department, the National Security Council, OCB.

3. There is no clear-cut assignment of responsibilities among various government propaganda agencies. This may be an insoluble problem:

   In a democratic society it is not possible to establish a general, strategic plan that would substantively outline the areas of concern with a timetable for the various government agencies. If that were so we would live in a totalitarian society. We have now veered to the other extreme. We hardly know about each other and have never come to a clear-cut delineation of responsibilities and priorities with regard to various military and civilian operations. There has never been an explicit understanding reached of the relation of the Voice of America to Radio Free Europe and

---

the [American] pledge on free passage through the Gulf of Aqaba. He neglected, however, to include USIA among the select group. Thus its editors did not know anything had happened until they read the newspapers Tuesday morning."

to Radio Liberation.[4] Never has a clear understanding been reached in Korea of what is the psychological warfare function and what USIA should do. We really act, in avoiding any totalitarian label, in an almost utopian-liberal way.

4. USIA's capacities are inadequately assessed: NSC may order "maximum publicity" on a question without regard for the fact that USIA's resources are inadequate to do the job that is being required.

5. USIA is inadequately guided by higher authorities. "Nobody is willing to say that, although the NSC is supposed to set policy, it does not do so." There is no continuous, central guidance. Speeches made by the President or the Secretary of State are now considered tantamount to policy guidance, whereas at another period of time these speeches were regarded as "contrary to national policy."

6. Policy is not clearly stated. Various government policy-making bodies work at cross-purposes. Foreign policy is so diverse that USIA cannot speak for more than one particular aspect at a time. "The government is always overtaking itself." [5]

RELATIONS WITH THE STATE DEPARTMENT

USIA's relations with the State Department are both intimate and complex, particularly in policy formation. Officially, the State Department formulates foreign policy. Information policy, implementing and explaining it, is the task of USIA. The State Department is charged with seeing that information policy agrees with foreign policy.

State deals with governments, USIA directly with peoples. Therefore, State has to make sure that USIA appeals that go over the heads of foreign governments do not substantially deviate from State's diplomatic position.

USIA-State relations are viewed by some as cordial, but less favorably by others:

1. State has been very liberal in explaining the background of its decision-making and in giving USIA advance warning of its decisions. The Agency is

[4] These CIA-funded broadcasting organizations purport to speak for dissident opinion in the countries to which they broadcast, rather than for the U. S. government. Radio Free Europe addresses Eastern Europe. Radio Liberation, broadcasting to the Soviet Union, was renamed Radio Liberty in 1963. In 1975 the two organizations were combined.

[5] The problems discussed here merely continued those already evident in World War II: "OWI policy planners had to make proposals for propaganda action based on the best information about our own national strategy which they could assemble; information which was often faulty and insufficient. Such proposals, when made to military or political officials, would be considered in a negative way; if they did not violate obvious plans or security, they would be approved if any action was taken on them at all. Even then, approved plans would often be so highly classified that they could not be put into effect. From its earliest days, OWI tried to relate its long-term effects to national strategy by developing long-term plans for propaganda to each main region of the world. These were drawn up and submitted to the other government departments for approval. This took so long that actual propaganda operations were carried on without much reference to such plans." (Charles Thomson, op. cit. p. 39.)

taken into full confidence, its advice accepted and taken into consideration. In fact, USIA helps set foreign policy.

2. USIA-State relations leave much to be desired. This critical view is expressed in two essentially contradictory forms: either that USIA is too remote from the sources of decision-making in State or that USIA is too much under State's thumb (in the sense that its representatives are unduly deferential and that output is designed to please the State Department rather than the ultimate audience).

> Often there's a feeling here, that I think is justified, that when our representatives do speak to State, they're good little boys and say, "Yes, sir" and "No, sir."

A strong feeling prevails that the State Department does not really accept the Agency as important and that State wishes that USIA did not exist or wants its target audiences to be limited to diplomats. A variety of explanations are advanced:

1. "Old-line Foreign Service Officers" believe the Agency serves no purpose in solving political problems.

> I don't think State Department people really believe in what is supposed to be done by the Agency. For the most part, I don't even think they know. I get the feeling that it's supposed to be a publicity outfit of the department. The department sends out a release and they're supposed to get it distributed everywhere.

2. State is snobbish—especially "the foreign service crowd"—and hence is distrustful of information program "newcomers." The State Department old guard come from the same social backgrounds. The similarity of their outlook makes them less flexible.

3. State is jealous and defensive.

> They are suspicious of us. We got too much money. We were socially not familiar with the niceties of international relationships. I don't mean that so many of us did not go to the right school, but in the field we were often hard-headed newspapermen and we tended to look on them as cookie-pushers. Their lack of hospitality toward us was matched by our inhospitality toward them. Information people are charlatans in foreign affairs.

4. The diplomatic tradition is one of secrecy. Diplomatic personnel resist the idea of a propaganda agency because it is incompatible with their function. They talk at the level of one government to another and report what that government has in mind. Because they keep formal lines, they can get along with anybody. But the information program goes beyond diplomatic channels.

5. Propaganda interferes with diplomacy. The State Department fears that USIA output may affect the course of diplomatic negotiations. If the Agency promulgates the theme that the Communists mistreat prisoners of war, this may jeopardize the chances of holding a peace conference. If the Voice of America takes the wrong tack, the Soviets may seize on it in their diplomatic bargaining. In talking to governments in the Communist world,

USIA must be careful not to smother possibilities—such as that the Soviets may enter into a limited settlement that is advantageous to the Free World.

The rejoinder of USIA's critics of the State Department is that propaganda does not hinder diplomacy. It is unreasonable to assume that a USIA error in interpreting official U. S. policy could ever be used in political bargaining.

> The policy people don't understand that Mr. Molotov does not come to the conference table and say, ''I've been listening to the Voice of America and we want to take you up on what they said.'' He wouldn't dream of using it. But in State, they think he would. They assume that the operator doesn't know what is really going on and that if he makes a mistake, the Russians will seize upon that for diplomatic purposes. I like to use the Voice of America with the truth, the way the Soviet Union uses Radio Moscow, without fear that Mr. Molotov will ever be handicapped by anything they say.

CRITICISM OF STATE DEPARTMENT GUIDANCE

USIA's grievances against the State Department are far greater than questions of self-esteem. They center on the kind of guidance the department gives the Agency and the restrictions it places on its news reporting and commentary functions. The charges range from lack of advance planning and failure to articulate definite policy on crucial issues (for example, the liberation of Eastern Europe) to being ''too tight'' on releasing policy statements, timid, and reluctant to make up its mind. State Department guidance is seen as unclear, unrealistic, and prolix; its documents ''too long and weasel-worded.'' ''A foreign policy position is often purposefully obscure, since it seeks not to join issue with embarrassing problems. However, an information operation cannot avoid the same problems in talking to its public.''

> Some of it is pretty unrealistic. Because we were for a long time getting daily guidance from people who had absolutely no experience with the media, we were getting such directions as that we could use only one paragraph or none of a given *New York Herald Tribune* editorial in spite of the fact that we knew the whole editorial would appear in their European edition. Similarly, they would edit *Time* magazine or the *Reader's Digest,* available on the newsstands in every country of the world. Except for that sort of criticism of the daily guidance, we found it useful, generally satisfactory for the most part.

At the same time, State oversteps the line by formulating information policy as well as foreign policy. It bypasses the Agency in releasing news.

> According to the setup now, the Secretary of State provides the Agency with general policy guidance. The Agency translates the general guidance into foreign information policy. On paper that sounds fine. In practice it seems to me that the following thing is happening. When the Turkish-Pakistan military pact was still very secret, the normal thing happened—the secret leaked out. There were press reports on it all

over, and our people in Washington went over and said, "What do you do, ignore it? Unless you can deny that there is a pact we better permit the media to pick up the story in attributed form." But the assistant secretary simply put his foot down and said, "No." In that case he was not forming foreign policy, he was forming information policy. He was fooling whom? Every chancellery in the world knew that this was going on. The Soviets knew it too. Then it leaked out. It's regrettable, but there it was. By not broadcasting it, we ran the danger of either looking as though we were unaware of an important development or hiding something that would then damage the important factor of credibility.

The information program was separated from the State Department in 1952 to give it higher stature. The Administrator gained more authority. There is, however, no general agreement as to how many of the Agency's problems have actually been solved by separating it from State.

It is argued that USIA, as a result of the separation, has lost certain advantages that go along with being part of the diplomatic operation, that the Agency no longer has sufficient contact with policy-making personnel in the State Department, and that it is getting less cooperation in the field.

To the degree that a Foreign Service man felt that our program was his program and that anything it did rebounded to the credit of the mission, he was terribly enthusiastic toward us; but now that our accomplishments are our own and are possible sources of danger or irritation of their problems, you have a slightly different attitude toward USIA overseas, or at least there is a danger of that.

Agency personnel agree that, as a diplomatic instrument, USIA must be completely sensitive to the Chief of Mission. How well the information program functions depends a great deal on the attitude of the ambassador.

You find ambassadors who like to use USIA as a personal organ and others who like to use it as a diplomatic instrument. On the other hand you will hit ambassadors who can see no value in any of its activities except for publicizing the ambassador.

Some consider it as an added administrative burden.

There are others who are not particularly interested, or who haven't any real knowledge of what the program is all about and is trying to do and can do if it were permitted to function, and there are still others who have no interest at all, and as long as you don't get in their hair they will permit anything. And there are a few, and they are rather rare, who take more interest in the U. S. Information Agency program and what it is doing than in any other single function of the embassy.

The information program can work best in a country if the ambassador is interested in it and is persuasive in his dealings with Washington. If he is a forceful personality, there will be a minimum of disagreement and dissent within the field post. If he has a "publicly accepted personality," USIA's task is even easier. On the other hand, operations can be inhibited by conflicts or strained relations between USIA personnel and the ambassador.

It has not been unusual for an ambassador to invite the seven key officers of the embassy and the seven key people of the government to dinner and not invite the

Public Affairs Officer at all. It manifested itself sometimes in the administrative side of the business in this way. The average ambassador was inclined to feel that the work of the embassy and consulates, aside from USIA, was far more important than anything USIS might do. No matter how urgently a particular element of the USIS program was being pushed at a particular time, it was still lower in priority than the lowest routine embassy function. A little jeep that could be used to carry a movie projector to the countryside might be used by the ambassador to carry mail more often or to move personal belongings.

In one instance, a newly appointed minister objected to the PAO's use of unattributed literature as "underhanded," although this was an established policy that had been approved by USIA in Washington.

Problems can also arise when the relationship of the ambassador and the PAO is too close.

We have had several posts where the PAO has become the principal political reporting officer, and that means he gets completely tied up with special assignments from the ambassador and of course his primary job is going to suffer.

THE FORMULATION OF INFORMATION POLICY

The Office of Policy (IOP) does not form or change political policy. Its job is to translate this policy into understandable terms, bringing to bear on the problem background information from the wire services, foreign broadcasts, intelligence, and State Department telegrams and information policy statements.

Information policy statements from State may be transmitted directly to operators without amendments or additions (as IOP personnel acknowledge). This procedure is regarded critically by operators who feel that the task of making information policy out of foreign policy should be a more "creative" one. IOP is said to have "so little initiative in developing policy" because, as part of the State Department, IOP was merely a "transmittal agency, and they too often still think of themselves in that same old role." (For this reason, many operators think of IOP as an extension of State, and their remarks about policy frequently do not distinguish between the two organizations.)

IOP's job is also to take the "overly long guidances received from the Department, boil them down, and submit them to operators in crisp, brief form." Other IOP functions are sometimes mentioned: to strike a balance between budget appropriations for various posts, to plan the use of program materials, and to set criteria for personnel selection. According to one definition, IOP's job is to determine what the resources of the Agency are for accomplishing a desired effect.

Policy must concern itself not only with program content, but with the quality of output. The main job of IOP should be to determine what emphasis an event or idea gets. Policy guidances should detail what should be emphasized in different areas, and what media should be used.

IOP must provide guidance on what should not be done. Guidance is often useful in preventing the Agency from "going out on a limb," with possible embarrassment to the State Department.

IOP should be concerned with policy only. But in the opinion of many operators, there is disapproval of the policy staff's reported tendency to get involved in personnel, budget, operational, and administrative matters, and other "housekeeping details."

There is no single agreed-upon definition of the role of policy itself. It is possible to distinguish a "directive" and "nondirective" approach.

THE DIRECTIVE APPROACH TO POLICY

This school of thought holds that the direction of output cannot be left to the day-to-day moves either of an individual operator or even of the whole desk; it must implement the policy line set by Washington. All planning should be done in IOP; the media must carry out instructions, and policy directives should carry the same weight as military orders: "It doesn't mean that every corporal would have to know the whole plan and at the same time there is a fairly coherent system of relating what he does know to the war plan." Those in IOP who take this approach couple it with a complaint that their instructions are often interpreted by the media or by the field as mere suggestions. This attitude in IOP has its counterpart in the position of some operators who say: "Mostly as far as we're concerned we would do like the people on high in policy tell us we're supposed to be doing."

Although many of its personnel believe that its authority should be implicit, IOP cannot execute policy. There is no "police staff," so it is impossible to control what is being said, although it is felt that IOP should be able to do so.

The argument for the directive approach is as follows:

1. IOP has access to classified information not available to operators, and is therefore in a better position to explain strategy. Policy decisions must often be based on behind-the-scenes activities. Operators cannot always be taken into the policy maker's confidence.

> We don't take our own people into our confidence. That's a security problem to some extent. How are you going to infuse into your general output the really high-powered political manipulations that the United States is attempting?

> Frequently negotiations in the foreign field are extremely complex, and we try to accomplish our national purposes by quietly talking to people on different sides of the question, trying to bring them together into a position that we think is good. Secrecy, then, is an essential element of success in some of these situations and secrecy is the thing we cannot very well live with because our business is public talk and the secrecy that is effectively imposed on us, and needs to be, is not adhered to by others.

Guidance to overseas posts cannot always be spelled out on delicate subjects (like the use of unattributed output) because of the danger that it might fall into the hands of foreign governments. (Nonetheless, unattributed material must observe the limits or criteria established by Agency policy guidance.)

2. IOP personnel are much better qualified than operators to think of solutions to policy questions. Having no other duties to divert them, they have the larger view in mind.

> We should get as much as possible to the point where your propaganda agency is a mechanism, an apparatus if necessary guiding public opinion somewhere, affecting an election elsewhere or whatever the objective may be. That means that your people who engage in propaganda shouldn't engage themselves overly much with policy, as has been the case in the past. They should know what the policy is but shouldn't give in to the temptation to alter policy along the way.
>
> That doesn't take away from the USIS man in the field the right or the obligation to report possible difficulties in the policy. That should be reported through the proper channel, namely the Chief of Mission. You may not personally accept U. S. Government policy. The man in the field may think he knows better. He should be indoctrinated before he goes out to the extent that he accepts this, not necessarily as a soldier accepts an order, but almost along these lines or on this basis. He is concerned with a certain type of mechanism and he's in a certain limited area where he doesn't have access to all the facts available to the men who guide him.
>
> Many of our people in Southeast Asia have felt critical of U. S. Government policy in or toward Indochina.[6] In almost all of the cases they haven't had the facts nor even given a thought to the situation in which the policy makers in Washington found themselves, namely thinking of what the United States does next in Indochina, which in turn affects your EDC [7] and NATO and perhaps air bases in North Africa. You can go on and on. If the policy maker knew what the man in the field was thinking he might agree with him, other things being equal. He is in a position to know that all other things are not equal. It's not really blind allegiance or blind faith. There are certain things that the man in the field doesn't know about and it's really not his business to know about them.

THE NONDIRECTIVE APPROACH TO POLICY

This school of thought contends that guidance should give background, not direction. The function of policy is to keep operators abreast of current government thinking and to suggest how this might best be conveyed to foreign audiences. (In this formulation, national policy rather than the problem of communication is the starting point.) IOP's function is to give guidance on the psychological handling of issues, but *not* technical instructions as to how news should be handled. This guidance must put the operator in the proper frame of mind.

> My religion in this business is that your operator who understands what you're after is a much better man than the guy who simply takes over because there are always

---

[6] The reference is to the cautious policy of assisting the French against the Viet Minh.

[7] The abortive European Defense Community, which was rejected by France.

problems on which you are not in a position to give orders and then you rely on him alone to do that. My argument is that an intelligent and informed operator does a much better job for you than one who will just take orders.

The best way to run an information program is to select the right media people and to give them maximum leeway, confining policy guidance only to major problems. Within the limits of basic objectives, talented operators should be given the widest possible latitude in preparing output. USIA's effectiveness will be limited in proportion to the degree to which the operator feels constrained in letting his imagination override the letter of policy guidance. Guidance lines should not be so rigid that they become dogmatic.

The "nondirective" approach is held within IOP itself. Guidance to the media should merely remind operators of problems that may arise. In news guidance it is not IOP's function to tell operators what to say, but to help them understand the possible repercussions of what they might say.

POLICY MAKERS AND OPERATORS

There is no disposition within the Agency to question the necessity to follow policy. Despite this universal belief, IOP personnel point to a tendency on the part of operators to think up solutions to policy questions which are "outside their sphere." This has its counterpart in operators' reports of reluctance on the part of policy makers to let them help in policy formation.

> I try, we all try to introduce ideas into the bloodstream of the Agency. Now it has been made pretty clear to us that they don't want such ideas introduced as projects even in the dummy stage. Sometimes the ideas do go into the mainstream in one form or another and come back to us as IOP ideas.

Instances in which policies were changed without consultation with media personnel are sometimes cited with regret or indignation.

IOP's alleged hostility to any display of planning initiative by the media may put IOP on the defensive. Informal meetings are said to be the best source of program ideas:

> We have developed an uncontrollable twitch when the question of programming comes up so we are being clandestine about the whole thing. We don't call it policy planning or programming or anything because other parts of the Agency are so damned sensitive to their prerogatives about it.

If guidances should be suggestive rather than directive, it follows that media operators should be called on for advice on policy, and that they, in fact, may initiate policy.

> Often the so-called operators lead the policy people. Take the subject of our trade policy. We kept after IOP to tell us what we could about U. S. policy on trade and they just declined to give us anything. We then went ahead and wrote several ar-

ticles on the subject and after we wrote the articles and the policy people saw them they abstracted these papers and sent them out as official guidance. It works both ways.

From the operator's standpoint, conferences and discussions of ideological issues are extremely valuable, but there are not enough of them, particularly meetings between policy and media people. The organization is not making proper use of know-how and expertise at the lower and intermediate levels in the media.

But the policy man's view of media operators generally is that, "No matter how much you tell them to write down their views, nothing is ever organized to bring them back."

The personal relationship between the policy maker and the operator is of key importance in infusing policy considerations into Agency thinking on an informal basis. One long-experienced policy man points out that, "When the operator seeks my views he does so because he regards me as a man who might have some good ideas rather than as a policy man."

When the Information Agency was smaller, it was possible to iron out policies informally, since everyone knew everybody else and decisions could be made on an interpersonal basis. The program is now too big and complex for such informal communication.

Policy is more effectively formulated and communicated by such informal methods as round-table discussions than by formal guidance. Much IOP guidance is transmitted verbally because it is "easier and more fruitful," and because there is too much material to reduce to writing.

There is frequently a clash between "policy restrictions" and the operator's awareness of his audience and his sense of obligation to it. Writers of guidance are concerned with the official U. S. viewpoint, whereas the operator faces the problem of communication and must start with an analysis of the audience's attitude. The conflict between operators and policy personnel may be seen as one between diplomats and propagandists ("friction between the cookie-pusher and the working newsman").

The only thing wrong with IOP is that they feel intellectually the way their bread and butter interest lies, in the field of diplomacy. The first thing a diplomatist thinks is, "No story; shut it up." The propagandist should think, "What can I do with this story?" We need part of the caution of the diplomatist's approach and part of the enthusiasm of the propagandist.

Why do you think the news room presses so hard for policy guidances? The news breaks. The diplomats are looking at it and you can't have a guidance until they're through looking at it. The whole world knows about it. It's on the press and the radio all over the world, and we don't carry the story. The people from whom we get the policy directives have one ambition in life—to wear striped pants and a morning coat. It's the difference between people who want everything to be diplomatic and people who are in the propaganda business.

The problem arises with particular poignancy for Voice of America broadcasters to the Communist world who feel that guidance makes them less vigorous than they would like to be.

The considerable amount of controversy and ill-feeling which exists between IOP and the media is evident in the adjectives often used by operators to describe guidance: "rigid," "petty," "unintelligent"; it is "a waste of time," "worthless," "overly generalized," "dealing with innocuous and obvious things," "piddling," "fatuous," "unrealistic," "sanctimonious." The result is "sterile," "soggy," "boring," "colorless," "uninspiring," "stilted," "deadly dull," "canned and hackneyed" output.

This hostility may be explained on the grounds that there are always bound to be differences of viewpoint between an operator and a policy man.

> Operators are allergic to planning. They are so preoccupied with the day's activity that they tend to resent planning.

Not all operators consider IOP guidances as "interference." Some commentary writers for the fast media (radio and press) feel themselves more or less independent in dealing with current news, and observe that few disagreements between policy men and writers are so basic that no adjustment of viewpoints is possible. (In practice, such adjustment does of course take place.) The commentary writer may accommodate: when Policy suggests something he usually goes along with it unless something else has already been decided on.

Policy makers don't stick to policy. They go beyond the bounds of their legitimate task when they criticize literary style or help write scripts. Implementing policy should be left to the operators. IOP's failings are responsible not only for a time lag but also for a lack of drama and imagination in output.

Policy advisors should give guidance, but commentary writers must adapt this guidance to the arts of persuasion. The operator should fight with the policy man, "not to subvert policy but to argue about it." However, he must follow policy even if he disagrees with the details.

> I believe our basic line is right. Where you disagree on the details you have got a job to do and you're paid to do it, and you follow the line on details.

Operators who may be critical of policy agree that a writer who tries to sneak in his personal view in opposition to the official policy position should be dismissed. An operator who finds that policy is in direct violation of his conscience should resign.

POLICY DISCUSSION AND POLICY PEOPLE

There does not appear to be much conflict or disagreement within IOP itself. A top official of IOP recalls no instance of "discussion, debate, or indecision in policy." Other IOP personnel acknowledge that disagreements exist but say it is always possible to come up with an "agreed position" which everybody by and large supports, although with reservations on the part of some.

Good policy results from controversial discussion. Lack of disagreement reflects insufficient communication and discussion within IOP and insufficient thought about the large issues covered by policy guidance. A policy man says,

> You don't fight up or sideways in a bureaucracy. You fight down. You have an illusion when you look for a discussion. You have to have it *inter pares*. It takes place not as a specific thing, but as a history. While you could get what you call discussion, you won't get a debate. There is no shop-talk here, not even at lunch. There is among operators in the media. There was lots of gossip, lots of political talk about national and foreign policies, and very lay talk, *New York Times*-informed talk, though it's the talk of experts who have nothing in common. We don't sit around and talk about "How do you persuade?" There are a few people who talk shop; but not enough.

And another reports:

> Around the hall are these other guys that I generally see only when I go breezing into their office saying, "Here is a terrible crisis, please help me," but I have no idea what they are doing day to day. I would probably do my job better if I knew what they were doing.

According to one IOP man, policy is "made up of general policy background, a little knowledge, and common sense." IOP has the responsibility to keep up with events. (Within IOP there are "people who know what issues are crucial in every country of the world.") They must be in a position to get information out fast. Policy people must be extremely reliable and careful in evaluating information on which policy is based since much of it comes by word-of-mouth. They "should be able to grasp things, have a broad view, experience in dealing with the intangible called policy, and exhibit evidence of creative thinking ability." Since they deal with abstractions, they must have a higher degree of judgment and perceptiveness than those who work on more concrete problems.

Human relations and social skills are also desirable, since IOP activity requires many meetings and much personal contact. IOP personnel are recruited never on the basis of their opinions, but on the basis of their qualifications.

Media experience is desirable. A policy advisor can be most effective if he is himself a writer and can produce output to be emulated.

But policy makers don't know the media, say the critics. They lack knowledge of the intimate technical details with which operators are familiar. (This complaint is echoed in every medium.) It is therefore "practically impossible" to translate guidances into operations.

The policy maker defends himself thus:

> Fundamentally the difficulty is a lack of understanding here of how much real thought and ingenuity and hard mental labor goes into policy guidance. There is so much going on behind the scenes that you cannot recognize unless you are exposed

to it directly. People here are constantly subject to a strong urge to go out and do something, are thinking not only of the problems and possible problems that will develop, but thinking out solutions to them; and they don't realize that at the same time that they're coming up with a lot of bright ideas that are based on a more or less firm foundation, that there are thousands of people elsewhere, coping with the same problems, but with a much better foundation, because they are being paid to do it, and because they are much better aware of more of the complexities that have bearing upon these apparently simple questions.

PROBLEMS AND CRITICISM OF GUIDANCE

Policy makers must think in terms of the long-range implications of U. S. and Communist policies. USIA should plan for emergencies far ahead of time so that it does not have to try too late to retrieve a situation. Guidance must anticipate events and Communist propaganda responses to events.

Policy makers point out that they do a lot of contingency planning. However, many contingencies never arise, or they arise in such a way that previous thinking is inapplicable.

The complaint of some in the media services is that IOP does no long-range planning. IOP does not provide guidance to help operators in the future. Its thinking is piecemeal:

It's a hell of a lot of little things. It's pretty much of a shotgun technique. You don't know what's going on upstairs. I do feel that we are living on a sort of hand-to-mouth basis. It looks like we are just moving from one small crisis to another strictly on a day-to-day basis.

As a result, media operators must "just improvise."

A great many things are done by planning, but the best things we do are spontaneous. We live from day to day and by our own wits.

IOP has never resolved basic questions. Unresolved policy conflicts (with respect to areas like Kashmir) inhibit the effectiveness of the media. IOP has not distinguished between what economic system is best for the United States and what for a foreign country.

There's never been any guidance, never a line written about how America should be projected, except for an ordeal we went through when they came in with a line that we should show people go to church in America to beat all hell. That's the only instruction we have got.

It is an enormous task to construct a general directive, and IOP men admit that not many are put out.

Guidance should be very general since it must try to cover a broad area. Focus on particular areas results in fragmentation of effort, which means that guidance fails to obtain acceptance.

The "nondirective" view of policy may lead to the position that it should be stated in general terms: Guidances should not handle day-to-day tactical considerations. They should define over-all policy so that the operators are clear as to what it is.

Guidance is worthless in generalized form, say the dissenters. Too often general guidances take the form of innocuous generalities.

Guidance proclaims the obvious, directing items to be played or not played, which any operator would instinctively handle correctly, and rarely suggesting stories or actions which have not already occurred to him. (But the same criticism is used to reason that guidance should *not* attempt to define things too finely.)

Guidance is misguided or unrealistic. The substance of policy directives (some based on decisions at the highest government level) may be criticized as inept or unworkable. Sometimes this may be a matter of timing: directives to "give wide play" to President Eisenhower's "atoms for peace" proposal were criticized as outdated and outweighted by events. Policy on the subject of the hydrogen bomb is said to lack effective propaganda appeal; it involves large complicated intellectual concepts less effective than the simple Soviet line, "ban it."

> When you're in a foreign office, you don't deal with flesh and blood. The closest you get to it is considering how many divisions a given country can put in the field—and there you don't think in terms of men, you think in terms of a big game. The more this attitude of high-level political thinking permeates a propaganda organization, the more it acts like that, the further removed it is from the general run of people in a country. It's taking a language talked by other people who talk in terms of foreign office abstractions, but it's not meaningful to the people who receive the media and must take the abstraction and personalize it in terms of their needs.

Directives are too broad, vague, and unclear. They can be interpreted differently by each operator.

> As it filters down from that broad directive it never gets filtered down to the point where it's realistic enough to be tangible. I don't think that it's a question of policy. I think it's a question of a more precise definition of policy and a more precise interpretation of policy.

IOP reacts too slowly to news. This is the perennial complaint of the news-oriented media, IPS and IBS, whose operators demand immediate guidance when an important news event or Communist charge comes up.

> When a situation like this arose a Communist would immediately come out with something. He wouldn't have to wait for orders from Moscow or even from the 9th Floor. He would know the line. But as a propagandist for the State Department, I am much more uncertain as to what it is going to be.

IOP operates like a committee; it takes a great deal of time to arrive at a decision. Operators themselves report a suspicion in IOP that their demands for fast guidance on news stories stem from the viewpoint of American newspaper-men striving to be out first with the news, although they deny that this is their purpose.

There is strong awareness of the need for speed on the part of IOP's news guidance personnel.

> A great many of these guidances are done before there are any policy statements, or in the complete absence of policy statements. We would never wait for a policy statement to come on a burning issue because our first duty is to the media to keep them as fully informed and as accurately as possible.

Yet guidance can often not be given quickly. Policy is set at a very high level. By the time it trickles down to the man who writes it, its influence may have diminished greatly. Guidances cannot be produced in a hurry when it is necessary to wait for the full text of a speech in order for a position to be formulated on an important and complicated issue.

There is continuous pressure on policy personnel from operators for simple formulations for which they can automatically determine what news items are usable. The policy man regards this as an impossible task: The continuous need for fast guidance can result in a breakdown of discipline. One reason why USIA does not have an organized system of implementing policy guidance is that it always "operates in haste." While the fast media complain that guidance is too slow, IOP is criticized in the library and motion picture services as a news-oriented organization uninterested in the problems of the "slow media."

News policy guidance should be concise, brief, and informative. It should be written informally in a standard form. A lengthy directive (of five or more pages) gets in the way of operations.

IOP is too prolific. Operators complain that they receive too much guidance.

> You get to a point of saturation. I get this much paper (10 inches thick) in here every day. Most of them I just glance at. I think there's a hell of a waste of government paper there.

But the opposite complaint is also heard: There is too little guidance (for particular areas and for the slow media).

Guidance is insufficiently coordinated, and sometimes even contradictory. This complaint is uttered by policy makers:

> We are constantly creating mechanisms for guidance that are unlinked. We lack circuits. We don't have a reticulated system of carrying out orders. We are always sending an embryo to do a man's job.

V

Targets

A PROPAGANDA PROGRAM with limited resources must address itself to only part of its potential audience. Although propagandists generally understand the value of selecting and concentrating effort on influential targets, there is in practice considerable approval of the philosophy of reaching people in the mass. The very nature of USIA's media operations determines, to a degree, the kind of audience that is reached. Those in activities like the library program find it especially difficult to characterize their targets. Desirable audiences may be defined in terms of their current or potential positions of political leadership, in terms of their capacity for influencing the public at large, or in terms of their existing political predispositions. USIA is internally divided as to both the merits and tactics of addressing Communists and anti-Communists, within and outside the Communist world.

WHOM SHOULD USIA BE REACHING? Wide differences of emphasis and theory exist within the organization on the subject of targeting, particularly on whether a mass audience is preferable to reaching an opinion-forming elite.

MASS AUDIENCE

Both in Washington and the field, many operators see their work as part of a mass program that reflects the will of Congress: "We are in a mass business. It's important to our program to reach as many people as we can." Limited to his own particular operational area, the man who works in Western Europe notes that mass media techniques make it possible to reach the whole mass of

Frenchmen or Germans, but that this extensive coverage is more difficult elsewhere in the world.

At the same time, the operator in Brazil, India, or rural Italy may also feel he should talk with "everybody," or at least everybody who is accessible. The very term "information program" assumes an appeal to people beyond the decision-making levels of government, to secure the broadest possible base of support for U. S. aims.

USIA should seek a mass audience where political decision making is diffused, where the leaders are dependent on articulate constituencies. This is true not only in Western Europe, with its far-reaching mass media, but also in a country like India, which is politically decentralized. By reaching the masses, operators hope to influence the leaders in every country.

> It used to be said that the Soviet government was not responsive to public opinion. But they're extremely sensitive to it, spending millions of dollars on jammers to keep our broadcasts out, and to censor the press. They probably spend more than any other government in the world in recognition of the importance of public opinion.

> The man in the street is still pretty powerful. The average American tends to think of people overseas, the people in Iran, let's say, as pretty powerless. But they can overthrow governments with greater effectiveness than we do through voting sometimes.

> The coffee-house listeners are the raw material of the mobs; we would not be doing our duty if we didn't make some attempt to meet them.

> You saw what the masses of India did. They got freedom from England. They *must* be important. There's considerable pressure from below. Ideally, you should reach ever-increasing numbers of people more often.

> In Latin America, the lower classes are getting the guns and doing the shooting.

> In Bolivia, trouble always starts with the miners.

These facts make it necessary for USIA to get its message to the most humble and illiterate. If the majority of the people in a given country favor the U. S., pro-American action will result, even if the ruling groups are anti-American.

Not every operator who thinks in terms of a mass program expresses this philosophy directly. He may imply this if he says, "Your principal audience is your average local individual." He may define his desired audience in such broad terms that almost no one is excluded:

> Women, youth, and labor are three of the most important targets.

> It is important to keep the middle classes and the ordinary workers friendly.

> It is just as important to reach workers as to reach intellectuals.

In any case, the operator tends to be a missionary who wants to spread the message he believes in to the widest possible audience. He may have little time to reflect on the nature of his audience and little accurate knowledge of whom his output is ultimately reaching: "The only thing we know about our audience is that it's a non-American audience and that the people can read."

Thus, the mass approach may arise by default—there is no clear-cut image of who targets are. Operators, in fact, sometimes comment that output need not be produced with an audience in mind. Its character may be determined by the subject matter or the techniques and tools at hand.

> The job almost describes itself once you get into it. You ask what should you shoot for and then will it work. You say this is a fat job or a thin job, it should be upsized or downsized, just by the feel of it. You suddenly realize that by doing this thus and thus you can cut it down eight pages. Or you might find it an advantage for the pace of a job to increase the page size for readability.

The distribution system may generate its own audience. Film distribution in France was at one time placed in the hands of a French organization that allegedly showed films without any apparent design or selection and that never provided a schedule. The distributor employed itinerant projectionists who were paid according to the number of people they got into the theater.

> It's a feeling we have to do everything in every country because we have everything for them to use. Take a country like India where a thin stratum of intellectuals on top basically make the political decisions. They may still be somewhere between 10 or 20 million people. For some reason which I never understood we take moving pictures and show them in the villages of India. We don't have enough movies for everybody in India so we show them to a few peasants who are not politically effective. Why do we make an effort to reach them? Why don't we try to reach the 20 million people and go after them? A new PAO gets there. He says, "What am I going to do? I come here and the mobile units are here and they keep sending me pictures."
>
> By the basic business of opening an office, the Public Affairs Officer automatically gets involved in certain operations. If you have got a library he's got to maintain it. He's got representation. He's got to mingle with the press and the government; he has got to mingle with the leaders. This is the way it's been done since OWI days and we are continuing to do it. If you ask them whom they are reaching, they have never thought of the answers. They're understaffed and they don't have time to examine what they are doing.

The very nature of the medium may determine its audience objectives. "All VOA operators are convinced that radio is a mass medium"—at least in the Free World. VOA is "the greatest mass medium employed by USIA." Therefore, it should be broadcasting to every area of the world as much as it can possibly absorb.

> You can't afford to tell a few million people to turn off their sets because you want to reach one special part of the audience. The opposite point of view is that you need to reach the leaders of the community and that they will reach the people. I say it's a very undemocratic point of view because this country believes that the people should decide.

SELECTIVE AUDIENCES

Critics of the mass approach use such metaphors as "narrowing the targets" and "sharpening the tools" to describe their objectives. Rifleshot, they point out, is more efficient than buckshot. They deny that USIA is in the "mass media business," and say that it is unwise to try to reach everyone (for both political and budgetary reasons). They maintain that public opinion has little influence on affairs of state.

Most countries in which USIA works are not democracies. The controlling groups determine national policy, and majority attitudes cannot change it. In Spain, for instance, it is of secondary interest for USIA to reach the workers because they are powerless to act. In colonial areas, such as French North Africa, political considerations often require USIA to ignore the native population and to concentrate on the European minority.

According to this view, in an area where illiteracy and poverty are rampant it is futile to reach the masses—"the guy with the loincloth in the jungle." USIA's financial resources are too limited.

> In Egypt you have got 20 million people of whom five percent are literate. One or two percent have any opinions on what happens in Egypt. As democrats we may deplore it, but we have to live with it. We would certainly be scattering our resources if we tried to win the good will of 20 million fellahin starting at the cradle with the hope that by the time they were 21 years old they would bring Egypt around to our way of thinking.

With the money USIA has at its disposal, it must direct its content to carefully defined priority targets. However, the size of the budget should not be allowed to determine the actual choice of priority targets.

> I have heard two principal arguments. One is that we have the techniques that we have learned from American advertising to attempt saturation that will reach right down to every village. The second one is a little more philosophical, that our hope lies in channeling a grass-roots moral revolution. We have got to get the man on the street to generate pressures that will rise up and suffuse the leaders. Neither of these arguments has impressed me too much because I think they're irrelevant on a $90 million budget. If we had $5 billion we could start arguing the merits of saturation. If we are going to be economical with what money we have the target has to be the correct one.

It is more efficient in democratic countries to influence the leaders of mass opinion than to go to the masses directly. Opinion molders can be identified. USIA's task is to determine who the most important leaders of thought are and funnel material to them. They will disseminate it to the rank and file. Even the masses of the Middle East may be reached indirectly through the "culturally top ten percent," making it unnecessary to have direct media contact with the people at large.

TARGET SELECTION CRITERIA

In deciding "whom to sock hard and whom to treat lightly," it is held that countries should be given priorities as targets in terms of the urgency of their political needs. Priority countries are those whose attitudes are of greatest importance to U. S. foreign policy objectives.

Also, target priorities represent areas of maximum program opportunity. But areas of program opportunity and political urgency do not necessarily coincide. (At the time Yugoslavia left the Cominform,[1] it represented a vital political target, but its doors were closed to U. S. information activity.)

Selecting targets involves such considerations as the urgency of the situation, the availability of funds and staff, and the focus of Communist propaganda.

The first step is to assess a society in terms of which groups make the decisions and help create the climate of opinion—a sociological, anthropological, and political analysis that identifies the political leaders who can help achieve immediate objectives and the leaders of mass opinion who can help win overall, long-range objectives.

Who are the principal people to reach? First are the members of the political elites that actually make national policy—a rather small group "who do the manipulating, the controlling." "Any given area, country, or city can be divided into 5 percent operators, 10 percent stooges, and 85 percent slobs."

There are also the literate and the politically conscious and the "top level policy people"—government officials, military leaders, and parliamentarians. In a country like Taiwan, where official U. S. contacts include many executives and military officials, it is important to maintain contacts with legislative and judicial figures who might not otherwise be reached.

Finally, there are the political "outs"; the "groups who may take over in a coup d'état"; junior officers in the military, labor leaders, and student groups ("the leaders of tomorrow"). These people must be approached cautiously so as not to arouse the ruling elite.

THE OPINION-FORMING ELITE

The theory behind concentrating attention on opinion leaders rests in the final analysis on conviction that public opinion is important. The argument for selective targets assumes a different complexion than the case made for addressing the political elite.

USIA must address itself to those in a position to influence others—to opinion leaders rather than to the masses directly.

[1] International Federation of Communist Parties, successor to the prewar Comintern. Yugoslavia left it in 1948.

We should think of our audiences as channels rather than as receptacles.

It is more important to reach one journalist than ten housewives or five doctors.

Those who are exposed to USIA output will disseminate it further. Even Communists can be reached through anti-Communist members of their families. Besides, a message that a local spokesman disseminates is more effective than a USIA broadside. His support lends credibility to the program.

If material is translated by USIA into terms that have specific particular meanings to the people that we want to reach ultimately, we may lose in such translations. However, a person who is a part of that culture and living there can do this well.

USIA targets include several distinct types of opinion molders:

1. Mass media operators—publishers, editors, writers, and radio and film people.
2. Directly influential persons—individuals whose views are considered authoritative by large numbers of people with whom they are in actual contact: educators, labor leaders, religious personages, including village priests or tribal headmen, and persons of high social position.
3. The cultural elite—those persons of prestige who set styles and are regarded as models: intellectuals, artists, writers, "professionals."

I would just as soon have a million intellectuals with our subtle propaganda being drummed into them every day in the year than ten million nonintellectuals hearing our less subtle propaganda, because they will get it from the others. I want the eggheads. If you can sell a line to them, you don't have to worry about selling a line to the people.

In backward areas, accessibility to a mass medium in itself may determine influence. The man who can read or who owns a radio is ipso facto a source of information and opinion.

THE ARGUMENT AGAINST SELECTIVITY

Those who oppose selective targeting may stress national differences, and point out that selectivity may be advisable for some countries but not for all. For example, if public opinion is a relatively minor factor in bringing a country to the U. S. side, it should receive less attention. If the people of a country are "subservient," only government officials should be targets; elsewhere, the rural villages may be a strong political factor.

In a country such as Kuwait there is one guy that lays down the law. Or in Iraq. And in Ethiopia. One man runs the country. And his cousins. At this point you just have the problem of getting to the guy that makes the decisions and persuading him. At the other end of the spectrum, as in France, there is a very large constituency upon which the leader depends. In France, it's worthwhile perhaps to run a media program to reach the constituents.

"The whole program should be aimed at the whole people." USIA should not worry about designating specific target groups in each individual country, since a country consists of people, all of whom have different reactions. If target groups are designated too specifically, much worthwhile activity may be precluded.

When the number of targets is limited, the gain in efficiency may be offset by inadequate coverage of secondary target groups. In a going country program, abandoning the bottom three of five target groups is often difficult or impractical and does not necessarily provide the manpower or money to concentrate more on the key people in the other two groups.

> When you have got a film program in South Africa, it's not good to say we will concentrate on the Afrikaner and not lend it to show to English-speaking people or to natives. If you have a library program and people call up, you don't ask them what group they belong to and say, "Sorry, we are not concentrating on you. We are concentrating on somebody else."

> There are a lot of people in this shop who see things in diplomatic terms. It sounds good to be talking to intellectual leaders. You can't by radio convince an intellectual leader of a target area of anything, while you can reach the masses. I would rather beam our Arabic broadcast at the crowd in one single coffee house.

"The so-called leaders do not lead," say the extreme opponents of targeting. Targets should not be limited to public-opinion molders. It is an undemocratic philosophy.

Concentrating on government officials is futile and politically dangerous; they may be out of office in a few months. Often the "leaders" selected as targets have no following.

> This business of talking to leaders in Asia, Europe, and Latin America is just a myth. Whom would you reach in France? Nobody trusts anybody. In my opinion, the only way is to talk to everybody.

The real leader may be a barber, a cobbler, an eloquent peasant, a priest, or a doctor. Where news travels by word of mouth, the most influential man in the community may be illiterate. Since these people are not distinguishable from the rest of the mass, it is necessary to go to the public at large.

> You don't hand a leaflet to a member of the Bundestag in Germany and expect that to sway his vote one way or the other. You distribute a million of them in Germany and hope they will have some effect.

COMBINING RIFLE AND BUCKSHOT

Not everyone in USIA takes a position for or against selective targeting. Some deem it desirable to reach both leaders and the mass—both the majority and the controlling groups. Such a middle path may entail a judicious combination of approaches.

> It's the job of the Agency to influence the ruling groups or those who are about to rule—the small groups. If the majority of the people are pro-U. S. and the ruling groups are anti, then you have the course open to you to make the ruling group pro. This can be attempted by getting the majority of the people to create or wield such efforts as to get the ruling group to change its attitude *or* to directly propagandize the smaller group to get this change.

> In the Near East and Far East, films are the principal mass medium. People can't read; however, we are not making films for masses of people. We are always making them for a target group. It may be that a village audience in a country can bring so much pressure that it is important. In another country you would only be interested in hitting government officials because the people are so subservient. I would say that film was a mass medium. It reaches large groups of people. I don't think you can specialize films except those that we do have as specialized pictures.

In the publications program also, the medium may dictate the audience assignment. A pamphlet can have the same effect on the semiliterate as on the government leader. A columnist should be understood by the ordinary person, but he should express himself in such a way that intellectuals with specialized interests are also interested. A magazine article reprinted abroad will attract the same type of reader as would read the original article in an American magazine. But a magazine that appeals to intellectuals in one country may appeal to the masses somewhere else. Thus, the operator must seek a common denominator, since his output will be used in many different places.

Since the Wireless File is intended both for reproduction in the press and for direct distribution to opinion leaders, operators must have both the opinion leader and mass reader in mind.

CRITIQUES OF TARGETING PRACTICE

USIA's targeting procedure is criticized for paying lip service to principle and for overlooking the limitations of mass media.

> People's gonads are too active. They insist on having 25 million people seeing their movies or seeing their pamphlets when 25 would be just as good. There is an emphasis on statistics, the number of people who see something or other. The opposition to the idea of the priority audience stems from an unwillingness to do any thinking—a fear of being constricted. You see you are trying to be all things to all men, and if you have a big broad beautiful set of priority audiences, anything you do is in line of duty, from drinking coffee all night with the Sheikh of Tabruz to addressing club women at the university.

Targets are frequently defined so broadly that they are meaningless. (Examples: "labor" and "youth.") Political and sociological factors are insufficiently analyzed in target selection.

A country paper [2] that couldn't be beat: The primary target group was all literates and semiliterates. The secondary target group was all illiterates and the tertiary target was all others. That amounted to two or three percent, and no one ever knew what they were.

I once saw a study of who comes into the library. One of the PAO's conclusions was that he had reached almost everybody in his target groups. 95 percent of the patrons were people listed in the country paper as target groups. Considering whom he had as target groups I can't imagine who the other five percent could have been.

Everybody made up his own listening audience to support his own prejudices. Nobody knew what the listening audience was. Down in Latin America they said, "Write your programs for the taxi drivers," but there are no taxi drivers in Latin America. The only people who heard us were intelligent. The possession of a radio was an economic badge.

Agency personnel let their own peculiar area knowledge or prejudices interfere with thoughtful solution of targeting problems.

It is suggested that it may be better to forget about targeting altogether.

The average program is not written with the spiritual image of the audience before the producers' eyes. If you ask the witty operator whom he is writing for, he will say, "for the Congress of the United States, and the Congress will like it if we have lots of letters." It is easier to write a program for a mass audience than to write a difficult program for a specialized or elite audience.

LIBRARY "TARGETS"

The USIS information centers around the world are heavily staffed by professional librarians who think in terms of service. Their thoughts on the subject reveal how media may determine "targets" rather than the other way around. The United States needs as many friends as it can get; libraries must therefore reach as many people as possible. Although ideally the program should not be reaching a mass audience, the nature of library activity makes it impossible to target with precision.

We don't mind their coming in. That's the purpose of display windows and hand-out bulletins—to get them to come in, but our targets take more than an open door and a welcome to everybody who comes by. You have to go out and get them.

Centers are not and should not be public libraries in the American service sense, but mass attendance cannot be discouraged. (This would contradict the concept of a free library.) The American library open-shelf tradition is impor-

[2] The "country paper" for each nation to which USIA output is directed represents the basic statement of political problems, objectives, and targets. In the Agency's Organization Manual, the Country Plan is described as "a definitive statement . . . of U. S. psychological objectives, tasks, themes, and audience groups in a particular country, supported by a detailed situation analysis."

tant to maintain. Books must be available on a wide range of subjects, appealing to all types of people.

> You can't be that selective and still maintain credibility. You can pack a library with works that would appeal only to certain intellectual groups, but you cannot make the horse drink once you get it to the water.

Children are important targets in their own right.

> We had a room where the children had come and they could take the books off the shelf and read them. It had never happened before and the children filed in. We had a small room and one time we had 250 children there in one afternoon. After that had been going on for a while, the National Library started a children's library, but they didn't lend books, they just had a reading room. In all school libraries the library consists of some cases with glass doors and they are locked. The books are arranged in the order they were received. . . . The library situation there being what it is, the children are a fruitful field because pretty soon they are university students, pretty soon they are adults.

> It was our feeling generally in any kind of book program that the earlier you reach children with any sort of ideology or information, particularly in cultural matters, the better results you have.

Others counter this view. The development of a children's program is a long-range project that can do little to advance USIA objectives.

> I have run into quite a few librarians who try to see to it as a first step that they have a good kiddy's corner running first thing, which makes no sense in many cases. . . . The minute we start pulling the kids in off the street to teach them to read English, the time, money and space spent on that is very definitely wasted. To begin with the two objectives are mutually incompatible. You can't run the library with the atmosphere of a center for thought and for the educated class while you're having cut-outs in the corner for a bunch of kids. The two cannot be done together. You have to have an aura of scholarship in which scholars or people who fancy themselves scholars work.[3]

It is recognized that the library program uses as source material publications intended for a wide American audience and not suitable for any explicit targeting that would require special printed materials.

> We are operating a program with very clear objectives, but the materials with which we are shooting are aimed at very different targets. We have to rely on the output of the American publishing industry. No publisher in the world could publish a book that might convince everybody. I think the only way we would have the materials we need would be to go into book printing ourselves.

Critics of the mass approach argue that it is wasteful and point out that it is essential to reach leaders of public opinion.

---

[3] In a report on Brazil by Raymond L. Scheele and Thomas L. Blair, "the investigators saw workers sewing, making cellophane paper bags for holding candy for a children's party, drinking refreshments, wrapping presents, knitting, and loafing while the borrowers were waiting to be served."

One of our librarians from India came back the other day. Her information center is the only public library in a city which is one of the biggest cities in the world. I hoped while she was here we were able to orient her into the thought that her object, for which she is being paid, is not to serve as the only public library in that city. She still has her targets and her library has very specific jobs to do.

In many parts of the Far East and Near East the institutions are for all practical purposes the only freely available public libraries to the educated—Indonesia, Pakistan, etc., where he can go to consult all sorts of materials—it's true by American authors—and see the workings and administration of a democratic library system. We deliberately try not to run public libraries. We try not to discourage them from using the centers but to point up the use of these centers by the opinion-molding, decision-making elements of the society.

Another viewpoint is that targeting is unnecessary. The very nature of the information center as a media service concentrates its impact upon the educated, and hence most desirable, targets. Book readers are a worthwhile target audience per se. They retain ideas better than any other media audience and spread them.

You get those who are the cream of the crop, those who are well informed, educated to read a foreign language.

Among my basic assumptions is that people who read books carry their ideas more effectively into a general social-political communications intercourse of a country than people who only listen to radio programs and read newspapers. I don't think a radio broadcast influences a soul.

Books are some sort of symbol of prestige in so many parts of the world. If the guy's got a book in his pocket, he's somebody who can read.

This is not in any sense a mass medium. The number of people who read books is low. The number of people who use our centers is lower. These groups coincide pretty well with the opinion-molding groups in a given area.

Library users have an intellectual curiosity that makes them particularly desirable targets. Similarly, persons receptive to musical activities are leaders in cultural and political life.

The location of an information center can determine its audience. Opinions diverge on whether the program should concentrate on political capitals, major urban areas, or the smaller towns that need libraries the most.

With your reference service you reach a higher percentage of highly influential people. We have a branch in Copacabana. I suppose the people we reach there are the idle rich, tourists. You can reach people at any level depending on the emphasis in the service you offer. The library we had in Amsterdam was deliberately placed near a poor residential neighborhood in order to attract kids in what is supposed to be a Communist voting district.

Book translation can be geared to targets by selecting appealing titles. Books suitable for translation have a specialized, intellectual appeal, and present a dilemma for those who prefer a mass approach.

We try to find books that will interest the largest possible audience, as so many of the books are not written for the lower level. . . . The books that are most useful to us program-wise usually are the poorest sellers. They don't attract the mass readers; they don't attract a commercial publisher. If you run down the list of our titles they are not—the majority of them—are not aimed at the reader of moderate intelligence, they're aimed at the opinion molder.

In selecting a book to translate, its popularity with the mass audience must be weighed against the reactions of the elite. A discussion on translating Horatio Alger into Thai points this up:

We said this was pretty corny. It helps their objectives for the following reason: it did show to these very primitive peoples at the lowest levels of literacy that poor boy makes good. Our objections were that it was so corny that any sophisticated audience would just laugh it out of court.

A similar problem exists with respect to selecting books for libraries. The division of opinion is clear-cut. Selective stocking makes it possible to concentrate on key targets. Centers should be stocked with books of interest or consequence for them. In general, however, technical books attract less desirable readers than those on social science and political subjects. Different books belong in different USIS libraries. There is no book that everyone would agree was a good selection for every place in the world.

Libraries have a responsibility to cover a full range of information of all sorts. Selective stocking is a bad procedure. This view stems from the traditions of librarianship. Any selective stocking of books by content, to promote selective targeting, makes the library less acceptable to the foreign audience. (Contradiction: "You never are going to get a wide selection of American books in any foreign language." Therefore, by implication, library patrons will never be aware that coverage is incomplete.)

POLITICAL CONSIDERATIONS IN TARGET SELECTION

Targets may be defined in terms of political groupings and beliefs as well as in terms of power and influence groups.

Parallel to the view that USIA should speak to the broad masses throughout the world is a political formula that covers everyone.

We hope to win over those who are on the fence and to keep favorable those who are already on the U. S. side, but we would also like to win over those on the other side.

USIA should not waste effort on the hard-core extremists or anti-Communists, but there are very few people at either extreme (so by implication, almost everybody is worth reaching).

USIA operators often see their audience as the same people the Communists reach—as people who are politically unconvinced. Analogous to the view of an audience without firm convictions of its own is the picture of the sophisticated opinion leader who wants to make his own evaluations of foreign policy moves, who likes to know things from the inside. He studies the full texts of both Soviet and U. S. statements before he draws his conclusions, and is not easily influenced by "propaganda."

According to another theory, USIA reaches an entirely different group of people than the Soviets do; and hence there is no "battle for men's minds"—at least in the Free World. Behind the Iron Curtain, USIA unavoidably reaches an audience under Communist propaganda pressure.

> The battle for men's minds does not exist. The Russians are reaching one group of people and we are reaching another group of people. I think the assumption probably is the opposite. If there is a stereotype it's probably of some mythical person overseas turning over in his mind our claims and Soviet claims and trying to decide between them.

COMMUNISTS AS A TARGET GROUP

Two basically different perceptions of the Communist Party exist within USIA. One is that communism is a conspiracy and that the conspirators are implacable enemies on whom any propaganda effort is wasted. The second is that communism is a mass movement with popular roots whose adherents can be influenced to change their allegiance.

Those who feel Communists should not be a target argue that this is a hostile and unresponsive audience that cannot be converted. Communists are "militant," "died-in-the-wool," "diehard," "hard-core," "dedicated," and "convinced." Communist sympathizers are just as dangerous as the hard-core members, so USIA should not "go after" them either.

Those who feel that most Communists are salvageable tend to more broadly define who "Communists" are; that is, they are either men at the highest levels of the party organization in the Soviet Union or they are the "zealous agitators and activists in other countries who are thoroughly persuaded that they are right." Those operators who want to reach "everybody" would address the Communist card-carrier as well as "the guy on the fence who doesn't know which way to jump." Some operators even feel that Communists should be the *prime* target for output and effort, particularly in a country where Communists have substantial voting strength: "Obviously, if we can get to the opposition, that's where the spearhead should be."

A group should be singled out as a high-priority target if Communist organizing or propaganda efforts have been directed at it. (Italian workers and Indian students are important targets precisely because of the strength of communism in their countries.)

If possible, contact should be made with actual Communist groups—such as scientists or artists who are sent on trips to the West from behind the Iron Curtain. Unfortunately, however, USIA field personnel are inhibited from making face-to-face Communist Party contacts.

There are, of course, degrees of involvement among adherents of any political movement, and not all Communists are true believers. Moreover, Communists use front organizations. So it is important that USIA targeting efforts differentiate between Communist leaders and the masses of Communist voters, sympathizers, or even Party members. Not much headway can be made with Communist labor leaders, but rank-and-file unionists, who may act and vote Communist, are not necessarily Communists themselves and may be very interested in USIA output.

The number of people who vote for Communist candidates is far greater than the actual Party members. Only a hard core of Communist voters in France or Italy, for example, are true Communists. The others do not know what communism really is and are not necessarily anti-American or pro-Soviet. They can be influenced.

But a distinction must be drawn between leaders and followers at any point below the Soviet Politburo level.

Many local Communist leaders in Western Europe are not doctrinaire and respond to their followers' wishes. Thus, even members of the Communist hierarchy can be influenced—if not directly by USIA, then by U. S. economic aid for their countries or through co-nationals whom they trust.

"NEUTRALISTS" AS TARGETS

While few USIA operators disagree that it is important to talk to people who are neither pro-American nor pro-Soviet, not all of them want the uncommitted listener or "fencesitter" to have top priority: "Time should not be wasted either on trying to convince those who cannot be convinced or on convincing those who are already convinced."

On the other hand, talking to those who are hostile may convince a middle group of comparatively open-minded persons with little extra effort. This group of "neutralists" may overlap with the Communist sympathizers, and both groups may respond to the same arguments: "The most important targets for USIA are those who are not convinced but can be convinced with a little effort."

In most countries, neutralism is especially strong among opinion leaders and the intellectual elite, both of which are critical targets. But just what is the neutralist position?

One view is that neutralism is a lack of position brought about through weariness, ignorance, distrust, disenchantment, or fear. For example:

Europeans are sick to death of contributing to defense structures, paying taxes, and so on.

In Asia, people cannot be identified as friends or enemies. The prevailing attitude is one of ignorance or apartness from the Cold War struggle.

They think Americans lack integrity and maturity in political affairs.

The worldwide reaction against propaganda has taken the form of a psychological self-defense in neutralist form.

There's an aversion to being dragged into a world war by either of the two giants, the U. S. and Russia.

Some people are neutralists basically because they have no guts. In every society there's the kind of person who is basically yellow, who won't fight for what he believes in and would much rather keep his mouth shut, stay out of trouble.

In the Arab countries, people are neutralist in the sense that they are tempted to do nothing rather than to go to the pro-U. S. side. Indians are neutralists in the sense that they can go to either one side or the other.

Neutralism is also regarded as a position. Neutralists think they can avoid responsibilities or advance their interests by avoiding commitment.

In small countries people want to let the two giants slug it out.

They want no more of Eisenhower than of Malenkov.[4]

Or neutralists are patriots pursuing an independent course of national self-interest.

The more reliable allies in case of an open conflagration are to be found in the so-called neutralist camp. I don't mean that the neutralists are all potential allies, but among the neutralists there are, and not necessarily among the expressed pro-Americans. The neutralists are the patriots. I am personally convinced that these are our allies who always go where they believe there is a higher chance for national survival, and I think that their chances for national survival will inevitably lead them to the side of the United States. These people can also read what is happening in Eastern Europe, and they are the audience whom we have to reach with the whole information program.

It follows from this view that neutralists can be reasoned with and persuaded of "the necessity of the American way in politics."

PRO-AMERICANS AS A TARGET GROUP

Many operators believe that it is futile to direct effort at people who are already convinced of the U. S. position. Friendly countries free of Communist influence such as England or Australia should not be principal targets.

We are wasting a hell of a lot of money and effort overseas working with people who are of the same opinion as we are, pro-democratic clubs—anti-Communist leagues. They already think the way we do. We ought to be working with groups that are doubtful and infiltrate Communist groups the same way Communists do.

[4] First Soviet premier after the death of Stalin.

The people there already like us and speak our language. They are fully aware of Soviet ideology and imperialism and need no convincing on that subject.

But USIA tends to select audiences that are already favorable to it. People who are friendly are more accessible and come to USIA for reinforcement, guidance, direction, and information. There are few curiosity seekers.

My view is that we should be letting slide, if we have to, those persons who are already on our side. But that's the hardest group to get rid of, the ones who are always knocking at your door for more motion pictures on America—the people who are already sold. The wavering ones, the people who are already on the other side of the fence, are the ones who never show up. There's the problem of the man in the field.

Similarly, Communists don't listen to VOA, except for professional reasons. Readers of anti-Communist papers are already anti-Communist.

This position is not universally accepted within the Agency, however.

My own feeling is that we are not simply talking to our friends. We just don't have that many friends.

I know of no instructions where the tone of any media product is predicated on the assumption that the people we are reaching are favorably disposed toward us to begin with. On the other hand, I know of no out-and-out examples where media products assume that the audience is going to be unfriendly.

There are divergent views on whether people who use USIA libraries are, primarily, already favorable. The centers are used by people who are not pro-American. If a Communist researcher wanted to get information to back up his charge against the U. S., he could very well use a USIA library.

There have been deliberate efforts made to supply materials to people known to be apathetic or antipathetic, perhaps in a roundabout way. If some member of the government is known to have certain avocational interests we can send him a book on his avocational interest if it comes in, rather than on his vocational interest. In my opinion the one thing in common that users of these libraries have is not necessarily friendliness toward the U. S. but interest in it or in some aspect of American accomplishment.

Those who believe pro-Americans are a major target point out that they are a channel to the unconvinced, so they should be given facts and arguments to fortify their stand.

We have to assume that the people for whom we are writing are favorably inclined to the United States. To a very great extent what we are doing is not winning them over to the American point of view, but strengthening their convictions and giving them thoughts and arguments which they in turn present to others who may not be so favorably inclined toward the United States. I don't think we are going to persuade many Communists to become anti-Communists directly. I don't think there are many Communists who read the *American Reporter* in India. But the people who do read these publications mix with others who are not so convinced of the American position.

Even if the users are friendly the program provides them with ammunition to arouse interest in those elements of the population with whom they come into contact and to counteract unfriendly ideas.

It is better to have English spokesmen for the American cause than have Americans speaking by themselves. If the British can be won over to the U. S. point of view, they will reinforce us and disseminate our message.

Favorable convictions must be reinforced.

We have to get people all over the world who are already passive on our side to act against the evil.

In the process of making our friends more stable friends, we inevitably increase our collective strength for whatever purpose it serves later.

Especially within the broadcasting service, the opinion is expressed that the VOA has overly emphasized its output to Soviet-dominated areas. It is in the Free World (rather than among the friendly listeners in the Soviet orbit) that the United States is in danger of losing its friends and should concentrate its broadcasts.

The Iron Curtain desks have set the tone of the place to a very unfortunate degree. One of the effects is to make it sort of axiomatic around here that the main audience is the Communist audience. Of course the Free World desk heads would disagree with that, but they usually don't come out and say so.

I think it's a pity that the Voice should ever be made to feel confined to Soviet-dominated areas. An enormous group in the Free World that needs the Voice is being denied the Voice. What do you think the BBC would give to have 10,000,000 listeners in America? Why shouldn't we invest time and money to talk to the English people? The solidarity of the Free World is the only quality by which it will survive, and that means understanding by a great many people, and overlooking this is overlooking an opportunity.

THE AUDIENCE IN THE COMMUNIST WORLD

VOA's great asset is that radio is the only medium for reaching people behind the Iron Curtain, their only free source of news.

One group pictures the audience as fiercely anti-Communist. (It listens at a risk, under conditions of great fear and extreme secrecy and with great penalties attached. Scripts must be written for the terrified people who literally listen under the rug.) Others proclaim that listening is as widespread and relatively open as in France under the Nazi occupation. (The typical VOA listener in Eastern Europe is "a wary but, inside his home, relatively open listener"; he is able to discuss the contents of broadcasts with his trusted friends.)

A third view is that in a totalitarian society—precisely because listening is a "dangerous adventure" made even more difficult by jamming—there is no great readiness to listen to foreign broadcasts. (Broadcasts can have little effect. VOA has merely "nuisance value" behind the Iron Curtain.)

The Russian desk is crazy to assume that it has a mass audience. The bulk of the Russian population lives in the country. If he's an individual peasant he doesn't have a radio. What he might have is a wired set that doesn't play the Voice of America. He's a member of a *kolkhoz*. They might have a tube radio, but it would be very unlikely that anyone there would be listening to the Voice of America. You know how people live in the cities, in the apartment houses, several families to a room. How could they listen to the Voice of America there?

VOA is heard by certain Communists behind the Iron Curtain. At one time or another, broadcasts must directly address them or take them into account. They are either official monitors, "opportunists who like to know what is happening," or Communists who have begun to experience doubt.

Some VOA personnel believe that broadcasts to the Communist world should sow seeds of doubt among top officials and Communist intellectuals. They see some opportunity for shaking their faith and arousing fear about the stability of their regime and their own fate in the event of ultimate liberation.

You do maybe have high officials or members of the military or people whose job it is to monitor our broadcasts, so they listen. I think that many military people listen. I'm convinced that in submarines, in military installations and airplanes that they listen. Then I am sure there are a lot of high-ranking officials who listen and then there are people who have to listen because they are monitors and that's their job. And those are the people we have to reach. Those people who listen to the Voice are great cynics. Those are the ones we should envisage as our audience.

But in directing output to the Communist Party hierarchy or members, operators must keep in mind the fact that the anti-Communist audience is also listening and should leave no room for them to infer that the Communists are more important to VOA than faithful, democratic listeners.

When there is a crisis in the Communist Party, we try to speak even to the Communists to weaken their loyalties to the regime and we say so, so that we would not offend our faithful democratic audience. Because this is naturally quite a problem, how to speak to the Communists, trying to at least mentally corrupt them and not to appear to the democratic audience as being without principles. We must avoid the picture that a Communist could be for us more interesting than a faithful democrat in an unimportant position, that we prefer Kravchenko [5] to somebody who has never been stupid or opportunistic, who has never been a Communist. But in my opinion our role is to overburden the Communist parties not only by helping the democratic resistance but by weakening them from the inside. This is why in particular moments of crisis we try to deepen the doubts of the Communist rank and file toward the regime.

In my opinion this cannot be and should not be addressed to the Communists only. The American government must speak to the people who are friendly to them. If we would like to engage in an operation where we address ourselves to the Communist rank and file, then it should be done by covert methods, by a secret transmitter that

[5] Igor Kravchenko was a Soviet defector, author of *I Chose Freedom*. New York: Charles Scribner's Sons, 1946.

would never be identified as the Voice of America. It should be done by other than open methods, though I admit it should be done.

The assessment of Soviet vulnerabilities is the subject of a fundamental schism within the Agency. The stated position of the government on this matter, adopted by the National Security Council, is that the Soviet regime is firmly established. It is the only government that the overwhelming majority of the Soviet population has known for its entire lifetime and is generally accepted by them.

I don't know how many convinced Communists there are. I think there are much fewer than most of us think, but they have a vested interest in the system which is frequently rationalized and justified in terms of the mission of Russia and Russian patriotism. It's been there for 37 years; it made out pretty well in the last war. It's there probably to stay for some time. If it's there the individual in the apparatus might as well serve the state in a manner which will give him as many of the good things of life as he can obtain, even though he may not like many of the features of the system. Actually he doesn't have a great range of choice. He can't get out. If he should somehow be able to get out, his friends and relatives are subject to reprisals. He can't retire to a farm in Vermont and cultivate his garden. He's there in the apparatus and he's got to keep going. So he keeps going.

Several corollaries stem from this basic thesis:

1. People in the Soviet Union are concerned with their own jobs, status problems, and other private interests rather than with world political issues.
2. They would not welcome revolution and upheaval that might interfere with these private interests.
3. Even among disaffected elements, Russian nationalism is a strong motive force with which VOA output must reckon.
4. Certain top leaders are, in effect, national leaders and command wide popular respect, in spite of grumbling about the regime.
5. It is silly to assume that there are millions of people waiting for liberation in the Soviet Union or China.
6. There is an elite bureaucratic group making up 10 to 20 percent of the population who have "no place else to go" and are firmly committed to the regime.

Many operators, however, feel very differently. They believe that the masses of people in the Soviet Union are against the regime and are waiting for the day of liberation.

Buttressing this position is the fact that millions of prisoners are in Soviet concentration camps. (Thus, a sizable percentage of the population bitterly hates the regime.) There is widespread disaffection among the peasants, and although a large part of the population is "neutral" in sentiment and concerned only with the problems of everyday living, they too have grievances. And efforts of the government to eliminate contact and communications with the outer world belie the theory that the people accept the regime.

These differing political assumptions lead to different definitions of the broadcasting target audience. One view is that with listening as difficult as it is, VOA output should interest the widest possible audience. The masses of the people in the Soviet Union listen to VOA insofar as they have the facilities to do so. There is a large audience for shortwave broadcasting in the Soviet Union because the great distances there make this the only feasible form of radio. To the extent that the Russian language program is designed to appeal to a particular target group, that is the group it will reach (by implication, it is possible to reach them).

A dissenting view is that it is impossible to reach the Russian masses. It follows from this premise that VOA should aim at actual dissident groups.

> There are 15 million people in the Soviet slave labor camps. Let's say each of them has three people who are close to him, mamma, papa, maybe a wife or child. They don't like it. That makes 45 million people who hate their guts. Let me broadcast to them and them alone, and I can guarantee that we can keep them off balance.

In contrast to the differences in appraisals of the Soviet audience, VOA operators agree that the people of the Eastern European satellites universally oppose their Communist regimes and hate the Russians. The historical friendship between the United States and these countries has survived the years of Communist rule. VOA's problem therefore is to determine not what the audience believes but "how far in their subconscious they have pushed their democratic beliefs."

This audience is in a state of emotional agitation. Soviet pressure is such a tremendous factor in the lives of Eastern Europeans that they are unable to think in rational terms about their predicament. The satellite audience is heavily politically-minded, and attention paid to VOA broadcasts reflects a desire to hear an expression of its own strong feelings.

A minority feels that the satellite audience is "on the fence." It includes many young persons who have never known democracy and whom the Communists have made strong efforts to win over. Life under communism is so drab, monotonous, and restrictive that young people cannot possibly escape boredom. They are no more vulnerable to Communist blandishments than their elders.

As time goes on the audience cannot escape a certain amount of contamination by communism. It will become somewhat "cynical and tough-minded" about the possibilities of liberation. It has already reached the saturation point with respect to propaganda. Already a good percentage of the audience consists of opportunists. Pressures to accommodate to the regime will increase.

VI

The Fight Against Communism

OPPOSING COMMUNISM both as an ideological movement and as a political force represents an important objective for many of USIA's propagandists. However, very different themes and tactics must be used in opposing communism in non-Communist and in Communist countries, and in dealing with non-Communist and Communist audiences. The Voice of America, broadcasting to the Soviet Union and its allies, faces difficult and unresolved issues that reflect the ambiguity of national purpose, for example on the liberation of Eastern Europe. Communist propagandists enjoy advantages over USIA, although they also have weaknesses that can be exploited. There is no unanimity within the Agency on how and when to respond to Communist attacks against the United States.

BECAUSE USIA USES many different media and reaches a widely varying audience, the ratio of its "positive" to "negative" (or anti-Communist) output is not fixed. But in the eyes of many persons in the Information Agency, the core task of USIA is to expose Communist atrocities, falsehoods, and injustices.

The media respond quickly to urgent field requests for anti-Communist materials and to every opportunity to "beat the Communists over the head." At the Voice of America, anti-Communist scripts are reported to be the most popular because they provide a common denominator. Anti-Communist propaganda is the same everywhere, whereas "Americana" have to be slanted for the target audience.

ANTI-COMMUNIST THEMES

In fighting communism, several arguments may be pursued:

1. The Communist idea is fallacious. A primary objective is to attack its basic concepts, symbols, and techniques. To make it appear unattractive as a philosophy, critical disbelief in the intellectual validity of communism must be induced. Communism must be portrayed as "not only deadly but ridiculous." The class struggle is not the whole answer to the world's economic ills.
2. Communism destroys human dignity and rights. Prick the conscience of the world. Alert everyone to Communist atrocities, such as the torture of American prisoners in Korea. Point up "crimes against humanity, perversion of truth, breaking of men's minds, violation of international conventions, and crime against natural law." "Show that since 1917, the implacable purpose of the Communist rulers has been to reduce all men to the level of animals."
3. The Communist system does not work. The difficulties that Communist regimes encounter should be stressed, particularly in output to anti-Communist areas.
4. Communism is aggressive. In exposing its imperialist ambitions, a parallel should be drawn with historical invasions that are familiar locally.
5. Communism menaces cherished institutions, values, and loyalties. People who are relatively unaffected by communism should begin to feel that if it did touch them, it would mean "the end of the things they are hoping for." (USIA scored in South America by reprinting an uncomplimentary biographical sketch of Bolivar that appeared in the *Soviet Encyclopedia*.)
6. Communism is alien. Counter the impression that Communist leaders and movements are indigenous nationalists.

In Asia, Ho Chi Minh is accepted for what he professes to be, as leader of Vietnamese nationalism. It becomes an automatic reaction to use material that counteracts that impression.

We had a very successful campaign in the Philippines where there was a great deal of support for the Huks.[1] We put out a series of films where we just identified the Huks with the Russian Communists. Every Huk in the films wore a hammer and sickle arm band, even though I doubt if any Huk guerrilla has ever been captured wearing such a uniform. I'm convinced that every loyal Filipino thinks that's the way the Huks are dressed. . . . We changed the film characterization of this international spy, this international Communist, by pointing out that he could be made more international, that emphasis was to be placed on the fact that he was an international Communist. He was originally just identified as a Communist. To people in a barrio in the Philippines the Communist might not represent an external threat but if you make him an international threat, then he may be identified.

[1] The Huks (short for Hukbalahaps) were a Communist guerrilla movement that threatened the pro-American Philippine regime in the early 1950s.

Since a hard-hitting anti-Communist item will be used only by friendly editors anyway, it should be stated in the strongest possible terms:

> We're trying to reach an elite group that reads newspapers in India, and we are trying to do that through the editors. The [Soviet] slave labor thing is our side of the story. My theory would be some of the editors are going to say, "U. S. propaganda, to hell with it." Those would be the antis and some of the neutralists. Some are going to take the material we give them, and they're going to publish it as is. Others may publish it with various reservations so that it doesn't look like a propaganda message at all.
>
> My theory says that since these friendly ones are the only ones who are even going to consider using it at all, we can form it more readily than if we aimed it at friendly, neutral, and hostile all at once. In other words, we can give them a stronger dose of propaganda to begin with. The hostile ones are not going to believe it anyway. The friendly ones are going to take a stronger dose and are going to talk to their friends about it and in that way we will reach the others through their friends and not directly.

But the exact opposite is also voiced: Communism must be attacked subtly. "Blatant" material sent to a neutralist country (like Indonesia) will not be read by local editors, and therefore will not be redisseminated.

> I think as a result of the McCarthy hearings and other developments here and various approaches taken by some of our former officials, we are tending, and this is all a matter of degree, toward more blatant, more patent propaganda, a little closer to the name-calling technique. The more obvious propaganda has been taken out since the Jackson Report, the more obvious insertion of material, the more patent effort to knock down.

Direct attacks on communism do not help achieve USIA objectives.

> The hard-hitting and anti-Communist approach just doesn't pay off. The more subtle you do it the better it does. The United States always comes off better when it does something in an educational way than in a horn-tooting way.

According to one report, those who have served abroad think that hard-hitting anti-Communist activity is ineffective or even detrimental. "The best way to fight communism is not by a direct knock-down, drag-out, frontal attack." "Wild charges unsubstantiated by facts or documentation" will be self-defeating. Anti-Communist output has no place in contexts where people do not want it, for example in India or Finland.

Fighting communism is "an expert's job." A problem arises because many Americans who know communism best have had past associations with the Communist movement and are security risks. Yet, because of domestic attitudes, USIA must protect and defend the best informed, militantly anti-Communist operators.

> Information and propaganda have very, very little to do with security. There is no security factor involved in the job of persuasion. If I can get tomorrow a top Communist to use an argument that I have injected into his system without his knowing it, I have violated every rule of security, but I have done a job of propaganda.

It is charged that the Agency does not know enough about the adversary.

We are doing less than an adequate job, because collectively the group is not sufficiently informed of the actual nature, and ethos, springs of action, tactics, and
strategy of communism. In talking about communism I can give the impression that
I'm a great expert because I'm fighting it every day. But looking at it with a little
detachment, it might be fun to ask in confidence, "How many Communists do you
know?" If the people in the Agency were to answer that honestly, without fear, I
think we know damn few Communists and we know damn little about how they
operate and are organized. The former chief of the policy and planning staff was
able to say in a public hearing that he had never read a book on communism.

Field personnel are "discouraged from making contacts with Communists."

While we say that we are going in for hard anti-Communist activities, in fact we are
not engaging the Communist Party at all, except for broadcasts to the satellites and
the Soviet Union. If you look at the activities of this Agency, where they are most
varied and on the firing line, namely in the field, you will find that the field staff is
not in effect trying to engage Communists directly—and again for domestic reasons
of security.

Questions are raised as to whether we should lend books to Communists or show
them our films, perhaps out of the fear that our people may be subverted. Our
officers are discouraged from actual meetings with Communists. So that on the one
hand we say that our chief activity is fighting communism and our activities on the
other hand are directed at people who are chiefly neutralists or are already convinced.

Attacks on communism should not be made on grounds that do not appeal
to important segments of the audience. For example, communism should not be
criticized for ending Islamic religious customs (like the unveiling of women)
that may also be opposed by intellectuals.

Emphasis on anti-communism builds up a picture of Communist might and
strength that may scare some people into acquiescence with communism or fear
of it. In some countries people are tired of anti-Communist propaganda or
resent it.

Principally in Europe, they are so tired of "communism is wonderful" from the
Russians and "communism is awful" from us. They don't want to hear any more of
it. It's the anti-Communist who is most tired, the Communist less. They are sick of
it. That's the opinion held widely.

People in Europe do not want to be educated by us except about America. They
would let us talk to them about Chicago but not about Morocco. It is not only that
there is a positive interest in hearing about America, there is a positive resentment
about having us talk to them about a good many subjects outside of our borders,
including communism. Many good anti-Communists resent being told by us why
they should hate communism.

Anti-Communist output may potentially cause riots or result in property
loss. A theater may be damaged in a riot over a film showing. It is futile to tell

people in Free World countries who have had first-hand contact with communism how bad it is. The Greeks, Austrians, and Germans have experienced Communist atrocities at first hand and do not have to be sold on its evils. In Taiwan, USIA output may be so weak in comparison with Nationalist Chinese propaganda that it looks "almost pro-Communist."

Others take the extreme view that USIA should not attempt to combat communism but should leave this tack to other agencies. USIA can be most effective by simply explaining America's role in the world.

USIA's attack on communism is thought to arise mainly from domestic political considerations rather than from professional judgment ("and any propaganda agency that has to wage its battle with one eye on its rear has a hard job"). Public Law 402, which authorizes the program, calls for a positive emphasis.

> You must do an extensive amount of interpolating and interpreting, you must have to engage in casuistry to justify a hard-hitting anti-Communist role for this Agency.

For example, the National Security Council is thought to appreciate the fact that propaganda must emphasize "the shared objectives of the U. S. and other peoples rather than attempt to impose U. S. values on them." This accords with a widespread feeling that operators themselves would prefer to have more output on life in America and regard this as more effective than anti-communism, though they are prevented by Congress from following this line. "The essence of a democratic information program is that it should not be an 'anti' program." "It should be more pro-American rather than less anti-Russian."

> There's too much of this stuff, "The Communists are bastards—we're good people." We have felt for a long time that we have to put up a positive philosophy for which we can stand, as well as saying, "The Communists are bastards."
>
> I think that if you present the current struggle as "They're bad, therefore you must be with us," you're still offering the person you are talking to an alternative. He still is able to say, "How do I know you're not both bad?" We must, I imagine, stand for something positive in people's minds.
>
> I try to avoid defeatism. I try to make the thing inspiring. If you continue on the dull, defeated angle, it begins to rub off after a while.

There are those who maintain that the program is strictly positive or that the terms "positive" and "negative" are two sides of the same coin.

An attack on communism should be made an appeal to self-interest. So, no clear-cut distinction can be made between "positive" and "negative" content.

Anti-Communist activity in a non-Communist country like Italy should not point to Communist evils, but to the possibilities of progress under a democratic form of government.

Communism can be fought by showing people how to better their conditions within the framework of law and order. USIA should reach the same kinds of people with anti-Communist output as with positive output showing shared aspirations.

PENETRATING THE IRON CURTAIN

The Voice of America's Iron Curtain audience listens under a strain, so it cannot be expected to tune in for two hours at a time. To promote regular listening, then, programming should be on a fixed schedule. And since the Iron Curtain listener is primarily interested in hearing objective news, news commentary is especially important. A bare, factual report may not be easily grasped.

Broadcasts that attempt to weaken the regime's hold over the rank and file must use the proper Communist terminology.

> Knowing that we were speaking also to the Communists, we were extremely careful in our choice of words so that there would not be any mistake that people experienced in Party history would detect.

Other points of consensus on Iron Curtain broadcasts are:

1. The lives of party and government officials should be contrasted with those of average persons to discredit Communist pretensions that theirs is a workers' state. Details of the power struggles among the ruling cliques should be reported if evidence is solid and not classified.
2. Output should show that life in the Free World, in contrast with "totalitarian monotonous dullness," is full of possibilities and adventure. An adventure program that stresses individualism is implicitly anti-Communist.
3. Iron Curtain youth is interested in films and in Free World technical and industrial developments.
4. People behind the Iron Curtain in general are interested in the activities of their prominent émigrés.

Other points are raised, however:

5. The Iron Curtain audience may be bitterly anti-Communist and yet accept the philosophy of collectivism. This should temper attacks upon communism that may imply that Americans are trying to foist an alien system upon them.
6. VOA should not advocate capitalism; it should stress that, as long as other governments are not aggressive and do not threaten world peace, the U. S. does not want to interfere.

But it is not always possible to assess easily how stable the Soviet Union is internally or to judge the nature of the Soviet audience. So there is no ready formula for what tone to adopt. Controversies arise, therefore, about both the content and tone of Russian-language broadcasts.

Those who consider the Soviet audience an amalgam of dissident elements bitterly opposed to the regime sanction the use of emotion. (Russian-language output is termed "strident and rebellious and prompted by émigré psychology.")

There are only two good reasons for listening to the Voice of America, one is it's interesting, and the other is it gives you courage and moral sustenance. This has been another tendency of recent times: to bleach out the color. In part, it's been due to fear. In part it has been due to the fact that the new Jackson Report directive is colorless. First is the attitude toward the Soviet people. The fallacious belief, which certainly the Soviet Government does not hold, that the people are used to the regime and they are generally accepting it. If that's so, why the jamming, and the prohibitions on ingress and egress?

An entirely different approach, following from the assumptions about the nature of the audience made in the Jackson Report, holds that:

Given the present internal situation in Russia, we are not speaking to a large group of malcontents, [but] to people who are relatively loyal to their regime, and the only thing we can do is give them facts that do not necessarily jibe with the facts that they can get from their other sources and let them draw their own conclusions. The people in charge of the Russian desk feel they should be emotional because they are addressing malcontents in Russia. The radio people also insist that the Congress wishes them to be propaganda and to assume that sort of tone.

Thus, VOA must restrain its emotional tone. A restrained, cautious, logical approach is more effective in talking to the Soviet audience, which consists mostly of government officials who can listen without being suspect. These broadcasts should not be argumentative or "slyly propagandistic." Name-calling is inappropriate; it would make VOA sound exactly like Radio Moscow.

Further, the official position is that satire in Russian output would boomerang. Russians are sensitive about their technical and material achievements and would resent having Americans make fun of matters of national pride. This interpretation is not shared by all operators:" I think the masses in the Soviet Union are against their leaders. The jokes coming out of any totalitarian country are very good too."

Another opinion, however, is that many Russians are fond of their leaders. Attacks on Soviet leaders should concentrate on their acts rather than on their personal vulnerabilities. Criticism should be focused on specific leaders, not "referred back" to Marx and Engels. "If you attack a man like Stalin it would backfire."

Operators are not quite clear as to the extent to which they can quote Communists against themselves:

1. Communists should not be quoted on the air. The audience may mistake the intention of the quote; it may follow the Communist line of reasoning without going on to hear its subsequent demolition.
2. The Communists should be quoted against themselves. If a top Communist can be gotten unwittingly to use arguments which serve the U. S. cause, this can be extremely effective propaganda. The inaccuracies and contradictions in Communist statements should be exposed.

THE LIBERATION ISSUE IN THE SATELLITES

There are two fundamentally different schools of thought on the subject of VOA's mission in broadcasting to Eastern Europe. The first is expressed in the assumption that the conflict between the free and Communist worlds is a struggle between implacable enemies.

> When I came there was a definite program. We had one unique goal. You could discuss the best methods to reach this goal, but you could not discuss the goal—the complete elimination of Nazism by war. This presupposes a deep conviction that you could not do business with Hitler. Just as our Russian desk has to know that you cannot do business with these people in the Soviet Union today. There was not the slightest doubt as to what had to be done. This means that the basic principle of a complete identity of political goals and acts and propagandistic goals and acts was given. Not a similarity or a congruity, but an identity. We fought not at the battle front, but at the propaganda front, to quote Goebbels.

VOA is in "the revolution business," actively trying to stir up discontent and political changes within the Soviet orbit: "I'm not in the radio business, I'm in the revolution business, the propaganda business. I'm for winning for the United States."

The opposing opinion is that there are great limitations on VOA's role as a revolutionary agent.[2] The United States is not prepared to go to war to liberate the peoples of Eastern Europe. VOA's task is to keep the enemy off balance through the pressures that can be mustered in people's minds, to the end that American diplomatic and political negotiations can create insecurity on the Communist side.

Reinforcing either assumption, VOA output to the Communist world serves the following allied purposes:

1. To undermine Communist control by sowing doubt about the activities of the regimes and driving a wedge between the people and the Communist cadres. It must overburden and demoralize the Communist parties by (a) awakening popular unrest, (b) by encouraging Communists to be suspicious of each other, and (c) inducing defections and actual flight of key personalities to the Free World.
2. To maintain morale and the will to resist on the part of the satellite populations. For example, in Eastern Europe VOA must maintain the hope of liberation by reminding the people of their bonds with the Free World. They must be made to feel that they are not alone, either in their enslavement or their opposition to it. It is important to convince them of the growing strength of the Free World.

[2] This became apparent during the Hungarian rebellion of 1956, which pointed up the inability of the U. S. government to back up the rhetoric of liberation.

Since liberation is not a popular cause in the U. S., goes one argument, VOA cannot satisfactorily answer the question of how liberation can take place without war. It is impossible to speak about liberation on the basis of vague hopes and no intention of going to war. If U. S. foreign policy calls only for containment and no more, there is nothing to say to the Iron Curtain countries.

Opponents of this position stress that the hope of liberation is strong among Eastern Europeans, who cling to it although they feel it is disappointingly small. Listeners live on the hope VOA gives them "as sick men live on the hope of recovery."

Another view is that because listeners behind the Iron Curtain are leery of the term "peace," since it implies continuance of Soviet domination, VOA must stress "peace with security."

There are differences of opinion on whether the people of the satellites hope for war as the only hope of liberation or would hesitate to risk atomic conflagration to overthrow their leaders, unpopular and hated as they are.

> We are losing the dissidents as we move away from liberation. It makes it very difficult for our desks to hold our audience.

> The minimum assumptions that you make are that the regimes are unpopular and hated and that they would go a long way to overthrow them, but except for the resistance elements my assumption is that the major part of those who are opposed to their regime do not want war.

While one group believes it is dangerous to assume that the Eastern European peoples want war and that the soft approach is less dangerous and still leaves some hope for the audience, other operators do not necessarily agree that liberation of Eastern Europe is impossible unless war is risked. A peace treaty with Austria and unification of Germany, for example, may increase the possibilities of liberating the satellites bordering on those countries. As for present VOA practice, these views are expressed:

1. Iron Curtain output that definitely promises liberation, but leaves the time uncertain, is criticized for hitting too hard—raising hopes that are bound to result in disillusionment.
2. The liberation theme is not spelled out too often, but the audience is reassured of liberation when the Communists deny the possibility. The word "liberation" should rarely be used. There can be tremendous boomerang effects if there are only words of hope and no actions. The "how" and "when" should not be discussed. Broadcasts must not give the audience the impression that the U. S. is ready to do something for them, and should provide no false incitement to revolt.
3. It may be enough for VOA to go on the air once a day and say, "we are still here" to an audience that is already on the U. S. side. This will remind them that there is still a political alternative.

An emotional tone is suitable in broadcasts to the Eastern European satellites. These people, already stirred up against their rulers, enjoy hearing someone voice the epithets and ridicule they would like to use. Yet, operators complain that they are not allowed to do "a really fighting job" by directives calling for calmness and objectivity. An audience that hates Communist rule and wants American support may resent a calm, cool presentation that creates the impression that the U. S. is unaware of its sufferings.

> Propaganda to be effective must not be obvious except where it is deliberately so, as in the case of satellite broadcasts. You know the audience hates the Communist rule, so you immediately let them know that you also hate it. Otherwise they say, "What's wrong with these guys? Don't they know what's going on?" During the "full and fair picture" stage we used to get that reaction from our listeners. "They in America are just waking up to communism." And then when we became overtly anti-Communist they were glad.

> When they begin to root these people out of their homes in Budapest I feel it. We have a reason for broadcasting to Hungary and it's not to tell them the news. It's to tell them that we know about those people they rooted out of their homes in Budapest, and that we think it is wrong.[3]

Dissent: The calm, factual approach is best.

> Why some poor son of a bitch would risk going to Siberia to hear you lecture Stalin I don't understand. He tunes in for somewhat different reasons.

VOA's task in China is "in broad lines" identical with that in Eastern Europe.[4] The hope is that:

> We can by sort of a double action drive some wedges between the victims of the regime and the cadres of the regime itself, and secondly between the Communist regimes in China and Moscow, by drawing attention of the Chinese to actions of their government which are costly to the Chinese people and obviously made in favor of the Moscow regime. They take food from hungry China and ship it to the Soviet Union. I think that's the kind of thing we can profit on.

It is especially important to maintain the patriotic self-esteem of the audience while they are being told that their regime is subservient to Moscow.

> The basic premise of this line of attack is that the Chinese have something to be patriotic about; they should have a national entity and dignity of their own. Therefore, you cannot talk in contemptuous terms of Chinese relations to Russia as a puppet or as a satellite. You have to confine yourself to the regime. You cannot say to the Chinese people as distinct from the regime, "why do you submit to the Soviet Union?" The question you ask is "just how patriotic are these leaders of yours?" This is based on long acquaintance with the Chinese habits of mind, their skepticism of the intentions of government. They're very realistic people, they have not in the past displayed the elements of emotional unbalance.

[3] The reference here is not to the 1956 Hungarian uprising, but to an earlier police action.
[4] This preceded the Sino-Soviet break.

COMMUNIST PROPAGANDA

The sources of Communist strength may be seen in two ways:

1. Communist strength is ideological. Communism is a religion to millions of people, which means that it carries an emotional force. "At the basis of any totalitarian system is a set of concepts which must be propagated and believed."

   · One of the primary problems is how are you going to meet a formal philosophically-based intellectual position, which is a theory of history and mankind and provides a definition of destiny and the dynamics that move society, with the fragmentary aspirations and literature and philosophy of peoples whose acceptance of these positions has never been able to find a text?

2. Communist strength is organizational. Communists in democratic countries are organized into a political machine which operates on the ward level of patronage and benevolence. Their voters are much more disciplined than any others. This highly organized political character of the Communist movement has very little to do with ideology.

What are the attitudes of USIA personnel toward Soviet propaganda? The vast sums of money the Soviets spend are often contrasted with the relatively small USIA budget. As for the caliber of Communist propagandists, USIA operators have high regard for their skill and intelligence. The Communists are called "infallible judges" of propaganda effectiveness. Their method is to promote a worldwide program with specific objectives and centralized direction. They know immediately what line to take when an event occurs, and can control events for propaganda ends, keeping in mind the vulnerabilities of USIA (for example, the paralyzing effect of the two-day American weekend). Soviet propaganda can push a campaign on many levels and with many different means simultaneously. It is geared to one major goal, such as the Stockholm peace appeal; the exploitation of symbols like the Picasso dove of peace; and use of simple themes, like that of "peace" or "Banning the H-bomb," that are hammered at repeatedly.

Soviet propaganda is flexible; it can deviate from the truth. Convenient falsification, concealed omission, manufactured evidence, and spurious consistency have been powerful weapons of expediency in totalitarian propaganda. The Soviets freely distort history and the developing news. They can make black white (show that the South Koreans started the Korean War, for example), distort or edit the meaning of official U. S. statements; or take sentences out of context and use them to ridicule the U. S.

The Soviets skillfully use the "slide-in" technique—starting with a factual item and passing unobtrusively into a factual-sounding statement that actually distorts the point. Moscow Radio supports its position by quoting incorrectly impressive sources not available to the reader. They freely bribe foreign newspaper editors, and are adept in handling propaganda so it does not violate foreign censorship codes.

The Communists use blackmail and threats to extort money and fealty from people. "They don't care whether people dislike them as long as they play ball with them." The Soviets are trying to neutralize countries by making them terror-stricken.

The Soviet propagandists have benefited from the fact that they operate their program under conditions of secrecy. USIA, by contrast, must reveal its objectives and plans in public statements and hearings.

The Communists start campaigns merely to raise tensions. They are satisfied if attention is focused on an issue. They make strong use of invective. Their motion pictures, for example, use a hate-love technique. "Everybody with them is good, everybody against them is bad."

The Communists talk in terms of immediate problems and objectives.

A lot of our criticism of Communist regimes, though meaningful to us, is meaningless to the people we are addressing. They can accept a lot in the way of horror and self-deprivation, government interferences in their daily lives, without being shocked by it. If you come up to them with two separate ideologies, they're more inclined to accept the one that offers them something concrete in the next couple of years rather than in the next generation or two. You go to the villages of Indonesia and an official comes along in a Buick. We come along and say, "In a generation or two your children will drive around in Buicks like that." The Communist says, "Let's knock off the bastard and take his Buick." He's going to appeal to them.

They successfully adapt their propaganda to local needs and aspirations, keeping international aspects to a minimum and relying on their friends to give their program an indigenous look. A favorite Soviet propaganda technique is to plant a story in a crypto-Communist newspaper in one country and then have this source quoted elsewhere as authority. The Communists successfully identify with local nationalist movements ("Asia for the Asians").

Since the Communists have Party workers in every country, they have no problems in distributing their output. The great strength of the Communists is their agitprop apparatus—"operators who know the answers," reach people personally, individual to individual and group to group.

The Communists show great interest in talking about people. Their propaganda is always taken down to the individual level; it is a curious anomaly to find "the monolithic state talking in terms of the democratic philosophy of the individual."

The Soviets balance doctrinal and policy material with output that shows that their culture is outstanding and their people happy. By using the Russian language and boosting their cultural and artistic talent, "they are trying to impress the Asians in particular that they have the same chrome-coated civilization as the U. S."

While Soviet propaganda is slick and lavish for prestige reasons, "when the Communists have a good, lasting message they put it out in the millions and sell it for two or three anna in every town in India.'' They publish material on very cheap newsprint to give it an indigenous look.

The Soviets speak arrogantly as if they were the leaders of the world. ''They are always saying that everything behind the Iron Curtain is perfect.'' Whether or not they are successful in this is a matter of debate between those who feel ''they are able to convince a lot of people that Russia is a paradise'' and those who contend that they are not even trying:

> They're not, except through certain minor groups, trying to sell the idea that Russia is a great and wonderful place. They're trying to sell the idea that if war comes it won't be as a result of an aggressive action on the part of Russia. Except with their hard-core membership, they're not trying to play up the idea that Russia is a big, wonderful place.

But Soviet propaganda has its vulnerabilities, too. The very emotionality and volume of Soviet propaganda, to some USIA observers, is proof of U. S. success and popularity. The volume and virulence of the attack on America by the Chinese Communists, for example, demonstrates that the Chinese people believe that Americans are interested in their wellbeing.

Another argument along these lines is that official Communist media are not believed in Communist countries. Even if the Communists caught USIA in a bare-faced lie, their statements would not be believed by their own people unless the evidence did not rest on Communist say-so. It is generally realized behind the Iron Curtain that the Communist radio does not tell the truth. Bold and blatant Communist film propaganda is not very effective either. Likewise, the violent distortions of Communist propaganda—such as germ warfare charges against the U. S.—are unsuccessful with intelligent Western audiences. Communist information centers—in Austria, for example—are highly unsuccessful compared with USIA centers.

ANSWERING COMMUNIST CHARGES AGAINST THE U.S.

USIA's attack on communism can only be discussed in the context of the Communists' ongoing attack on America and Americans and their charges that America is warlike, undemocratic, doomed economically, without culture, and immoral.

1. The Communists seek to show the U. S. as an imperialist power desirous of waging war on the rest of the world and run by people who do not understand Europe, are hysterical about communism, and need war or heavy defense efforts to save ''a rotten economy.''
2. All opportunities are seized to demonstrate that the U. S. does not practice the democracy it preaches—that it is ''a class nation.'' All violations of civil liberties and minority rights are magnified. ''McCarthyism'' is ''American fascism.''

3. Capitalist countries, particularly the U. S., are headed for economic disaster. War is necessary to save the U. S. from another depression.
4. The U. S. is culturally backward and has "nothing to offer except dollars." Its popular literature and motion pictures are evidence of barbarism.
5. The U. S. would stop at nothing to achieve its ends. Therefore, America engages in germ warfare and commits atrocities in Korea.

The problem of how best to reply to Communist charges is a crucial one for the Agency. It is commonly accepted in USIA that in conducting propaganda "it is a disadvantage to have to answer somebody else who has taken a lead." Nevertheless, USIA operators stress the desirability of taking the initiative rather than merely answering Soviet charges. This approach is recognized by the National Security Council and by the State Department. The President's atomic energy proposal is often cited as an example of American initiative in the Cold War. The issue of free elections in East Germany or the Austrian Peace Treaty are examples of how USIA has taken the lead.

In treating a major controversy, such as the Korean prisoners of war issue,[5] it is important to emphasize a positive theme. USIA would have been placed on the defensive if it had answered Communist charges that releasing the prisoners violated the armistice.

An offensive position enables USIA to build its own "frame of reference" in world opinion on crucial attitudes rather than to accept the Communist frame of reference.

Every issue on which Moscow has said little or nothing should be examined as a possible opportunity for us. Put the enemy off balance, so that he has to use up time, energy, and effort to counteract the move.

Thus, USIA must also anticipate possible Soviet propaganda campaigns and be ready to reply. An event that is damaging to U. S. public relations, such as a race riot, must not be ignored until the Communists have made capital of it.

TALKING BACK

While it is agreed generally that USIA should take the offensive, there is constant pressure from both home and abroad to answer Communist attacks swiftly, particularly on the part of operators who feel, in a sense, in competition with their opposite numbers in Moscow.

The positive is harder to come up with. It's easier to criticize, and, too, the Russians are always coming up with something that we can counter. It's a screwy business.

Soviet charges, however preposterous they may seem to Americans, may acquire widespread acceptance abroad, particularly among intellectuals who do not know the U. S. or are unfamiliar with the issues.

[5] The many North Korean and Chinese prisoners who refused to go home were permitted by the United States respectively to remain in the South or to go to Taiwan.

It is a basic function of the Agency to answer Soviet falsehoods as quickly as possible.[6] The Soviets are always coming up with some propaganda move which can be countered. The most effective anti-Communist approach is to demolish Communist defensive arguments.

Part of the news job of the press and broadcasting services is to show "what facts and actions lie behind Communist words and pronouncements which appear quite reasonable and logical if taken at face value." Answering the opposition is particularly necessary in radio programs beamed to Iron Curtain countries "which are deluged with Communist propaganda."

In talking to a Communist-dominated area VOA must make certain that it is not forfeiting something to the gain of the other side by ignoring or underplaying it. When a Communist regime prepares a campaign, a counter-campaign should be planned for the same period, and, if possible, should anticipate it.

THE ARGUMENT AGAINST TALKING BACK

Some operators feel there is a danger in becoming purely defensive. "We must guard against the temptation constantly to answer hostile propaganda blow by blow." A reply need not be made to "everything unfavorable about the U. S. that seeps through the communications channels of the world."

1. "Refuting an opposition charge never makes propaganda. A propaganda battle conducted to score debating points is a waste of time." To reply to Communist charges directly gives the Communists control over output. The job of USIA is "not to talk to the Moscow Radio but to the Russian people."

2. USIA will be beaten if it engages the Communists in direct combat. The Soviets do not fight according to our rules, and we do not have the party line necessary to wage "their sort of political warfare." They launch propaganda campaigns to create diversions, without any particular desire to win the argument. Even if the U. S. "wins," the Communists still profit.

   This business of answering propaganda charges is highly debatable. My own theory is that it is not ever going to do us much good to answer a propaganda campaign launched by the Communists, even successfully, because our success is apt to be from our own point of view. Such campaigns are launched by the Communists to set up a difference, simply to raise tensions. Their needs are served if tension is focused on an issue. They don't care about achieving it. To do so enables them to set the frame of reference for the debate. In my mind it's much more preferable not to accept their frame of reference but to build one of our own.

3. Denials do not catch up with original charges.

   It's not a good thing to answer directly, because then you turn over to the other guy the control over what to say and what you treat. The Communists with their accusations and distortions could keep us busy full time just answering them. Also there's

---

[6] The techniques of rebuttal to Communist charges are discussed in Chapter X, "Truth and Credibility."

another psychological consideration. To say, "They said this and it's not true; the facts are thus and so," is not a good technique. The charge is usually more sensational than the facts and to repeat the accusation is to give it reemphasis and greater currency. The sensational accusation sticks in the mind better than a statement of the facts. Also if you answer directly and say, "It ain't so, it's this way," you set up in the mind of the listener the impression that you are going to answer a charge, "so they have to propagandize their own point of view," he thinks.

4. "Skeptical thoughts that do not already exist in the listener's mind should not be stirred up unnecessarily." (This is also an argument for ignoring unfavorable news items that may otherwise be ignored by enemy propaganda.)

5. The most effective anti-Communist approach is to argue in black-and-white terms, stressing the U. S. position and ignoring the Communist argument. This rule applies also to instances where the Communists catch USIA in a contradiction: in such cases no reply should be made.

SOME CHARGES REQUIRE REPLY

On specific issues, such as the Rosenberg spy case,[7] there are often sharp differences of judgment on the course to be taken. Some operators believe the case requires full USIA treatment and rebuttal of accusations in a country like France, where it can be used as a point of departure for describing the American system of justice. Others are equally convinced that USIA should remain aloof.

> We are talking about selling the idea that our judicial system has integrity when we talk about the Rosenbergs. Believe me, there is no possibility of selling the people of Europe that it was a good idea to execute the Rosenbergs. My idea was that we should not too much fall into the trap of answering them at all; just keep our head covered and hope it doesn't do too much damage.

In reaching a resolution of this question it is suggested that an attack should be answered if it is already an issue in people's minds—if it has caused a sensation and is going to "really hurt" the U. S.

> If it's a major propaganda campaign like bacteriological warfare, we go to all lengths to document and disprove the charges and bring them up before the UN. If they are pulling a campaign, as they did in France, to link the Rosenberg case with the Dreyfus case, we will send volumes of stuff to get the answers across. If it's the usual crazy ranting we usually ignore it. We don't try to counter every screwball claim they make. We would rather be on the offensive than on the defensive.

Another rule of thumb: Take issue with the Communists only when there is a good chance of coming out a winner. However, it may still be desirable to

---

[7] The trial and execution of Julius and Ethel Rosenberg for the theft of U. S. nuclear secrets became the subject of major Soviet propaganda efforts.

answer charges behind the Iron Curtain where the Soviets control the communications media. In broadcasting to this area, however, VOA need touch a subject only if the Communists have raised it for their own purposes.

> Behind the Iron Curtain where the Communists have the first and last word and access to all facilities and can argue more strongly than we can in an argument, in a matter of assertion and counter-assertion, it's worthwhile to answer directly only when they have made a specific charge or accusation about something that can be undermined on the basis of what the audience itself knows. Then the audience doesn't have to say, "He argues this way and the other fellow argues that way. What is correct?" Where we can say, "The Communists said this and you yourself know from seeing this tree or this street or this building that it's not correct," then the listener himself knows that the Communists have lied.

The argument against hard-hitting techniques often encompasses not only the tone of anti-Communist output but content as well; "merely attacking communism does not achieve program objectives. It merely holds the line." Too much anti-communism will cause the audience to regard all USIA output as propaganda.

USIA's anti-Communist output strengthens unfavorable stereotypes of the U. S. as a belligerent nation that cares only about beating Russia. Further, doctrinal attacks on communism or exposés of Communist atrocities may backfire in economically impoverished areas where the audience may refuse to believe that communism can be any worse than what they have known.

> We cannot attain our aims anywhere in the Far East merely by saying that communism is bad, because the people in those areas have never had anything approaching the democratic society that we are trying to tell them about.

VII

Projecting America

IN CONTRAST to its Cold War adversary stance against communism, USIA dedicates a substantial part of its activity to cultivating familiarity (and by implication friendship) with the United States and its institutions. While the Agency's operators generally agree as to what aspects of American life are most attractive to other peoples, they are divided on the question of whether they should tell the world about the unattractive aspects too. America's strength, its high standard of living, and its foreign aid are all considered to be of ambivalent propaganda value. The foreign view of this country is to a large extent shaped by commercial media, like Hollywood films, that convey a very different picture than the Agency's.

As SUCCESSIVE DIRECTIVES have made clear, an important part of USIA's mission is to provide foreign audiences with a picture of American life. Behind this effort to project America lies one of USIA's most basic assumptions: that familiarity causes friendliness. ("You inevitably like someone a great deal better after you know him.")

> People are more apt to listen to a person with whom they have something in common than to someone remote from them.

> The more information someone has about the U.S. the less misconceptions he will have and the less subject he will be to opposing propaganda.

> The basic assumption underlying any information program is that to understand is at least to appreciate this, that or the other position, and assuming that the United States government represents the American people's basic desire for a better, more friendly world, many of the same positions which we adopt, they will adopt, when they understand the underlying philosophy of the American people on world affairs and presumably that's the reason for any information program at all.

The point is not to get everybody to think like Americans or to do like Americans but to have them get confidence in the United States and to show them what has been done here and what can be adapted to their way of life.

Yet, the exact place of Americana in output remains uncertain. It is argued, for example, that familiarity does not always lead to friendship. Foreign leaders who have been here on the Exchange Program may be highly critical of our policies and actions. American prestige and influence in a country will not keep mobs from breaking in or destroying a USIS library.

Norway, after the first World War, was full of Germans who lived in Norwegian homes and yet, when the war came, did it do the Germans any good? Who are the people who knew the Japanese best, and whom did the Chinese know best? The Japanese.

Those who say Americana receive too much emphasis point out that "Congress sneers at VOA for broadcasting trivial Americana at times of major social and political crisis." Americana serve no propaganda point. Besides, it is wasteful to describe America to an area like the Far East, where the U. S. plays an insignificant role in the average person's daily life.

But many field personnel particularly reiterate that projecting America is USIA's biggest job. Americana show the identity of interest and cultural heritage between Americans and the target audience. They should portray phases of American life and history that create confidence in U. S. leadership.

We try to stick to the things that people will appreciate—family life, morals, religion, culture. Those are the things about America that they'd want to know.

In the Broadcasting Service, too, it is said that audiences are interested far more in everyday life in America than in American foreign policy. Presenting Americana is VOA's greatest audience-building device. Europeans do not want to be "educated" by VOA, except about life in the United States. While they have a positive interest in hearing about the U. S., they also have an aversion to hearing VOA talk about subjects outside U. S. borders. (This contradicts the view that people listen to VOA to find out what the greatest power in the world has to say on *all* issues of the day.)

What themes should be developed? Operators suggest an emphasis on positive traits and values:

1. Americans are nice people.
2. America is generous and altruistic. U. S. self-interest is enlightened.
3. America is democratic. Americans believe in freedom of thought and expression. In a democratic U. S., all races and creeds live happily together. The U. S. comes close to being a classless society. Americans don't consider it beneath a man's dignity to work with his hands.
4. Americans believe in freedom for other people. The government and people have never swallowed heavy-handed colonial policies. The U. S. is not an imperialist power.

5. American life has a spiritual quality. USIA must build respect for the ethical values and high moral quality of American aims, overcome the foreign stereotype of U. S. society as completely dominated by materialism and self-interest.

6. Americans are a cultured people.

   The U. S. has art, ballet, and a creative cultural life; there are serious books available here at prices that people can afford; we have writers of noted achievement and a young but developing literary tradition.

7. The U. S. economy is successful. America's material well-being rests on its freedom. American capitalism is unique, but is often confused with the European kind "that is cartel-like or feudalistic." Since people overseas do not understand how the American economy works, often thinking of the Marxist concept of capitalism, USIA must emphasize that the U. S. actually has a "mixed economy" that provides the ordinary consumer with a high income. It has changed since the heyday of American industrial expansion and the "robber barons."

8. America is a peaceable country. USIA must show

   that the United States was interested in peace, that the United States was not just a fortress arming itself for defensive war but that it was interested in pursuit of peaceful aims for itself and the whole world.

Language is a bond. There is intrinsic value in gaining wider acceptance and familiarity with English. A people's language cannot be separated from its culture and civilization. Learning English increases familiarity (and presumably friendliness) with the U. S. People are drawn to those whose language they know. "They may not develop great love for them, but they become interested in them."

It is desirable for English to be accepted as a major means of communication throughout the world, and to make it the predominant language in foreign countries—a substitute for such other international languages as French:

   Any nation that can get its language accepted as a major means of communication as the French have for so many years is in a strong position. The Bi-national Centers support this in large part through their English-teaching program, making them use American materials with American content rather than British content materials.

THE PLACE OF CULTURE

Cultural activity is an important part of USIA's effort to project America for the foreign audience. "The civilized character of American social life" can be shown not only through emphasizing the contribution of talented individuals to the fine arts but also by showing the widespread diffusion of artistic interest as reflected, for example, by museum attendance.

Evidence of American intellectual achievements is of value even if it deals with an esoteric subject of relatively little interest to the target audience.

I can see that in Washington they wondered why we should order *Speculum* (a Latin publication) for all the libraries. A very esoteric, scholarly periodical that probably will not be read, but it's the kind of thing the cultural officer thought ought to be there as an example of American cultural life.

Those who value cultural activity stress these points:

1. The unfavorable stereotype of Americans as cultural barbarians must be counteracted. Americans are regarded throughout the world as uncultured boors and crude, materialistic people "who have no time for the finer things in life." This impression stems from a lack of information, Communist propaganda, and "sour grapes." (Countries that have lagged behind the United States may salvage their national self-esteem by maintaining the myth of our cultural inferiority.)

   The Europeans attach greater importance to the subject of culture than we do. As a matter of fact, they have a tendency to fall back on that because they have lost their rank in world affairs. They fall back on the fact that they are the center of world culture.

   Over and over in the Italian press we have references to the immaturity of the United States. Your Italian intellectual, while he is perfectly ready to accept that we have technological progress, if he admits to himself that we have culture too, it tears him down. One of the main factors in the evaluation of the picture in Italy is the tremendous national inferiority complex that colors every attitude toward the United States.

2. Cultural activity raises U. S. prestige in backward areas. It demonstrates that the U. S. can compete with European colonial powers that have traditionally been culturally dominant in such regions as the Near East, Africa, or Latin America.

   This country is cutting its own throat in not allowing an official agency or private interests to do more in demonstrating more about the cultural life about this country in all its forms, to put our best cultural foot forward.

3. Cultural activity creates a favorable response because people are grateful for the entertainment or inspiration it gives them.

   It may be simply a feeling that they need more cultural information to enlarge their horizons. To the extent that we identify ourselves with the satisfaction of that need it's to the advantage of the program.

4. Cultural activity is a means to the end of supporting U. S. foreign policy. It impresses people abroad with the fact that American foreign policy can be trusted and accepted because it is made by cultured and civilized people.

   Democracy is the highest form of civilization that has currently been attained in the world. . . . I believe we should try to overcome the impression that we are a bunch of wild people and have none of the refinements. They will be less inclined to believe in us and to agree to the wisdom of our conduct on foreign affairs if they continue to feel that we are a bunch of barbarians. I don't think the American taxpayer would want to spend money just to impress the Europeans with the fact that we have museums. I think we ought to impress them with the fact that when Secretary Dulles gets up to recommend EDC, their reaction is, "The man is a sensible person, he's a wise person, maybe there's something to it." Because he comes from a civilized country, civilized in terms of being able to think clearly and wisely.

Some operators minimize the positive impact of cultural activity, believing that it rarely has immediate policy applications and that it involves such a vast body of material that it is difficult "to get a handle on it."

Since cultural activities in the field frequently cannot be planned in advance, according to one USIA field officer, Washington often "sneers" at special-events projects that are not part of an integrated program, or considers it a waste of time for a field post to exhibit the work of American artists who are less accomplished than the leading artists of the host country.

I don't think we should preach culture. It's a very uncultured thing to do. A cultivated human being doesn't talk about his culture. I don't think we have any more culture than the other fellow.

Culture has no place in the information program, because "the American taxpayer is not interested in spending money to impress Europeans with American cultural achievements." He expects information activity to relate to concrete foreign-policy objectives.

USIA output emphasizes the spiritual and moral content of American life to impress overseas audiences that "our people are not completely materialistic." Among those who believe that USIA should publicize American church attendance and religious practice, it is considered valuable to show, even to people who do not share the American religious heritage, "the important part played by religion among persons high in government and among great American industrialists."

Others dissent: The religious theme has been overstressed. "Can we really conquer the forces that make people distrust us by telling them that we have religion?" Hindus, Moslems, and Buddhists are not interested in the faith of American Baptists and Methodists.

USIA: MIRROR OR SHOW WINDOW?

Should USIA be a mirror of American life or a show window offering a selective and admirable picture of it? The question is answered pragmatically day by day as output is selected and treated. Two major attitudes toward story treatment may be distinguished. The first is that the "full and fair picture idea is silly," and that instead of being exhaustive, output must be selective. It is not enough merely to inform people and count on them to react favorably. It is necessary to promote a point of view, to present a picture of America that is favorable, and stir other countries to emulate U. S. accomplishments and institutions. This edict applies particularly to the American standard of living and freedoms. Otherwise, the audience may not absorb important information, or it may draw the wrong conclusions.

Opponents of this view maintain that without a "full and fair picture"—a true, documentary picture of life in America—the audience will not have a basis for understanding the U. S.

> Take all the magazines distributed in those countries—*Time, Life, Ladies' Home Journal, Collier's, American, Reader's Digest.* Are they doing any good for America? I believe they are, because if they do nothing else than show our ads, they show our standard of living and how people get on here.

It makes sense to show people behind the Iron Curtain that Americans live better than they do, and that under a free economy it requires less working time to buy a pair of shoes than under communism.

On the other hand, it's ill-advised to boast. There is criticism of output that is "provincial," telling the audience "how bad they have it and how good we have it" and that therefore implies that "everything in the U. S. is newer, bigger, and better than anything else." USIA should never gloat over an obvious victory. America must exercise humility.

> My feeling is that going into a world's fair where we will have one exhibit among 30 countries we should underplay our hand. We should put a type of foot forward that will not make it seem that we are tooting our own horn.
>
> We can't any more beat our breasts and say, "We Americans are the greatest people of the world." Now we want to show that we appreciate how much we have learned from them.
>
> I'm not sure that it's necessary to sell the entire American way of life to the English or the French or the Hottentots. I don't think that in all respects our American way of life is superior to everybody's. Politically I think the American way of life is the greatest in the world. As far as the message of freedom is concerned, we don't have to preach it to the English who are just as free as we are.

These attitudes reflect the view that U. S. material strength is not necessarily a propaganda asset.

> I don't think you're going to conquer the forces that make people distrustful of us by selling them on the idea that we have religion or refrigerators or a high standard of living for our working people.

Foreign audiences already know of U. S. material progress; so depicting the American standard of living accurately and in a matter-of-fact way may arouse the same hostile reaction in a foreign audience as actual boasting. A film that shows the plumbing in an American worker's home may be rejected by Italian laborers as propaganda. It may be necessary to minimize the truth in order to insure credibility: "You cut out anything that makes the U. S. look foolish, luxury things, tremendous food and dinners."

The "green-tiled bathroom" image should be counteracted, wherever possible, by showing that some Americans live under simple conditions, or by stressing the survival of handicrafts in the Appalachian highlands.

Still, it is thought that a lot of operators are oversensitive and have over-compensated. "They're always too afraid of showing too high a standard of living in this country."

An analogous problem is how to depict U. S. military strength without exaggerating the picture of two giants, the U. S. and the U.S.S.R. "slugging it out." Since propaganda emanating from a great military power like the United States is viewed as dangerous by many people throughout the world, some operators state that USIA should avoid themes or techniques that may inspire apprehension, films showing violence, Americans acting as thugs, atomic explosions, or anything else implying that "here is the American steamroller ready to move in."

DEPICTING FOREIGN AID

There is controversy over the question of whether U. S. foreign aid is a proper subject for propaganda and, if so, how it should be presented. Some hold that it is an important information program objective to publicize economic aid and technical assistance to the beneficiary countries and countries that may be candidates for aid, and that it is desirable to "let people know what the U. S. is doing for them." Implicit is the belief that when people know about American aid programs (even in countries that are not directly benefiting) they will be grateful or sympathetic.

Others believe that foreign attitudes toward the U. S. have been deteriorating because America insists on showing how much aid it has given. Aid should not be a major USIA theme.

> We have a tendency of always talking about our charity, and no one wants to receive charity. Lots of times in our efforts to please people or to do good we are constantly recalling what we have done for them. That's something that has to be done very carefully.

> We seem to assume that just giving other nations things, whether goods, ideas or services—we think these things are good for them, they ought to have them—once we have given them, somehow or other there's going to be a strange alchemy by which they wake up some morning and find out that they're lined up on the Western side.

Rather, the U. S. should emphasize mutuality of effort. In the case of cooperative activities, USIA should stress what the beneficiary nations are doing. For example, accounts of American help to Korean rehabilitation should point to the joint character of the effort but make the fact of American aid unmistakably clear.

> We can say, "We learned from you people, we improved these things. We invented our tractor but we are shipping it to you so you can take advantage of our experiences as we have taken advantage of yours." We must not "give" them anything. The moral of all these stories is to cooperate. In all these countries now we are giving them help. They get suspicious. "Why are they doing this? Are they trying to get something out of us for themselves?" These films explain, "We want you to be strong, we will gain from this. We are willing to give you advice and financial help."

People are receptive to contributions, "if their pride and dignity as human beings are not trampled upon." Any accounts of U. S. aid should be made under local auspices by local leaders. If they are grateful to the U. S. they would rather tell America about it than have Americans tell them. However, this has its dangers.

> In most of the aid agreements so far, we not only give it with the knowledge that it's supposed to accomplish specific needs but we make these guys get on a soapbox and say, "I have just accepted charity from Uncle Sam and I hereby acknowledge this great and wonderful gift from overseas. I had nothing to do with it." I personally feel that this is one of the psychologically most inept steps that we have taken in this whole aid program—to expect people to make public acknowledgment of it to their own neighbors. If we want to accomplish something, we shouldn't try to posit these relationships so bluntly as to expect them to make public acknowledgment of it. There, again, you will run into a storm of protest right away.

AMERICA AS PORTRAYED BY ITS MASS MEDIA

Nonofficial media, flowing through commercial channels, play an important part in shaping the foreign image of the U. S. American popular literature—particularly sensational magazines or comic books—is frequently cited as being harmful to the U. S. and inconsistent with USIA purposes. Nevertheless, American popular literature should be spread abroad. If some magazines carry stories that are detrimental to USIA objectives, the agency may exercise some control by holding back its usual routing procedure.

There are mixed reactions to using Hollywood films as a propaganda device:

1. Many commercial films can advance USIA objectives, because even people who are antipathetic to the U. S. get generally favorable impressions from them.
2. Commercial movies have a mixed influence.
3. Hollywood films are harmful, and wipe out much of USIA's effectiveness. They give a distorted picture of the U. S. Gangster films and bedroom

farces have inspired the idea that Americans are all millionaires—"a bunch of rich boors"—and that American women are all gold diggers or career women. If these negative views are accepted, it follows that USIA must counteract unfavorable impressions created by Hollywood. Field personnel must go out of their way to combat these attitudes. Yet, their personal contacts are limited, "whereas thousands of people overseas are exposed to Hollywood motion pictures." It is difficult for USIA output on American life and its "cultural side" to correct the dramatic stereotypes of Hollywood movies.

If Hollywood film output is harmful, partially or in the aggregate, then USIA should not merely counteract these harmful effects; it should prevent harmful films from being produced. This thesis arouses controversy: One view is that while it is desirable to modify the content of commercial films, it is "political dynamite" to do so. USIA cannot and should not control what Hollywood produces. Another view is that if USIA cannot exercise control over Hollywood's output, it must get the industry to cooperate by organizing "high-minded citizens" to "pass on" films for export.

We have been successful in a number of cases in getting the industry to withdraw or delay distribution of some films. I have thought for a long time it would be very worthwhile if three or four times a year someone of the stature of the Undersecretary of State would go to Hollywood with three or four top experts to run a briefing session.

VIII

Adaptation to the Audience

USIA FACES A WIDE VARIETY of target audiences in a great many cultures. It must reconcile its tactical needs to be intelligible and persuasive with the broader goals of supporting national objectives on a consistent worldwide scale. Adaptation to the audience involves both what is said as well as the style or technique of saying it. Elite targets must be approached differently than the mass. In both instances the skilled propagandist seeks to identify himself and his cause with the interests, outlooks, and even the familiar media format and language of those he addresses.

TARGETING IMPLIES that program content and techniques have been adapted to the character of the audience—its aims, interests, prejudices, and sensibilities. One of the most widely held, freely stated assumptions in USIA is that the audience must be kept in mind in the preparation of output.

> You cannot start with what you want them to do or what you want to order them to do; you must start with a consideration of what they are.
>
> What is sometimes seen as a worldwide program is often resolved as a purely local religious or cultural or ethnic matter.
>
> I don't think we can do an adequate job until we write with a specific audience in mind.

"ACROSS-THE-BOARD" OUTPUT

A minority believes that output must be planned for the widest possible audience to make full use of talent and materials—materials that seek a common

97

denominator for all target areas and groups. "Full use should be made of those motives that are known to be strong and universal: the desires for peace, prosperity, democracy, social justice, and truthful information." People are similar around the world, although their values are different. Everyone likes human interest stories on children, animals, and women's fashions. "There is no such thing as a nation; there are only people." This means it is possible to design "something that is intelligible to everyone who can read, and it may have the same effect on the guy who spells it out word by word as for the member of parliament."

Another argument in favor of across-the-board output is that many subjects do not lend themselves to adaptation from area to area. But news about American political and economic trends is important all over the world.

> Some things have to be for everybody. The threat is universal. Communism exists everywhere. You have to fight it in universal terms. I am just sap enough to believe that you can find a common denominator in everything, though it's the job of the area expert to discover what's unique about his area, and it should be the job of somebody else to find the common denominator. Some of these area experts now argue in effect that there is not any one thing that Dwight D. Eisenhower can safely say to everybody in the world. I think it would be a sad state of affairs if it were true.

In addition to being a more practical, economical way of handling materials, across-the-board treatment permits USIA to use major themes that represent U. S. interests rather than to defer to the audience.

> I don't think we should ever make the mistake of giving them what they want to hear.

> We sometimes transpose our interests to the Middle East. We can also make the mistake the other way and say, "Because they're not interested in it let's not give it to them." There are certain things we've got to make them understand. Most Arab countries were not concerned about Korea at all, and one of our big jobs was to make them concerned about Korea.

> We can have quite a number of films in our program that the audience would not like because they presented new ideas which were at variance with their fixed prejudices. Popularity should be a poor criterion for judging our films.

THE NEED FOR ADAPTATION

Counterposed to the view that the Agency's objectives are worldwide is the position that, "USIA cannot have a country-by-country program based on glittering generalities." Output broad enough for the entire world is "not saying anything." There is no place for output that is essentially "all of one piece, without variation." USIA would actually defeat its own ends if it presented the same picture of America to every country.

The hard-hitting pamphlet that brings 50 Huks out of the hills might be bad in England, and the Huks are not interested in American trade policy.

Human interest material [such as a feature on bathing beauties] cannot be used in every country.

I think that people are similar around the world but people's values are different. The things that are important to people are different. For example, death in many countries is relatively unimportant, human life is very cheap. In some parts of Asia, people actually laugh when they see someone killed.

For some areas, you will start an idea by telling a fable or quoting from the Bible. In other areas, people will laugh if you start that way.

Foreign audiences differ in their norms, values, and methods of reasoning. The operator must recognize that there is

the existence of a logic different from ours, the Oriental logic. They simply don't accept the same premises that we do, and therefore when we present what, to us, is a very well-reasoned argument from an acceptable premise to a well-reasoned conclusion, it doesn't hold water, because they don't accept the premise we start with. That doesn't mean that their logic is wrong, because if you go back 3,000 or 4,000 years you do see certain things which lead them to accept certain premises as parts of their daily lives. From a propaganda standpoint it doesn't mean that you cannot argue, but it means that you have to learn some new syllogisms.

Product tone must be adapted to the audience. In some places, atrocity stories may receive full-page spreads in the local press. Elsewhere, they may raise objections. The motives that are strong in a particular audience should be stressed: Desires for freedom of speech, freedom of religion, national independence, and individual land ownership.

While output must obviously be comprehensible to the audience, it should not be so elementary that it arouses ridicule.

We felt that exhibits as a big thing didn't really pay off because the kind of exhibits that brought in thousands of people brought in thousands who couldn't react to what you were showing. You were playing to illiterates—you couldn't simplify it to the point where it was really meaningful to them. . . . All they did was wander through. An illiterate peasant wouldn't know what he had gone through. A brightly lighted room with things on the wall he couldn't read or even a movie he couldn't understand.

Romain Rolland does not give a damn about the Chicago stockyards.

Different points must be emphasized to different areas when explaining a complex policy, such as the U. S. position on atomic weapons inspection. In broadcasts to Western Europe, the U. S. plan may be stressed as the only possible control vehicle. Different things must be said to an Iron Curtain audience. If an Arab League official is visiting the President, three different film versions may result—one for the Arab world, one for neutralist countries, and a third for the Far East.

But in selecting centrally produced material and adapting it, operators who specialize in regional output must have autonomy. Their emphasis depends not only on existing notions about the United States in a given country, but also on the activity of the Communist opposition and popular conceptions of it.

> People who are drawing up the broad policy can't possibly think in terms of the particular regions and what is going on there at a particular time. For example, they cook up the word "Free World." We have been told many times that it's a very unfortunate term. To an Egyptian the imperialist is not the Russians, it's the British. To an American it really has a meaning. It does in Europe, but in some other places it does not.

> Whether or not there is an international Soviet conspiracy is irrelevant for planning purposes. The deciding factor in terms of program content is whether or not the people in a particular target group think so or not.

Even a very specific argument must be presented in nationally individual versions.

> Actually we need two Far East (news) files. We need one primarily calculated for neutralist countries and another one for the countries that are overtly and strongly anti-Communist—Korea, Indochina, Thailand and the Philippines, and Nationalist China. A more moderate approach for Japan, Malaya, and Singapore. Thailand wants all the anti-Communist material they can get. Indonesia says it's impossible to make any use of anti-Communist material. The file for the strongly anti-Communist countries would include whatever material we could include on the difficulties the Chinese Communists were having in establishing their regime. In contrast, the file to the neutralist countries would concentrate quite heavily on material designed to show that the United States has no real economic imperialist attitudes in Asia.

A complex series of political considerations are seen as underlying basic decisions on program content. For example, countries in the Western democratic tradition require a different approach to the themes of liberty than countries without this tradition. Countries on the border of communism and directly threatened by it need more output "on Communist aggression, on the 'no appeasement' theme, and on immediately available Western strength." Output to U. S.-occupied countries should emphasize American occupation policy.

In summary, USIA would tend to have the same targets from country to country in Europe, even if it were not forced to follow this course because of lack of funds, since at least one or two of its major objectives are identical in every European country.

THE AMERICAN SLANT

Operators see a difficulty in adapting material so that it addresses itself to the audience's viewpoint. USIA personnel are Americans, and USIA media often use outside publications, articles, and books that were originally prepared for an American audience. How can USIA overcome the American slant?

A news story must be gauged from the standpoint of its significance to the foreign audience. A story that is important domestically is not necessarily important abroad. Or a story that has been buried by the domestic U. S. media may be ideal abroad. A position that may be popular with the American people or press may be quite unsuitable for output to certain areas. For example, a story on U. S. military aid to Indochina should not be sent to India. A book that is well received by domestic U. S. reviewers is not necessarily suitable for overseas propaganda. In other words, many things that are meaningful for Americans have no meaning, or the wrong meaning, for others.

How far should adaptation to the audience go? U. S. policy cannot always be in the national self interest of all countries everywhere. A minority holds that it is possible to say different things about ideas or events to people in different geographical areas. Content should be altered to avoid argument with a foreign country's position: If the Arab countries oppose the U. S. stance on Morocco, the position should be "softened."

> Maybe we shouldn't say too much to the Indians about Indochina because it's hard to make a good case to the Indians. A statement that we are sending planes to Indochina may be very popular with the press over here, yet to the Indians all it means is that we are helping to bomb Asians. You have got to find another way to approach that.

There is a strongly held position that USIA should never make the mistake of giving its audience in a given country exactly what it wants to hear.

Conflicting interests of the U. S. and other countries should not be slurred over. Problem areas should be admitted. This has a very wholesome effect on the audience, sophisticated or not sophisticated. (It is alleged that USIA, in practice, does skirt issues of conflicting interest between the U. S. and other countries.)

It may be necessary to feed an audience output on a subject in which it is not interested; there are certain things it must be made to understand. Latin Americans may not be interested in NATO, but it is part of USIA's job to make them aware of all the ramifications of U. S. foreign policy.

The idea is not to please everybody, but to get the facts to them even though the facts are unpalatable. According to one view, Agency personnel often overestimate the degree to which they must worry about foreign sensitivities. Much important USIA output is disliked because it presents new ideas that are at variance with the audience's fixed prejudices. USIA should buck the tide and make an effort to spread beneficial new ideas.

Even an action taken by the U. S. that is not in the interest of a target audience should not be soft-pedaled. An accurate account of an action like the Pakistan Treaty should be given to India, for example. The problem is to win understanding of a U. S. position that runs counter to local interests rather than to gain acceptance of it. The audience should be convinced that the U. S. position is at least sensible: "Neutralists in the target countries must be shown the necessity of the American way in politics, even if it clashes with what they want."

It is often not easy to associate American self interest with the self interests of other countries (for example, with the Arabs in the Arab-Israeli dispute). However, if over-all American policy is good, that fact can be used to take the sting out of specific elements that may be undesirable from the target country's standpoint. Favorable material makes a longer lasting impression than unfavorable material. Unfavorable material can be used because it will be forgotten.

AVOIDING OFFENSE

It is axiomatic that, insofar as possible, no one in a potential audience should be offended. These rules of thumb apply:

1. Avoid taboos. The colloquial use of "Mecca," Shriners in fezzes, pigs, kissing, low-cut gowns, the slaughter of animals—all are regarded as possibly offensive to particular cultures.
2. Avoid criticizing the audience, government policies, or a respected leader, unless major objectives depend on it.
3. Consider national pride. The Chinese cannot be addressed in contemptuous terms as Soviet puppets. The Russians don't want to be told they did not invent radio.

Concern with national pride may be carried to extremes, as this discussion of a film treatment for a Middle Eastern audience of a soccer match lost by Egypt reveals.

Why not leave out the final score?

You have to say it just to complete the story.

Can't you say, "Italy won but Egypt did this or that?"

What happens if all Egypt thinks the Egyptians did a very poor job?

I don't think anyone is apt to feel left out if we leave out the final score.

By the time we get it back into Egypt it's not going to be a news story.

Can't we put an ending in there about international good will?

4. Keep in mind the physical appearance of persons in the target country. Since Asians are generally shorter than Americans, a mixed group should be photographed sitting down.
5. Avoid subjects about which the audience may be sensitive, like American wealth. Much Americana from U. S. magazines may offend foreigners' sensibilities by making Americans look "hardboiled or also terribly mushy."

Depicting the U. S. standard of living may be offensive.

One picture showed the American in the foreground, prominently played up, and the native was standing partly behind the ox. The American was dressed simply, a white shirt and what we would say regular slacks and socks and shoes. There was talk about first of all his prominence in the picture. Secondly, there was a little bit of fear that perhaps the reader, particularly in the Far East, might think we were trying to show how well off we were, how well dressed. So we scrapped the picture and got one with the American in the background and the native in the foreground.

Even using certain media may be considered patronizing in highly civilized countries.

A lot of the things we are doing range from innocuous to harmful. We have sent lots of film units and bookmobiles rolling down the highways and byways of countries all over the world, including highly civilized countries. Imagine looking out of a window here in Washington and seeing a bus come rolling down the street here reading on the side Finnish Information Service or Spanish Information Service. There would be hell to pay. We would resent it, and those people resent it. We have aroused irritation and given the opposition proof to use as a handle to show our bad intentions or own low culture.

It is wrong to stress U.S. accomplishments in a field at which the audience itself excels: "The Germans laughed at the TVA film because they said, 'We have electric projects of our own.' "

Avoid strong anti-Communist output to areas where it would be resented. The national interests of a target audience may make them look askance at "indiscriminate attacks on Communists." In dealing with a group which is sensitive to propaganda, begin by exposing them to information material which is not "propagandistic" in character.

Do not stress sympathy for nations that are disliked by the target audience. A film showing Japanese farmers in California is unsuitable for areas where the Japanese are unpopular. This viewpoint may be carried to extremes: "If you put a Beethoven symphony on a film and sent it to France they might say, 'We have our own composers.' "

VOA reports of Chinese difficulties under the Communist regime may backfire in areas of Southeast Asia where the Chinese are hated (the audience may be glad to learn of Chinese sufferings).

A picture of a Negro beating a white man in a boxing match should not be shown in South Africa.

ADAPTATION TO THE ELITE AUDIENCE

USIA output may be geared to a high-level audience for one of three reasons: these are the people it wants to reach; these are the people who are attracted or available; or output designed for a sophisticated audience is more acceptable to others (for example, it must attract the highest rather than the lowest common denominator).

If it is assumed that the audience is above average in education and sophistication, it automatically follows that they understand the political facts of life. They "instinctively understand the meaning of the Beria [1] purge as an overturn

---

[1] The dreaded head of the Soviet Secret Police was deposed after Stalin's death.

in a monolithic power system, or of the East German revolt as disproof of Soviet claims to be a workers' state.'' Such understanding can be assumed in preparing output. They have the essential factual background and a more differentiated picture of Western civilization than might be called for in broadcasts to a mass audience. This means ''more marshalling of facts instead of simple assertion.'' Explanations of such relatively dry subjects as U. S. foreign policy or the doctrinal structure of communism are suitable for this group. Full textual statements must be supplied to them. They want to draw their own conclusions from the available evidence.

Thinking in broader, nonmaterialistic terms, they require a *less strenuous* effort to relate everything explicitly to the interests of the listening country as such. There is less need to translate everything into concrete and personal terms, and more appeal to ''the values of educated people,'' such as freedom of speech and press and academic freedom.

> The motive we can most strongly appeal to—the desire for freedom of thought—is more often strong in intellectuals, while the motive our opponents can most strongly appeal to—the desire for redistribution of wealth—is more often strong in peasants and unskilled workers.

They must be approached through the intellect.

> There are not many intellectuals in the world, and therefore an intellectual is flattered by intellectual approaches.

> You cannot keep an intelligent audience except by discussing things seriously.

They can be approached with more subtle arguments, greater candor, more direct *discussion of the opponent's* ideology, longer commentaries, more discussion of the relative credibility of sources, and distinctions between what is certain and what is merely probable. There should be less repetition of the main themes and more variety of subthemes, fewer slogans or cliches.

They react negatively to crude, emotional appeals. This means less name-calling and fewer lurid, hard-hitting, unattributed pamphlets. Religious appeals should not be evoked, although religion can be discussed.

They have strong cultural interests. It is important to demonstrate American cultural achievements in dealing with sophisticated audiences.

APPEAL TO THE MASS AUDIENCE

Just as some USIA output limits its audience to an educated elite, other output (such as films on general Americana) lends itself to the widest possible mass appeal. The mass audience is sometimes assumed to be not only uninformed or unsophisticated, but unintelligent: ''Audiences in the Middle East and Far East have very low I.Q.'s; we estimate about eight years old.''

Accordingly, certain rules must be followed:

1. Output must be simplified to be meaningful and to avoid misinterpretation. Sentences must be relatively short and words familiar. If a film is not clear enough to be immediately understood, the audience may turn for explanation to its own leaders, who will not necessarily represent the American point of view.
2. Impact is lost unless a message is confined to only one point or idea and is repeated.

   Any script that has more than one major idea in it is no good to us in the first place. In speaking to a largely illiterate audience such as we have in the Far East, you have to confine yourself to one point. You tell them what you're going to say, you say it, and then you tell them what you have said. To muddle them up with a lot of thoughts you lose the value or impact of what you're going to say.

3. If content is not geared to the audience's own experience it will not make sense. "A man who has never seen the ocean will not understand a steamship; one who has always lived in a kraal would find a film on New York City incredible." Any description of U. S. institutions must be written in terms of the rudimentary understanding of mass audiences overseas. It is a mistake to describe gadgets and technical developments which are beyond the scope of the audience's comprehension. This may arouse suspicion or disbelief. In dealing with science and technology, emphasize concrete innovations, not theory.
4. The backward audience is less capable of abstract thought. Themes must be expressed in personal terms (for example, Horatio Alger as a demonstration of American economic democracy). Political radio broadcasts are of no interest to the unsophisticated radio listener. Factual material, like speeches and statements that appear dull and overly long, must be condensed, illustrated, and brought to life.
5. To avoid possible confusion, do not use disguises. Descriptions or photographs of life in the United States may divert a foreign audience from a central theme.

   In looking at a film, particularly in your less developed areas and with your less intelligent and literate audience, they're liable to miss certain things or focus their attention on something that you had no idea they were going to. An audience may become fascinated by some little operation and be less attracted by what you were trying to give them over-all.

6. Don't presume they have the factual background to understand democratic traditions. News requires context and interpretation to make it meaningful. In translating American material, the translator must put his subject matter in proper perspective (if only through a footnote).

   The European reader can put Jefferson in his place, but if this went to an Asiatic reader and he reads such and such a passage that Jefferson said about England or about Europe and doesn't realize that this was written 150 years ago, it may shock him.

Allegations about slave labor in the Soviet Union make no sense in Asian countries, where there is no highly developed sense of the dignity of labor.

7. Stick to the broad picture. The audience will only be confused if told about every tactical move in American politics. Each move will thereby be magnified to the status of an issue. Instead, American events should be reported in broad outline.

8. Don't create issues. Don't talk about communism in a country that has never heard of it.

9. Use slogans, but these must be meaningful for the mass audience. "International conspiracy" is an empty phrase to Greek peasants.

10. Stick to popular tastes. Music (for broadcasting to the Mideast) should be selected "with the taste of the coffee house audience in mind."

11. Use emotional appeals. "Lurid, hard-hitting" pamphlets (resembling Communist propaganda and over-simplified) may be appropriate for semi-literate people.

12. Pictures and cartoons should be used when possible. However, a picture must clearly tell its own story. The mass audience overseas is not accustomed to reading picture captions.

One medium may have to serve both mass and elite audiences. A country may on the whole be as primitive "as darkest Africa," but its cities may be highly developed. Production must often cover both areas because of the language factor.

A somewhat analogous problem arises in directing broadcasts in a given language to two different audiences (for example, "intellectual" and "coffee house" programs in Arabic). Hopefully, the timing and character of the program will find two different audiences. A product may be intended ultimately to reach a mass audience but may have to get the approval of an elite (editors or officials) to reach them.

UTILIZING AUDIENCE SELF-INTEREST

A widely accepted premise in USIA is that people are governed by self-interest. Thus, they must be addressed in terms of their own aspirations, wants, and needs. The degree to which a target group's actions can be influenced depends on how much they feel they are personally affected—the degree to which informational content is useful to them. (A visitor to an information center looks for things that will benefit him personally, socially, or economically.)

Political appeals should be translated into personal terms: "Will bombs drop on your house, and if so, why?" "Will you be awakened at three in the morning by secret police taking your son for slave labor?" "Why do you have to pay three weeks' wages for a pair of shoes?"

If you can figure out a way to make him see that the approaches the President has made do have a very direct application to him personally and to his kids, maybe he'll sit down and take notice.

The Iron Curtain audiences who are "risking their necks to listen" must be given information that makes the risk worthwhile.

American contributions to European defense and economic and technical aid are of moment to people in the countries affected. The state of the U. S. economy is a subject of universal interest. U. S. tariff policy is a subject of life-and-death interest to the Japanese.

But again, news should be given a regional or local slant. If the most important point in a news story concerns some other area, and that point is retained as the lead in the story, another point of direct area interest should immediately follow it. Questions are raised about the degree to which audiences are interested in U. S. domestic issues and in news of areas other than their own. It is held that purely domestic legislation, day-to-day routine developments in the American political scene, are of no interest abroad. Nevertheless, coverage of bills of overseas interest must be provided. On the question of area interests, operators ask whether the Far-Eastern audience is interested in European news.

The Indian government has taken a neutralist position. Their primary interest is certainly not in what's going on in Europe; they are more interested in what's going on in Asia. However any position that we would take with respect to EDC or NATO, whether they are interested or not, forms a part of the pattern of issues and events which are important beyond a limited geographic area. There I think we should make the material available, and to a great extent the dissemination of material, how it is disseminated, should be determined by the man on the grounds.

There are common ties to be strengthened by stressing subject matter paralleling the audience's vital interests or characteristics. Highly religious countries, like Poland, the Arab world, and Turkey, require more output dealing with religion. Countries with a strong military tradition should have more output on military matters; agricultural countries require farming subjects. There are also strong ties of kinship that the U. S. can promote by including more information on daily life in America.

In broadcasting to colonial peoples, USIA should "play up speeches and public statements by U. S. officials which show that the U. S. supports their legitimate demands for orderly progress toward self-government."

Or the U. S. can tell foreign audiences how it has solved problems they now face, such as business monopoly or in the areas of health and sanitation. (But if a foreign audience is shown how to build a house, the house it is shown should be the kind that exists there, not here.)

Going one step further from the thesis that appeals should be made to the audience's self-interest is the thesis that output should be interesting to the audience—although what is "interesting" may go well beyond self-interest. The information program can survive only if it interests the target audiences.

Thus, policy must be enunciated in terms that have popular appeal. Output must be lively or picturesque. The foreign audience is interested in aspects of American life that resemble its own. Pictures of summer gardens interest the Japanese. Scientific developments have wide interest overseas. Publicity photographs of the latest model cars can always be placed in the local press.

These subjects can be treated selectively to parallel audience interests. A specialized interest in music, like the preference for stringed instruments in India, calls for stress on the musicianship of American violinists and cellists.

Color is a bond among peoples. Feature stories dealing with Negro progress in the U. S. are good output for West Africa.

People are interested not only in the affairs of their own country but also in other countries who share their cultural heritage. (Filipinos are interested in Latin American features; the Arab countries are interested in Spain; Indians in Britain, etc.)

FOREIGN NATIONALS IN THE U. S.

An important bond between the U. S. and other countries takes place in the actual contact of peoples through visits or through immigration. Foreign audiences identify themselves with visitors or immigrants from their country to the U. S. Immigrants who have achieved outstanding success are particularly choice subjects of USIA output directed at their country of origin. This is true both in the case of countries of mass immigration (like Italy or Poland) and for countries of relatively sparse immigration (like Far Eastern or Middle Eastern countries).

The personal experiences or statements of an American of foreign birth (or descent) are a most effective way to convey information about the U. S. to his native country. In dealing with nonwhite people it is particularly important to stress American traditions of racial tolerance and equality of opportunity (as in the story of a Chinese-born woman in Maine being named "Woman of the Year").

The Iron Curtain audience is particularly self-centered and anxious to hear news about its nationals abroad. Straight Americana are of no value for it unless some definite connection is drawn with its own nationality. The impression that the country has been forgotten by the Free World may be contradicted by showing that its prominent people are still well-known. Refugee activities are also useful subject matter.

Overseas visitors should be played up, particularly from countries whose visitors are infrequent. Pictures of foreign visitors should be taken in front of U. S. historical monuments, so that the accompanying article or caption can bring in historical background material. "There's always a little shirt-tail mentioning 'the Jefferson Memorial erected to the memory of this great American who did so and so.' '' The Washington mosque makes an excellent backdrop for pictures of Moslem visitors.

Other subjects of interest are: sporting matches in the U. S. in which foreign nationals, students, or notables participate. (In keeping with motion picture traditions, visits by foreign royalty or officials appear to receive heavy emphasis in newsreels. Pictures of royalty are considered of interest to other countries than their own. The American tour of the King and Queen of Greece is thought to be of interest to Asian audiences.

Visits by foreign diplomats to American officials should be covered by USIA media to show the respect with which they are treated. Audiences, especially in underdeveloped areas, are proud to see pictures of their outstanding nationals in a social meeting with high-ranking American personages.

Foreign audiences are also interested in activities by nationals of other countries. For example, Thai soldiers in Korea are of interest in Turkey because Turkish soldiers also served there.

But merely stressing "foreignness" is not enough: "Do you think the man in Saudi Arabia would believe it if he saw Chinese faces? He doesn't know where China is. He will think it's all propaganda."

MUTUALITY OF INTEREST

Since people are motivated by self-interest, their mutuality of interest with the U. S. is one of USIA's leading concepts.

What we are looking for is a community of interest, common aspirations with these peoples. We want to stress that the things which we want they want.

The total impact that USIA tries to create is one of belief that if the U. S. and the target country work together, the future belongs to us.

But contradictory opinions emerge on the question of whether the U. S. should be shown as selfish or unselfish. One view is that the audience must never think that the U. S. does anything for selfish reasons. It must be shown as completely altruistic, "sincere, not self-interested, but motivated by a desire for their regimes to acquire stability."

Others believe that foreign audiences will not accept propaganda unless they see that America is acting for reasons of self-interest, since they can understand this. The message that the U. S. will protect them and is interested in their well-being should be based on mutual self-interest: "Your being in good shape helps us. We want you to be safe and healthy and educated because we can deal better with educated than with ignorant people." To preserve the self-esteem of the audience, collective security must be shown as a matter of partnership with the U. S. rather than of following America's leadership.

How can mutual interest be demonstrated?

1. Support international agencies. Mutuality of interest carries over into matters which involve the U. S. only indirectly, such as efforts to promote Eu-

ropean integration or such international bodies as the North Atlantic Treaty Organization or the United Nations.

2. Bring the U. S. into the picture wherever possible. USIS field personnel must quickly capitalize on any local events in which the U. S. has interest or involvement, even though they are quite remote. In an Arab country, for example, USIS arranged an exhibit on the Philippines. This capitalized on local interest in a tennis tournament that was won by a Filipino but in which no Americans were entered. Content should stress:

A similarity between his country's history and American history, difference between his country's customs and those of America, a relation between American foreign policy and his country's future.

3. Emphasize shared tradition rather than something that either the U. S. or the target country has derived from the other. In other words, show that American art and French impressionism are derived from the same tradition rather than that one is derived from the other. Stress the common cultural heritage of the U. S. and the target audience to destroy stereotyped ideas about the U. S. People can meet Americans on common ground if their interests and desires are divorced from their political positions and if stress is laid upon occupational techniques and problems, matters affecting their children, school and home life, culture, art, and music. These form a bridge. It is even possible to stress the basic similarity between the U. S. and the Arab world by showing that Americans, like Arabs, are individualists.

Mutuality of interests. "We like to box, Americans box too." It creates an interest. There's always an angle that if they become interested enough in one aspect of a country they might be interested in some other aspect.

4. Show similarity of problems. Reports of American technological advances or of American conquest of natural obstacles should show that America has encountered the same problems as the target audience, particularly if American institutions are described in a historical setting.

There's not a problem in the realm of man against nature that anyone is encountering today that we have not encountered, and some of them are not licked yet; but this is how we've tackled them. I think this book will probably go farther in making a young student from Denmark or Brazil believe that we are not a super race and not particularly favored by God, that we are more like him than he had any reason to suspect.

Drawing parallels suggests a continuous effort to show aspects of American life which resemble things familiar to the audience. This sometimes leads operators to emphasize the atypical in order to make it appear that Americans are really not "different."

We have a gal here who is very proud of herself because she had done a picture story about a little old doll of a woman in New Mexico who kept a wood stove. Because it showed that not everybody in the United States has an electric stove.

5. In addressing a target group stress the achievements of their opposite numbers within the United States. Women abroad want to know "how women thrive in this country." Foreign students are interested in the life of American students.

To persuade workers abroad that their interests are tied up with the U. S. and opposed to those of the Soviets, two points may be made: (1) labor-management cooperation is superior to Communist concepts of the class struggle, shown by the American trend toward settling industrial disputes by collective bargaining; (2) American workers have the highest standard of living in the world because their unions are free, support private enterprise, and have higher productivity.

The value of stressing common group interests may also arouse skepticism. It may be possible for a foreign audience to develop sympathy with particular groups within the U. S. without developing sympathy for the U. S. as a whole. A foreign labor audience for the International Ladies Garment Workers Union film, "With These Hands," may develop sympathy or understanding for the American labor movement without necessarily feeling friendly to America as such.

USE OF LOCAL FORMS AND REFERENCES

The media patterns and forms to which the target audience is accustomed should be followed. Where output is unattributed it must resemble the native product in production and format. USIA print output should be rewritten by local writers before it is produced. Drawings should be made by native artists. Wherever possible, reference should be made to familiar persons, places, and things, and to native proverbs or fables.

Evidence of familiarity with the target audience supports its self-esteem by showing American appreciation of its national heritage and accomplishments.

> The Indonesian says, "Gee, here's this great big American newsreel putting in an Indonesian story." The Indian says, "Gee, they're interested in colored people just like us."

USIA must assuage foreign feelings of inferiority and self-consciousness. The audience's respect for America will rise if it is persuaded that Americans know and respect their own culture.

LANGUAGE

The governing assumption in the agency is that, whenever possible, media output should be in the local language. It reaches a larger audience, is best understood, and inspires more confidence because it is familiar. A radio or film script in the audience's own language creates the flattering impression that it has been written especially for them.

Writing for translation is "the exact opposite" from writing for an American audience. American colloquialisms must be translated into the idioms of the language in question. American placenames or references should be minimized or eliminated. If part of a script rests on language which cannot be translated, it should be omitted.

Some languages take longer to say things than others, causing problems in preparing publications set up for a given size, of films whose soundtracks must synchronize with the scenes. Many languages do not have the technical vocabulary of English, lack abstract terms and ideas, and do not have the same political terminology.

To minimize the chance of error, translations should be made in the field. To avoid sabotage, several translators should be used and a balance struck among them. If possible, output should be written in the local language, to get "the feel of it," rather than translated or adapted from English.

The use of local languages is a problem for the library program. Few books that meet program objectives are written in other languages. In most areas, few translations of any American books are available. There are also objections to translations themselves. A book should be written in the original language (English) to convey all the nuances of meaning.

In USIS libraries, the ratio of English to foreign-language books varies enormously. To set up an arbitrary ratio of translated books to English books would limit the number of English-language books to be effectively used. The number of languages into which a book is translated does not necessarily indicate the size or character of the audience it reaches. It may be possible to reach as many important people with three languages as with sixteen.

Personal contact is limited by the language barrier. An American speaking to a foreign audience should be accompanied by an interpreter so that he can cope with an unexpected situation. The actual sound of language on radio or film presents difficulties. What goes on the air or into films must be checked, to avoid faulty translation or a wrong inflection of the voice.

Anyone who goes on the air for VOA should have a perfect command of the language spoken, to remove any reminder of foreignness. Pronunciations should be the colloquial speech of the well-educated. In the case of languages which are international in character, like Spanish or Arabic, acceptance may not be forthcoming in countries other than the speaker's. Some VOA announcers are criticized as émigrés who speak an "archaic" language.

Voicing of films in foreign languages should be done locally, if possible. An authentic local accent carries credibility. (A man's accent changes after he has been away from home "for even one day.")

Dissent: "An American accent is often expected in an American program; while a too perfect native accent suggests that a renegade is talking."

English-language broadcasts are the most important and valuable in VOA, according to some. They have particular value as a channel to opinion leaders. The audience for this program is better educated than that for vernacular broadcasts. They carry a note of authenticity to listeners abroad. (Since they are in English they are presumed to be close to domestic standards of reporting; moreover they include rebroadcasts of domestic radio commentators.) This is "the only program that top management can understand," and therefore is a showpiece for the entire organization.

The important targets know English anyway. Output in English automatically selects the principal targets, the educated elements. Opinion-molders read English; intellectuals in most countries read it.

> Just as in this country there is no market for a translation of a German work on medieval music, because all the people who want that information are sufficiently cosmopolitan to read it in the original.

> We will not today translate a highly technical book on the principles of aerodynamics. We assume that a person interested in so highly technical a field would have the educational background necessary to read it in English. It would not pay them to invest in a translation of such a book.

> There's another thing which we have discussed for a long time, and that's this feeling, taken over from anthropologists, that you have to talk to these people in their languages, according to their customs, in their idiom. And then you find that the people who do listen to us or read our material by and large speak English or know English and have a pro-Western orientation or approach. They're not really part of a tribe in India or a cult and don't have to be spoken to in those terms. Perhaps the mistake is that we try to do the translation into the terms of that country rather than let the audience do it for us so that when they disseminate that information they will do it in terms that their audiences will understand.

Therefore, it does not matter that there are no local language books in USIS libraries. But the belief that the target audience itself knows English is sometimes carried to excess: "Nearly everybody in the German cities can read English." "Fifty to sixty percent of the people in Lebanon understand English."

IX

Attribution

IN ADAPTING ITSELF to its various target audiences, USIA can present its output openly and directly, or seek to secure other, more acceptable, auspices. Nonofficial American media or individuals can be more believable than officialdom; and non-Americans (not necessarily those of the target country) can be even better. An argument can also be made for completely concealing the official U. S. sponsorship of Agency output, although this can be dangerous if the American hand is detected. As a branch of the American government, USIA carries a unique responsibility for the presentation of an official viewpoint. Its audiences may look to it for this very reason, but if it sounds too official, it may be a bore.

SHOULD USIA OUTPUT be attributed directly to its source? Or is it more effective to carry on activities under other sponsorship, real or apparent?

The importance of the attribution problem is underscored by the fact that it arises in a number of distinct operations that involve decisions on (1) encouraging local voices to support the U. S. position, (2) securing local sponsors for USIA output, (3) disseminating USIA output directly without local attribution, and (4) arranging for nonofficial U.S. sponsorship.

NONOFFICIAL AMERICAN AUSPICES

To many operators, it is not desirable to attribute statements to U. S. agencies because the foreign audience will suspect they are biased. People abroad are impervious to official propaganda, but activities may be conducted under nonofficial American auspices.

If it's only published through American information media, it immediately runs into all the great resistances to propaganda. People today are overtired of propaganda.

Within the Agency this viewpoint is reinforced by these assumptions:

1. People can be appealed to through a common bond other than nationality. Therefore, information from a nonofficial American source that resembles the target is more acceptable than output coming directly from USIA.
2. A statement by a well-known American, such as a newspaper editor, not a government official, carries more impact than an official spokesman's.
3. USIA should try to get prestigious American organizations abroad to adopt statements supporting its themes and objectives so that, wherever possible, expressions of opinion are attributed to some other nonofficial source. Anti-Communist material emanating from American labor organizations is especially effective.

Those within USIA who are strong advocates for getting private American institutions and individuals to conduct supplementary activity argue that the great value of private, cooperative projects is that, once they are started, many of them can continue independently. Being nonofficial, they can spread information about American capitalism more effectively than the U. S. government. To induce private American firms and industries operating abroad to supplement USIA activities, the Agency should convince them that "it is their patriotic duty." USIA's "big mistake" is not sufficiently exploiting this potential resource.

> Sometimes broad-gauge businessmen working in an area have achieved this effect, and we should not blindly go operate in a situation where they need support. Give them a lift. We shouldn't be rigid. We shouldn't be afraid to give even a Standard Oil man money to advance our interests.
>
> Let's say he's an off-shoot of the Standard Oil Company in a particular country. They have set up a little local school system and sanitation, and the local company doctor might be the one—he might need materials. Some of these big corporations overseas want an improved labor market, they want people who will know more. It's my belief that on occasion we could legitimately give such a person materials to use in broadening the program he conducts from this selfish company viewpoint.

It is considered legitimate to support the private interests of American business if they coincide with USIA's. Although it was once considered inadvisable to cooperate with private firms overseas by showing product promotions or sales films—to avoid accusations of favoritism—present policy is to collaborate, if possible. American firms with overseas investments, as well as religious and missionary groups, should be encouraged to produce films or literature.

Foreign audiences attach more credence to broadcasts from private American radio stations than to the official VOA, whose rebroadcasts of American radio programs may seem more objective than specially prepared scripts. The listener knows that "no one is trying to put something over on him."

In the same vein, acquired films may run under their original credits, and propaganda films included with straight entertainment may be unattributed. In some countries it may be politically necessary to have nonofficial attribution of films.

> It's an excellent medium in which to expound our foreign policy to foreign audiences without these audiences knowing that the U. S. government is doing it. It does not stamp it as a propaganda medium as long as people think it's private enterprise and not a government operation.

Books, magazines, and newspapers that the foreign audience knows are on sale at U. S. newsstands are particularly confidence-inspiring, so they should be distributed abroad.

> In 1942, there was a very good article in *Newsweek* on the actual facts of Pearl Harbor and how the naval war was going. The people in OWI in New York saw this, put it in one of their reprint series, and sent out an airmail paper with a number of copies. We translated it, though we did not specify that it was from *Newsweek*. I personally took it around to the editors of a half-dozen leading newspapers in Chungking. They all thanked me profusely and not a word of it was published. Then a month later a single copy of *Newsweek* arrived in our infrequent pouches. We put it in our little reading room which was heavily patronized. Three or four of the newspapers published the article, clipped from *Newsweek,* although they had turned it down when it was given to them before. At first they were suspicious that this was written especially for them, that they were the target. When they saw that this was in a magazine for other Americans, they were sure that this had not just been written for the Chinese—it must be the real dope.

People abroad (especially opinion leaders) are interested in the editorial views of the American press, so it should be quoted. When an influential American newspaper scores a propaganda point in supporting U. S. foreign policy, it should be disseminated.

But the foreign audience may not consider even nonofficial American organizations as reliable sources of information. A local labor organization, for example, may consider American labor unions untrustworthy or too conservative. Thus, any ideological output with U. S. attribution may be immediately discounted, whether it is a private or government enterprise. As USIA uses more nonofficial U. S. sources, these sources become identified with the USIA's official position and their value diminishes: "The more we use the *New York Times*, the less value it has for us. Since most countries have a semiofficial paper, they assume the *Times* is our mouthpiece."

NON-AMERICAN SPOKESMEN

A message from a familiar source is more apt to be accepted than one from a strange, unfamiliar source. USIA output should, if possible, be placed through indigenous media or by local organizations or spokesmen, especially if they resemble the target group in nationality, culture, or creed. Therefore, USIA must determine who is pro-American or accepts American policy on a particular point.

It's more effective if a local leads a discussion than if the American does it, except for the peculiarities of certain countries where they would not believe their own people. Usually it's better if there's a teacher or someone from the government. It's not we who are telling them something. They feel it has the approval of their own leaders whom they know and recognize.

Where there's an ideological message, we much prefer that they be by foreign authors. They would expect an American author to be more dedicated to fighting communism, whereas an author from another country would look at communism and democracy a little more objectively.

A Swede can talk about Swedish self-interest with a hell of a lot straighter face than we can talk about Swedish self-interest.

It is best to use a person who comes close to sharing the audience's characteristics or opinions. "A child is more influenced by children than by adults." Talks of escapees from communism should be scheduled so that workers speak to workers, intellectuals to intellectuals.

If I wanted to convince an Italian left-wing Socialist that he ought at least become a right-wing Socialist, I would use someone with whom he would be apt to come into contact. He's not apt to be influenced by a Christian Democrat or Liberal. He might be influenced by a right-wing Socialist. If I wanted to contact a Communist, I would not ask a Monarchist to carry the ball. I might get a left-wing Socialist to carry the ball.

Even skin color is relevant. White Americans' views are less readily accepted when they speak to nonwhite foreigners. Negro Americans can answer charges of race discrimination more effectively than white Americans can. Any favorable description of Americans or America should be written by a foreign national since his account will be more readily believed. Output should be presented by people who are "human bridges" between the U. S. and the audience.

It's always better to have somebody else say you're a great guy than to go around blowing your own horn. I would much rather have *Paris-Presse* and *France-Soir* going down the line for us. We can supplement what they say but I think the important thing is to get other people to say the good things.

As far as the French and British are concerned, we are speaking only from hearsay. They say, "What do you know about the policy of the Communists and satellites? What do you know more about it than we do? You're just giving us the propaganda line."

It will be considered propaganda if we sponsor them. We should let these people tell what they have experienced. If they can't speak the language, that makes no difference. It's the sincerity in his voice that will count. This should be the spearhead—the actual escapees. They should be face to face with Europeans with their stories, and all the other information which we get from these areas every day should be behind them. I agree with the Europeans that we are not in any better a position to know than they are about what goes on behind the Iron Curtain. We really are not. But the escapee is.

Some local spokesmen are, of course, more effective than others. Since intellectuals carry prestige everywhere, in certain countries even labor groups can best be reached through them. (This emphasis on influential and intellectual spokesmen does not jibe with the position that it is best to have spokesmen from within the target group itself.)

USIA themes should be reinforced by support from friendly foreign government officials, who in turn should be supplied with information that will help them seize suitable occasions for statements.

Since a book published locally is more acceptable than one published in the U. S., even if the author is not an American, respected local individuals should be brought directly into the information program as authors or film narrators. Local media are effective channels. The Chinese are impervious to official propaganda, but they will absorb material appearing in the Hong Kong press. A good local editorial that backs up an American point of view can be more helpful than a dozen USIA stories.

> I think the Arab will resent very much someone sitting in New York and telling him not to play ball with the Communists, but if he reads the same thing in an Indian socialist newspaper, then he's talking with someone in his same general situation in the world.

It is more useful for a European paper to correct or amplify a point involving anti-American propaganda than for an American source to issue a denial. Financial support from local sources may also relieve the burden on the American taxpayer. Also, cooperation from local organizations is valuable because officials then become involved in the information program, particularly in distributing its output. Permitting a hall to be used for a USIA film showing may mobilize and commit them to action.

FILM ATTRIBUTION

Films that do not deal specifically with American themes should, if possible, not be attributed to USIA. Open USIA sponsorship is particularly unwise in presentations to an unfriendly audience. But it would not seem strange for a friendly local film producer to appear as the producer of USIA-sponsored films.

Local attribution also assists in distributing output. A motion picture distributor is more apt to use an American newsreel if he does not know that it is officially sponsored. Local attribution is especially important in neutralist areas and for material from Iron Curtain sources.

A film program is more effectively handled by the local government under its own label and auspices than the USIA, since it can reach the audience more consistently. Once foreign government agencies cooperate in making films on subjects of great national interest, such as malaria and TB control, it is easier to get the films shown. Foreign governments should sometimes be provided with funds for making films. However, when American film-makers have been sent overseas, the American touch may be obvious in their motion pictures, and local attribution fools no one. According to some reports, the lavish budgets and technical proficiency of Hollywood are clearly evident in such films, especially compared with films locally-made in Asia, which are technically primitive. (It follows that a local crew could do a more effective job on a fraction of the funds expended by Americans making a similar picture.)

DEALING WITH LOCAL SPONSORS

Operators acknowledge that local spokesmen have their limitations. It is dangerous to seize on an Indian's anti-Soviet statements and relay them to Indians, who may expect USIA output to be anti-Communist anyway. This may be the "kiss of death" for the Indian making the statement. A better approach would be for such a story to come through the native press, with the information funneled through official outside channels, such as press associations. Another assumption is that, wherever possible, USIA should get local organizations to perform or sponsor its work.

An existing organization that is doing work of interest to USIA should be given the wherewithal to be effective. It may require an economic incentive to cooperate. Pamphlets and publications should be placed with local groups that can use them to best effect. Local organizations such as labor unions can distribute unattributed USIA material to their members. It can even be channeled through pro-Communist or Communist organizations. Committees of local anti-Communist government officials should be used.

> In all publications we are trying more and more to get indigenous nonattributed use of our material. It means a lot more if it has the seal of a local group in these neutralist areas, because then the person reads it without having him feel that, "This is just part of the battle between East and West, and this is just America blustering with its point of view and tomorrow we will have Russia blustering with her point of view." They're more apt to believe it if our hand is completely out of it.

The direct interest of the groups with which USIA works places constraints on what it can hope to accomplish.

> You could get a good deal of help, a lot of approval, but in evaluating what you could really accomplish it was clear that you were really moving ahead of their interests and there was a limit as to how far you could go.

Some cooperative groups may not want to work with each other, or be willing to spend the money to produce desirable output, because they lack

American appreciation of the value of advertising or public relations techniques. Public officials may be reluctant to be associated with anything foreign or American, even though some of them may be flattered by personal associations with Americans. Local organizations may "botch up" USIA's ideas. Or their efforts may boomerang.

> You have the case of a Bi-national Center [1] in Buenos Aires which is actually a strong center of anti-American activities. They turned the tables on us under the guise of using this hyphenated term. They're using it to sell us a bill of goods.

It is difficult to strike the right note in dealing with foreign groups. "There are always leaks which reveal the American hand."

> If we didn't put enough effort into the relationships people who had asked us to do it were insulted. If we did a really good job the reaction was that we were trying to overwhelm them, that this was America at work again.

The most effective local groups may not always be those with which it is possible to identify. Or they may be afraid to cooperate fully.

> At this particular period we were being moved back in Korea and in a fence-sitting Asian atmosphere the nationals you are working with would not say, "No," but they would not work with you. If they were overcommitted to the United States' side, they tried to indicate that they were in a sense being pressured. The posters being generally produced would first go up around the American Mission and then in the rest of the town. Sometimes it was done out of simple lackadaisicalness, sometimes it was an effort to show they were not completely behind it. You can't prove that, but you felt that in case the Commies took over they were preparing themselves so they could say, "Oh, the Americans forced us to do this." Operationally you learned that lack of interest and efficiency meant that distribution would not be fully effective. There was stockpiling; materials were thrown out of train windows.

UNATTRIBUTED OUTPUT

Using local organizations to disseminate and sponsor USIA output is only a shade removed from "gray" activity involving either unattributed or fictitiously attributed output. It is widely believed that USIA's "most effective things are those for which we don't get credit."

Fictitious attribution is better than no attribution. A piece of paper with no sponsor may be suspect, while one bearing the name of a fictitious organization may not be because, as far as the audience knows, it is possible that the organization exists.

A propaganda operation works most efficiently in complete secrecy. USIA should function "in the dark more, along the lines of CIA." The only test of

---

[1] These Centers, ostensibly under joint sponsorship with indigenous organizations in the host countries, stress English-language training as well as the usual USIS activities.

how far it should go toward covert activity is whether the consequences will advance U. S. interests.

For example, it may be necessary to deviate from the stated objectives of Public Law 402, if the situation requires it. A number of sub rosa techniques are recommended: hiring speakers to talk to crowds outside the mosques in the Middle East; infiltrating Communist groups; smuggling materials into Communist strongholds; addressing the Communist rank and file in Iron Curtain countries through covert radio transmitters; subsidizing pro-U. S. elements in Western Europe by creating "slush funds"; influencing elections, and creating political parties that the U. S. could control.

> My own philosophy of a real propagandist is basically this. If you put me into a country with a maximum of two other Americans and give me a million dollars in unvouchered funds, with a shipload of white paper sitting in the harbor, I could damn well deliver any country in the Far East to our way of life. That implies going almost totally black and gray with the program.[2]

To fight communism, USIA must use some Communist weapons (infiltration, nonattributed placement of materials). USIA should have its own "agitprop"[3] apparatus to encourage discussion and spread word-of-mouth propaganda. It should set up pro-American "agitprop" schools in important countries.

In one opinion, it would be best for the Agency to maintain a surface operation devoted to "the full and fair picture," as a cover for other clandestine activities. But this would require complete support for USIA from the public, Congress, and the executive branch of government. In countries needing internal reforms, a good argument may even be made for moving USIA underground, free to stimulate reform movements.

Another suggestion is that USIA get out of direct propaganda to Western Europe and move purely into indirect work—financing or facilitating the work of Europeans—since there are very few political causes of importance to the United States for which USIA, as such, can successfully agitate in Europe.

PITFALLS IN COVERT ACTIVITY

Not everyone in USIA regards unattributed or undercover activity enthusiastically. Objections are on two grounds: it is not within USIA's province, and often results in discovery and embarrassment. Objections are seldom raised to "gray" activities on moral grounds, although it is acknowledged that any propaganda with no holds barred presents a problem for a democratic information program.

Part of the problem is that "neither Congress nor the USIA administration

---

[2] In the intelligence lexicon, black propaganda is wholly deceptive in source and sometimes in content, while gray is ambiguous, and white is open.

[3] A Soviet neologism for agitation and propaganda cadres.

has ever been honest in telling what the job of propaganda is supposed to be. They have always done it in broad generalities like the 'Campaign of Truth.' "

USIA's task can be distinguished from the total propaganda mission, however. It plays a limited role as an official government agency, whereas "some of the rough things can be done by other agencies." (One suggestion is that another agency between USIA and CIA take care of "gray" activities.)

The USIA administration wants the program to be open and forthright. Some ambassadors oppose any USIA activity that is not above board.

> We had a Public Affairs Officer who was a very energetic guy. The country was not high in the order of priority, but there was a good deal of feeling in labor ranks against the United States and evidence of Communist efforts to infiltrate. It was not a world-shaking problem, but the PAO figured it was his greatest single responsibility. So he started making contacts with local organizations, arranged with some of them that he would make information available that they might use to promote common purposes. He got out a lot of information that was prepared in his office and made it available to representatives of these organizations. It wasn't of course identified as USIS distribution. This was reviewed in the Department, it was endorsed, and lo and behold—change of administration, new ambassador, an energetic fiery guy, who gets on the scene and gets wind that the information program, which is subject to his policy control, is conducting activity which is not forthright, overt, and openly identified as American. Unfortunately at the same time there was an incident in which an organization that used some of the PAO's information had a change in leadership from a strong anti-Commie one to a neutralist one, and they disclaimed a pamphlet that had been put out by the previous officers and attacked the role of the American PAO in supplying it. The ambassador wrote a scorching letter saying that he would not be responsible for underhanded dealings with anyone and ended up with a demand for the recall of the PAO. This all precipitated a nice little problem.

The U. S. government cannot afford to mask its participation and support of its international information program activities.

> I think some PAO's have reached the conclusion that unattributed material is not always good. Material attributed to fictitious organizations has been a source of embarrassment.

> Obviously this is a ready handle for the Commies anyway. If they can prove or infer that the United States Government is active behind the scenes, they can make quite a cause célèbre of that.

Activity should never be such that it would result in an unfavorable reaction, if uncovered.

> A long time ago they arrived at a sensible conclusion, never go further than to fake an attribution that you are willing to admit to if discovered and won't be hurt by too much if you are. Black is a field that our kind of organization cannot get into, or even grayish. It will always show up in the *Congressional Record* or some harassed official will be bragging about it. We start by saying that our story, told by somebody else, might in some cases be better or more acceptable than our story told by ourselves. If you can, on any given point of American policy, put the argument into

the mouth of a citizen of a country rather than admit it yourself, it might improve your chances. People who read it would theoretically not have the barrier that they have against your argument, knowing of your vested interest.

But if the operation is so handled that you are really embarrassed by the ultimate revelation that you have suggested the action, that he has been talking to your point, then you might as well keep away from it, because this kind of organization is just not structured to do anything that it can't admit openly to have done. Local employees somewhere along the line have the chance to become aware of it. It's a job for other organizations that have money to spend on obscure details like that. I am sure in Siam they're doing a lot of things they think are secret but everybody knows about it because it's the damnedest gossipy country you ever saw. There is in a sense a public relations angle involved, since we are not equipped to run secret operations. We can so easily get established as two-faced bastards. "I know this man is really an intelligence agent and not a friend of the people."

A different line of thought is that people abroad do not give any particular thought to the possibility that certain activities, such as Bi-national Centers, are U. S. "fronts." They are simply places where they can go to read books about America or attend social activities. Rank and file patrons of the Centers, for example, do not care whether or not they are U. S.-run, since they are concerned primarily with reading English.

It is also unimportant whether the USIS label appears on press output that is reprinted locally. What matters is that the material is printed at all.

Similarly, it is difficult for most people to determine who is behind an unattributed film. Entertainment may be a legitimate rationale for showing a film.

I don't think that they necessarily believed that it was an American organization, and in many cases they wouldn't have had any way of knowing that the films were American-made films, since many of the films were made in Italy or in France and contained bits from Italian newsreels. It was very difficult for them to know who was behind it. The locally-produced films usually carried some attribution to a local organization which wouldn't mean anything to people who saw the films. Those people who realized that the purpose of the film showing was to fight communism—that I believe was sufficient explanation to most of the folks. In the case of the rice workers there was a further explanation. We were trying to entertain them, and that had a legitimate rationale because the films were shown through the labor union organization that was trying to organize them.

The character of the output as well as the character of the audience determines whether or not attribution is desirable. The prevailing theory is that "hard-hitting anti-Communist" activity should be unattributed or attributed to a local source.

If you're going to do an aggressive negative anti-Communist job where the matter is subject to refutation, it may be pretty nasty, pretty dirty; you don't want U. S. attribution.

You certainly don't want U. S. attribution on anything too tendentious, too hostile in nature, anything that makes it appear that the United States is carrying on an aggressive cold war against the Soviet Union. That's a thing that almost has got to be played by ear. You have got to think, would it discredit the United States? Would it be more effective unattributed? So much of this thing is a matter of flying by the seat of your pants. You feel that this is right or that it is not.

Anything put out under U. S. government imprint should be calm, factual, and noncombative. The stature and dignity of the United States are not heightened by ridiculing the Communists. Anti-Communist propaganda reinforces the feeling abroad that Americans are overconcerned with the problem.

Still another way to view attribution is a selective one—neither intrinsically good nor bad, but a matter of spontaneous judgment in a local situation.

Generalizations may be based on geography:

> In Middle East countries, in countries that tend to be neutralist, you lose by having the USIS label. In countries where the U. S. is highly respected, like Turkey or West Germany, it adds to have U. S. attribution.

The American label may be removed for one audience and put back for another.

> If he's just broken into a workers' quarter in a city where communism is highly virulent and he wants to get these pictures shown and sees that those labels handicap effectiveness, he will take them off. But the next day he may be showing the same film to a highly educated audience very favorable to us and he may leave it on.

> If it's anti-Communist, it should be indigenous. Most of the world thinks of two collossi fighting a cold war. They will lay off the stuff if it's American. If it carries the impression of their own local group, they won't know it's American so they'll not be afraid to read it. There's an instinctive aversion to being propagandized.

Where USIA output resembles the lurid style of Communist propaganda it must be unattributed. Satire, broad humor, and ridicule are suitable only for unattributed material. The same material might be very successful as nonattributed clandestine output (baby pictures with captions satirizing Communist rule) but creates a childish impression when directly attributed to USIA.

Where the anti-Communist case is stated with sufficient dignity, U. S. attribution is appropriate.

> If someone like Dulles, Ike, or Ralph Bunche personally exposes a fallacy of communism, it should go out over his name with a USIA attribution. Particularly if it's from sources behind the Iron Curtain it should always be indigenous, but if you have a slave labor pamphlet compiled in the main from AFL sources it may be good to do one version with AFL attribution, where they wanted to handle distribution, and in other countries put it out indigenously.

ADVANTAGES OF OFFICIAL ATTRIBUTION

There is no unanimity in USIA on the superiority of unattributed output to official output. Several arguments may be advanced for official U. S. attribution.

1. It cannot be avoided on official news and press releases and does no harm.
2. It is necessary if it is important to make the U. S. position clear. For this purpose, indigenous media cannot be used.
3. In such areas as the Far East, U. S.-attributed publications are essential to carry material that is too anti-Communist or otherwise politically unacceptable to be printed locally. Such publications can circulate freely, while unattributed or locally attributed output saying the same things would be censored or outlawed.
4. Voice of America programs should originate in the U. S. and carry its official stamp. "If you are talking about America and its way of life, you talk about it from the U. S. and not from Timbuktu."
5. A U. S. official's statement should come from an official source, since it is "straight from the horse's mouth."
6. Foreign audiences do not mind Americana when they are U. S.-attributed. They expect USIA explanations of American institutions to be more accurate than a description by their own nationals. (This is at variance with the opinion that they prefer a description from a non-American and presumably more objective source.) The Western European audience may go to its own news sources for data and opinion on U. S. foreign policy, but may turn to the Voice of America to get authentic glimpses of American life.

Anything obviously about American life and customs should carry our imprint abroad if it's a prestige piece. If it's a thing you can give to government leaders and place in schools, let the kids borrow it on a rotating basis and let their parents see it.

Anything that's a history of the United States, Americans at work or play, any and all of these subjects should be USIA. It gains us goodwill in that we have given them a prestige item to explain our people in a good light. Nobody minds propaganda like that. It's official.

7. U. S. attribution is desirable when trying to convey the impression that Americans respect the target country and its leaders. One example was a visit to the U. S. made by the president of Turkey:

IOP suggested that inasmuch as the Turkish government had certain funds set aside for covering the trip on its own, that perhaps it would be a good idea for the United States to approach the Turks and offer them our assistance on it; then it would not cost us anything but a nominal sum. Under the plan, the picture would have been shown back in Turkey without any credit to us whatsoever. This office disagreed with that view. We felt that we ought to put enough into this picture and have a large enough hand in it so that when it is shown back in Turkey it will be attributed to the USIA. We would be more or less the laughing stock of the Turks, if they had to come over here and make their own motion picture on him. We thought that it was most advisable for them to know that the Information Agency had a hand in it.

8. Official output does not have to be considered "propaganda."

There is nothing particularly bad with having it known that a man has some general connection with his government. I don't think people in all countries are ever as edgy about government representatives as opposed to private representatives as we are led to believe.

9. The very fact that Americans are working or thinking along a certain line may influence people abroad positively. Even Communist scientists may be influenced by what U. S. scientists say.
10. U. S. attribution may actually make output more acceptable in areas where the U. S. is favorably regarded. Why should USIA conceal its work on Taiwan when the American label gets a positive reaction there?
11. U. S. attribution is desirable where the audience is aware of U. S. sponsorship. "Everyone who uses the Bi-national Centers in Latin America and Turkey knows that the U. S. government supports them, so it is valuable to admit this support."
12. Some activities achieve their favorable effect by their association with the U. S. The fact that USIS libraries are openly under American auspices is all to the good, since they provide patrons with good, rapid service.

This last viewpoint raises the question of how "official" USIA should be. One view is that since it is regarded as an arm of the government it must place its primary emphasis on official U. S. news and commentary. Many people tune in to VOA precisely because it gives them the official U. S. word.

Because leading Americans like the President or members of the Cabinet personify the U. S. overseas, their pictures should be exploited in news output on any possible occasion, particularly when they go on trips or make statements.

> We do that wherever we can. Eisenhower going to church, Eisenhower going to a concert, Eisenhower the family man. That's good for us.

USIA must not just reproduce and disseminate speeches and statements, but give them a "full media treatment." (The President's atomic energy speech [proposing a sharing of peaceful applications] was regarded as "worth more than all the money we have spent on the program this year.") [4]

But there is also a feeling that USIA is "too official" and that official statements and speeches do not usually make important and useful program output, unless they deal with matters directly affecting the target country.

> We put too much attention on international conferences, on editorials, on what Congressmen have to say. I'm just thinking of myself sitting in Poland and hearing a Congressman reading he would not consent to a tax cut of more than 5 percent. If I am sitting in Poland what do I care? I feel we give a great deal of attention to things that are not of immediate interest to people abroad.

Reprints and pamphlets based on official speeches and statements produced several months afterwards may be overshadowed by interim events.

---

[4] Eisenhower's "Atoms for Peace" plan was hailed by USIA's head, Theodore Streibert, as a "master stroke," and his aides told a Congressional committee that over a billion persons throughout the world had been informed of it.

In my opinion the sort of thing you could cut out is maybe reprints of speeches by Eisenhower. They wouldn't be interested in speeches that he might give unless it was a tremendous policy declaration that might tremendously affect them or the countries behind the Iron Curtain. We had about three of them. For example, there were two different reprints of the same Eisenhower speech. I remember my German chief pointing out to me that one was much more successful because it had a terrific cover and format. The other was duller, in graphic presentation, and was a complete waste of money. I don't think that's the sort of thing we ought to risk people's lives smuggling into East Germany.

X

Truth and Credibility

HONESTY IN REPORTING is defended in USIA both on the grounds that it is morally right and because it is the best policy on entirely pragmatic grounds. Yet, the truth comes in many shapes and forms, and a strong case is made for selecting from it, tempering it, or even disregarding it. USIA's Communist adversaries are not handicapped by any concern for the truth, which raises serious questions about the proper techniques for countering Communist charges. The task of appearing believable is even more challenging than the handling of unpalatable facts. Special difficulties arise in reporting domestic political controversies in the U. S., especially when the Administration's own position is strongly challenged. USIA's fast news media, radio and press, must strike a balance in defining their function relative to the commercial news wire services with which, in a sense, they feel themselves in competition.

ALTHOUGH THE SLOGAN, "Campaign of Truth," is no longer in vogue, discussion continues within the Agency on how important it is to adhere to the truth in fast media output.[1]

The moral argument for truth as a cardinal principle is that USIA is the agency of a democratic country. It must tell the truth because to do so is morally right. If news were slanted, single deviations from the truth would inevitably lead to other distortions. The professional code of operators requires honest reporting.

A pragmatic argument is also advanced. Completely accurate and objective reporting is best in practice as well as principle. The more objective the operator tries to be, the more objective he appears to be.

[1] As USIA's "Statement of Strategic Principles" puts it, the Agency "is deprived of the devices of convenient falsification, concealed omission, manufactured evidence, and spurious consistency

It seems to me that the greatest evil I know is the Hitler-Stalin type of thinking, and I think that there is no more basic ethical value than to say the truth as you see it. I am not the kind of absolutist ethically who feels that, regardless of a big difference in terms of the East-West conflict. The conflict with the Communist power system seems to me so urgent that if I were convinced that there was a big difference in favor of slanting, distorting, card-stacking anywhere, in terms of that being better for the struggle against Soviet communism, I would favor it. But I'm not convinced that there is a very big difference in favor of card-stacking and distorting.

Self-criticism and admission of faults are democracy's great virtues.

What better way is there to combat lies than with the truth? Why get into name-calling and ranting and raving? This is the Moscow technique which, it has been proved around here, is not well received. Truth is our only weapon. It's a pretty good weapon.

A strategy of truth contrasts effectively with Soviet distortion:

If we were initiating a new propaganda venture, many arguments could be advanced for careful disregard of the truth at times, but in the present circumstances, where you have this 30-year record of Soviet propaganda and misrepresentations, counter-propaganda that exposes the falsity of this is the preferable method, and to emphasize the Communist technique of falsifications we should maintain our record of accuracy. If the Secretary of State tells Germany and France to go ahead and commit suicide, there will be a temporary reaction for three or four days. But if the editor of a European newspaper saw us leave that out, he would say, "The bastards are no better than *Pravda*." We have to maintain that reputation for credibility.

Honesty and candor are the most effective ways of dealing with essentially unfavorable subjects. Domestic news that may be received unfavorably abroad must be covered in a strictly factual manner, not "explained away." Statements of American officials must be reported, even if they leave an unfavorable impression.

The news guys are competing in a sense with AP and UP. You can't have our story coming out saying one thing and AP saying something else with another angle to the picture.

No information that reflects adversely on the U. S. should ever be omitted. Credibility requires rapid and full treatment of news that is available to the audience through other sources.

But those who favor adhering to the truth are sometimes criticized as "naive."

You have some people in the program who feel that the sole Agency mission is to provide information to the peoples of the world, and they assume that if you give all of the information, the people will automatically select the proper course.

---

which have been powerful weapons of expediency in totalitarian propaganda." However, the "Statement" goes on to note that "USIA is under no compulsion to provide all the facts, to disseminate all the news, or to report events merely because they command public attention."

Instead, it is suggested that USIA must strive to appear objective rather than actually to achieve objectivity. The following rebuttal illuminates some of the problems raised about this position:

> You can get away with stacking the cards most of the time and you just have to be careful not to stack them when the news you are suppressing is so conspicuous that he [the listener] can notice your suppression of it.

> In our inner councils, the basic criterion is always assumed to be the appearance of objectivity. How much propaganda can you get away with and still sound objective? I'm not too dissatisfied with that, because all the change in the direction of objectivity that I think there's any hope of getting can be very cogently justified on that ground. All-out objectivity might well be more effective than even the intermediate degree of it that I am willing to argue for and settle for, even in the situation that exists here with its little preconceptions and axioms—one of them being that you have got to be cagey, you have got to fight fire with fire. There are a couple of epigrams that I have heard to support these axioms. One is that there is one danger in white propaganda and that is that it becomes lily-white propaganda. Another is that you cannot fight black shirts and brown shirts and red shirts with stuffed shirts—stuffed shirts being idealists who don't believe in hitting below the belt.

The need for deviating from the truth is sustained by seven basic arguments:

1. A full exposition of the truth may be embarrassing. Some problems can be treated best by ignoring them. Or the situation may call for deleting items harmful to USIA objectives or major officials' statements, particularly material that makes the U. S. appear "two-faced" or self contradictory. (Example: a film for showing in Europe that urges lower tariffs but appears to contradict American tariff policy.)

> If somebody makes a charge that certain basic liberties in this country are being endangered, we just don't treat these subjects. We don't treat McCarthyism. In the economic field, we select stories that indicate a dynamic and growing economy, probably downplaying the idea of possible depression. We would not put out a story reporting a guy who said the United States economy is going to hell next year. In labor, our treatment is basically to show that cordial relations have been developed between labor and management and that there's relatively little strife. Strikes are mentioned, but they're not played up.

2. Output must be selective. All possible news or information cannot be included. "We always tell the truth, but we are not morally obliged to tell the complete truth to everyone."

> You're doing a story showing that Americans are becoming interested in the Arab world culturally. We're not forced at the same time to show that we are giving more aid to Israel than to Egypt. We don't have to point it out in that context. We can show in a story that the Middle East gets so much of American aid and we won't stress the fact that Israel gets as much as the Arabs in the lead, though we would give the breakdown in the body of the story. There is no stressing or denying the fact. We are not the only ones sending news abroad. There has got to be a constant awareness of what other people are sending abroad. Then we operate within that context.

Selectivity, of course, can be interpreted as distortion:

We got into a hassle when the Yugoslav U. N. delegate, [Vladimir] Dedijer, delivered a speech, the burden of which was an attack on the way the Russians have perverted their own press and the satellites' so that the newspapers of each satellite country look exactly like *Pravda*. But before he got into that, he was criticizing the big powers for their monopoly of the machinery of information and news, and he had an unkind comment, not against the United States government but American news services for their monopoly, particularly in Latin America.

This seemed to me to be very minor and not the burden of the speech. In writing my story, it seemed to me overwhelmingly an attack on the prostitution of the Soviet press and I was not going into this minor comment that was not vicious or angry, but was critical of the fact that the American wire services controlled the news-gathering machinery in the Western hemisphere. I didn't even make reference to it and the fellow who edited the text had eliminated it from the text.

We got a hot comment back from Germany, saying that the American wire services were also cutting out this criticism of them, and the DPA [2] was calling back *Amerika Dienst* asking questions. I said we wrote the story as though it were a news story and we had not considered it important enough to mention, although it was critical. If I had written a much longer story, I probably would have included it. HICOG's[3] contention was that for credibility we should have included it.

3. Truth in itself is not enough. Propaganda requires "a truth that registers as a truth." USIA output will always be regarded with a certain amount of suspicion. Unslanted news may sound slanted to a foreign audience.

We are not slanting this news at all, not consciously, but it will sound slanted to the Iranians because the American viewpoint on world news is not going to be the same version that the Iranian gets. The facts as we see them and as the Communists see them are two different things. They may be the same but they don't sound the same.

Facts don't always speak for themselves and may lack the "necessary spark" to change attitudes. They may have to be put into perspective.

Where does credibility lead us—to the mandate of objective and factual news reporting? I go along with "factual"—that it has to be. "Objective" is another thing. It's our mission to press the American point of view. We are, as a matter of fact, very subjective. The term should be rather factual and selective, because I don't think we are under obligation to broadcast anything simply because it's news. I think we should broadcast information if it's factual and promotes our objectives, and is in line with our credibility, but "objective" is simply meaningless, because it would mean that if Mr. Molotov presents his proposals in Berlin and Mr. Dulles answers we would have to report what Mr. Molotov says, what Mr. Dulles says, and let it go out without weighing the pros and cons on both sides. But we are in the business of showing the rightness of what Mr. Dulles says and of showing that what Mr. Molotov says is not sound.

USIA is in the news business only in order to get and maintain an audience for the American foreign policy viewpoint.

---

[2] *Deutsche Presseagentur* (German Press Agency).

[3] High Commissioner's Office, Germany—U. S. headquarters during the postwar occupation.

Ninety percent of all news should have propaganda relevance. The only exceptions to this should be those few carefully chosen items which are included in order to heighten the impression of candor. . . . This means that we should not pretend to perform the newspaper's function of supplying a representative or complete survey of the news.

4. The "truth" may be misleading. A foreign policy position that really makes sense may be harder to propagandize than a dishonest or unsound position. It is apt to be more complex, hence less plausible. It is not objective or competent handling of the news merely to state that a development has taken place without interpreting its real meaning through background information.

If you accept Soviet announcements at face value, which BBC does, and make no effort to give them their real meaning, then it sounds naive. You may call this objective reporting, but I don't think it is, because it hides the real situation. It's not enough to handle as straight news the fact that the Soviet Union is having elections for the Supreme Soviet and that they won by 99 percent of the vote. Those are the facts, but it's also part of the business to show that candidates are selected by a small minority, that it's a one-party slate and that people who want to vote the other way have to go into a separate room and that their names are taken down, that they're herded to the polls.

Films or books that are "overly realistic" about American life, such as [James Jones'] *From Here to Eternity,* may be all right for an American audience but unsuitable overseas. Presenting a problem may (a) eclipse the solution and (b) serve the ends of Soviet propaganda. (Example: publicizing a magazine article that describes how the mayor of Cincinnati rooted out dope peddlers.)

5. USIA is in business to demonstrate that American foreign policy is correct, a position inconsistent with objective reporting. News must be factual in the sense that it deals with true events. But there is no reason for it to be objective in the sense that it does not take sides.

6. Deliberate slanting and selectivity are simply part of the art of propaganda and admittedly are part of the USIA operator's job.

We have no set of ethics. It's the practicality of the thing.

The only test is whether the consequences of what we do will advance United States interests.

7. With an audience that is already strongly persuaded, objectivity is unacceptable. In addressing a very friendly audience, such as in Greece or Turkey, VOA can "get away" more readily with a one-sided news presentation.

To the Free World, you definitely want to appear objective. There is little argument there. The only argument is, should you really be objective or only appear to be objective? To the satellite world, which after all is a captive world, appearances of objectivity backfire on us frequently. Defectors say they listen to us rather than to BBC because there is more meat to us.

Taken at its most extreme, there is a position that holds that nothing that can be identified with the U. S. should ever be shown in a bad light. "Play down the unfavorable without ignoring it," is the prescribed mode. A balanced picture on some subjects "might be very bleak." Comment and interpretation must put bad news in perspective and make it look less serious.

> We don't want to hide that we have slums, but on the other hand we show that we are clearing up slums or juvenile delinquency. We have got citizens who are attacking these problems without pay. We are all proud to be Americans and we all want to look at the right side. We want to throw in just enough gray to give it credibility.

Others hold, however, that unfavorable domestic events cannot be written off with direct commentary that shows editorial disapproval. Any rationalization will backfire. A lynching should be reported without comment, but the following week, when memories of it have faded, there should be a general report on progress in U. S. race relations.

TECHNIQUES OF REBUTTAL

There is strong faith in USIA that truth is the most effective weapon the United States has to answer Communist lies. But it is not easy when the truth requires a simple denial of a Soviet fabrication, like germ warfare charges, where "there is no evidence." It may be necessary to use different techniques to refute the charges—possibly quoting an outside, internationally credible authority.

While it is generally agreed that the best way to answer Communist charges is quietly and dispassionately, some operators feel that this does not rule out emotional appeals completely, particularly if they throw the enemy off balance. In making a rebuttal, how should the original charge be presented? Several different suggestions are made:

1. Don't refer to Communist charges directly.

> We don't engage in a propaganda battle with the Soviets solely for the sake of winning a propaganda battle. After they make wild charges we try to unmask those charges. We try not to do it as a propaganda battle but just by giving the facts, not referring to a Soviet broadcast.

> If you can present a fact which has to stand by itself and is not just part of an argument, then the establishment of that fact in the mind of the listener will stand in his mind without your being involved in arguments.

When the Soviets exploit an evil in American life, this should not be answered directly by an attack on Soviet evils, but should be dealt with obliquely by contrasting the American and Soviet systems. Soviet-fostered misconceptions about the U. S. should be attacked in a roundabout fashion, and not frontally. A positive statement of the American position usually answers the Communist line by implication. The best reply is to present a "full and fair" view of the U. S., to show that "Americans are friendly and anxious to help other people," to show the American standard of living, and to show "how hard Americans work for what they have."

2. Report the Communist charge only as a starting point. The Communist position should be stated in such a way that it sounds accurate but deliberately should not be presented "in its best light."

We would state the Soviet position only in a prelude to a rebuttal. I'm not going to give publicity to the Soviet position. That's standard propaganda practice. You talk about it only enough to make the situation clear. If you have to quote them out of context, that's OK too, as long as it's to kill a phony.

An argument cannot be won if it is conceded that the other side has any case at all: "I don't think we would go so far as to admit anything good about the Russians."

3. Give both sides. A two-sided presentation is much more effective than a one-sided one, particularly with a skeptical or hostile audience.[4]

It's better to align your statement with the original statement. Where it's a question of different positions on an issue, it's effective to contrast the two and then by compelling logic prove that one is bad and another good.

Distortion of the opposition viewpoint would undermine credibility if the audience learned the actual position. Moreover, disproof of an incorrectly stated position is not of much value in discrediting the real one.

We have to maintain the appearance at all times of fairness. We are news reporters and a reporter does not go out and get just one side of the thing. If you are telling a story, you want to be telling a comprehensive story, even though it's slanted in the sense that you show us in a better light.

"Nonessential points should occasionally be conceded to the opponent's case." These "should be points on which many listeners are already convinced that a concession is necessary."

ACHIEVING CREDIBILITY

To convince anyone, output must first be believed. What devices produce credibility? The following list includes the suggestions of a number of operators:

1. Stressing a single, well-known fact that is easily recalled.
2. Avoiding an explicit conclusion (as in the Communist "peace" campaign).
3. Generalizing, to imply that no one in the world would sincerely challenge a statement or theme.
4. Delivering a message in a calm, sober tone of voice.
5. Including self-criticism that produces the impression of candor.

[4] This proposition represents a major subject of investigation in experimental social psychology both before and since this study was made. As with other sweeping propositions on the art of communication, the evidence leads to restatement of the conditions. For example, an informed, skeptical audience with a strong interest in the subject, reacts differently (and more favorably) to the two-sided approach than a naive, uninterested, and already favorable audience. But this was well understood in 1953 by social scientists like Leo Lowenthal and Ralph White within USIA.

BBC strikes people as objective because they report things critical of the British themselves. It's a phony in a sense, because you can include an item that's self-critical, but the rest of the program may be self-praise.

It was a good idea to throw a rock at yourself and show it could happen in your country also [by describing the Ku Klux Klan in an exhibit].

We sent out a cartoon that showed Americans seeing Communists under the bed. After we sent it someone objected, and we wired the field to kill it. Manila came back and said it was too late, it had already gone out and made a good impression, because editors said it showed Americans can laugh at themselves.

6. Admitting self-interest.

I have seen some of the dope that said this whole thing was just for the benefit of mankind, and people know better.

7. Not always pursuing the same line on a subject. An analysis of economic problems in the Soviet orbit need not always be identical with other broadcasts. The object is to give the audience food for thought rather than a final position.
8. Clearly distinguishing news from commentary. USIA's fast media should practice the kind of "approximate objectivity" maintained in American newspapers, not editorialize.
9. Organizing facts so logically that the audience draws the desired conclusion.

Both USIA's official character and its need for credibility create strong pressures for authenticity in news reporting. An unauthenticated ("soft") story may be used occasionally if it backs up a U. S. position, but only if it surely will be accepted as true.

News stories carried by USIA media must be "hard" (or confirmed). Unvalidated stories could easily result in loss of credibility. VOA cannot afford to send any "soft" (unvalidated) news to the Iron Curtain countries. It can be easily uncovered and exposed by the Communist radio. (This contradicts the assumption that Iron Curtain listeners can be told virtually anything, because they have no basis for evaluating what VOA tells them.)

USIA must be candid in talking to friends.

I don't think by radio we ever change one person's mind. We keep some of our friends. I think fundamentally our friends listen to us and I don't think we would lose them if we didn't broadcast to them, and I sometimes think we lose some of their friendship because of our lack of candor. I think if I were abroad I would not listen to the Voice because why should I listen to this canned crap that comes out when I can read the French press or the *Herald Tribune?* I don't want to listen to a radio that avoids things, that doesn't talk about the key issues.

The bad news should be given along with the good; on balance America has nothing to be ashamed of.

I would certainly think that the best value would just be to show what really is. We always talk about distortion of the picture of America. It's not only distorted by enemy propaganda, it's distorted by the internal contradictions in American propaganda. I would not hesitate to show the bad aspects and to expand on them. I would present a picture of America, but not just in a rosy, propagandistic light. I don't think that the presentation of America should be tendentious. You lose every propaganda value, and that's exactly what gets me mad, that everything has to be projected to some propagandistic end.

I'm just thinking what are the very bad things—what would I include? If I were in Malenkov's services or in Goebbels', I would not include the concentration camps. Bad things are things for which there are no justifications, and it occurs to me, I am surprised myself, that I cannot think of a very bad thing which could not be justified by the process of American life itself. Take slave labor in Russia. There's no justification for it, except the maintenance of terror. Nothing can help you. There's no explaining it away. And such things I don't think are in American life. Take the fact of discrimination. You can still deal with this fact because as it is now, it is not a real bad thing because after all things happen, and it is changing.

To achieve balance in news coverage the "freakish" aspect of special events output should be counterweighted by semiofficial and official statements and by coverage of conventions and group meetings. (If special events coverage were confined mainly to sporting events, odd or special things, this would not give a genuine picture of life in the U. S.)

Any audience is unreceptive to any degree of overt propaganda. People have "an instinctive dislike" of being propagandized. Audiences "want information but won't touch propaganda with a ten-foot pole." Obvious propaganda lacks credibility and is unconvincing. According to one observer, the only difference between psychological warfare, propaganda, and international information is semantic. Many operators reportedly think of propaganda as "a nasty word," equated with lies. They prefer to think of USIA as not propagandistic.

Anything that carries a government label is commonly regarded as propaganda, at least by a sophisticated audience. An unsophisticated audience does not necessarily identify it in this way. USIA's object is to have its propaganda not identifiable as such. This implies an emphasis on the pro-American rather than the anti-Communist aspects of the program. (It is desirable not to have "a lot of propaganda" in U.S. libraries.) The audience is less suspicious of output on a relatively innocuous subject, like European political affairs, than of comment on a momentous matter like the hydrogen bomb.

TREATMENT OF DOMESTIC CONTROVERSY

A severe test of USIA's concern with credibility arises in its treatment of controversial domestic issues. Opinions differ as to how these issues should be handled.

It is a generally accepted principle that, for purposes of credibility, it is useful to show that there are a variety of views in the U. S., freely expressed.

Nothing tends to convince a listener more of your reliability than to hear over a government radio something said in criticism of the government.

Where the United States takes a position officially, and much public opinion—at least vocal public opinion—seems to be critical or opposed, you can always fall back on the proposition that this variety of views illustrates the freedom with which Americans can speak up. It's different from totalitarianism.

Controversy is always attractive.'' It should be taken for granted and interpreted. Columns and commentary should deal with important and controversial issues. By reporting domestic American political news as fearlessly and colorfully as a domestic news commentator might, VOA broadcasters can turn controversy to advantage, illustrating how the American system of government operates.

There are those who debate whether every big domestic issue in the U. S. must be commented upon. They feel that objective reporting may make it necessary to point up ''confusion'' or friction among branches of the government, even when this may not serve American interests.

Should USIA take sides on domestic issues? The accepted opinion is that discussion of domestic controversy should take place in a clear-cut fashion so that the pros and cons are delineated, without having the Agency take a position.

News and commentary should be strictly balanced between opposing viewpoints, centering on ''what's under discussion and why.'' Domestic debate should be given a fair, balanced, calm factual treatment: ''It's gotten down to the point of word-counting, where if you say one paragraph on one side you have to give a paragraph on the other side.''

American foreign policy should not be interpreted so as to serve the administration's ends in domestic politics. The Agency represents the whole nation rather than any particular administration. But a case is also made for approaching domestic controversy from the administration viewpoint, ''because the administration is the spokesman for all the people of the United States as far as people abroad are concerned.''

The continuing controversy over Senator [Joseph] McCarthy has provided the Agency with ticklish questions for news treatment. There are several ways of looking at the matter:

1. Equal amounts of press comment should be quoted on both sides of this controversy. Reports should stick ''to the facts.''
2. Truthful comment on the McCarthy hearings would not reflect credit on the United States. (This opinion has its counterpart in the criticism that ''the Agency pretends that McCarthy does not exist.'') To ignore the controversy damages credibility.

The exaggerated importance attached to McCarthyism abroad is due to the fact that his credit has been permitted to grow without any explanations from VOA.

It is advisable to broadcast U. S. comment preponderantly unfavorable to McCarthyism because of foreign concern with the subject. The foreign audience wants interpretation as well as news on this subject; it is reassuring to them to know that a large segment of U. S. opinion agrees with its own assessment of a domestic situation.

3. "The McCarthy phenomenon" might be handled in a dignified way, so as to diminish its importance, and "to keep the foreign audience from thinking that America is on the road to fascism." USIA should show that "the so-called American hysteria over communism actually represents a legitimate conclusion that it is necessary to be on constant guard against it."

REPRESENTING U. S. PRESS OPINION

How far should USIA reflect the official views of the administration? To what extent should it be representative in reflecting the whole array of American opinion? This question is particularly crucial in reporting, by the fast media, of domestic press opinions.

In reporting domestic editorial comment opposing the official position, the Press Service runs into a dilemma in its desire to give the foreign editor a good reflection of editorial comment in the United States.

Domestic press comment should be a cross-section. Such a position is particularly useful in dealing with issues where a sizable bloc of American opinion supports the views of the Administration. Treatment of a problem is easiest when official policy and public opinion concur.

> There are times when the bulk of American opinion is right on the beam of what official policy is. Then we ride high on it. There are times when the official policy is opposed by important segments of the American press. That's when we have our troubles.

When the official American position is opposed by much vocal public opinion, comment should be made along the lines that this variety of views illustrates the freedom of the American press.

On some controversial issues of foreign policy, it is desirable to show the actual balance of American opinion, so that changes in official policy will appear consistent to the foreign audience.

The basic objective of quoting the American press is to explain foreign policy. Press opinion selected must represent the administration position. Quotations must be items that support policy directives. USIA is under no compulsion to reflect the exact balance of public opinion on foreign policy. Opposition viewpoints must be quoted. However, they should receive "representation but not play."

> We tend to put most weight on those editorials that support the administration and American foreign policy. We will also include some of the opposition, but we don't quite frankly give equal space to anti-administration editorial policy.

It would not be to the national interest to give equal treatment to the isolationist and internationalist viewpoints in American opinion, although both should be quoted.

No domestic press opinion should be carried that questions a fundamental objective of official policy, but it is permissible to carry opinion that criticizes details of the policy if it agrees with the basic premise. The picture presented of domestic opinion on controversial subjects should be multisided, but with emphasis and weight of logic on the side of the official American viewpoint.

How can foreign editors be given a complete reflection of American editorial comment in cases where it might show strong opposition to the administration, particularly on a point of foreign policy? One way to provide a rounded picture of editorial attitudes and at the same time insure a balance favorable to the administration is to file additional editorial comment to those special posts that might require additional opposition comment, allowing the PAO to make the decision to use them or not.

Quotations to illustrate a dissenting opinion on a point of controversy should come from conservative rather than from sensational newspapers.

Does the audience distinguish between press and official opinion? The answer may be different for press and radio. While one view is that foreign listeners can distinguish between unofficial and official opinions expressed on VOA broadcasts, there is also a dissent. The average listener does not distinguish clearly between unofficial and official opinions. Balanced editorial comment reported by VOA may leave listeners confused as to what the U. S. stands for. Therefore, excerpts from domestic radio commentators should not be broadcast: "We hope the foreign editors do not notice that the editorial excerpts sent them are weighted in a pro-administration direction, but they probably do." The audience is not fooled. They recognize when USIA's quotation of editorial opinion does not reflect true differences of opinion but only the official line.

THE WIRE SERVICES

Commercial press associations and wire services are an important source of information about America overseas. USIA's relationship with the services is of considerable importance not only for this reason, but also because the Agency's fast media use them as source material.

The wire services serve commercial clients. Because their objective is to sell newspapers, they do not present American news or policy in the way USIA wants. They do not have any definite aim as to the kind of impression of the U. S. they want to create.

The primary responsibility of a wire service is to cater to the market it is trying to reach. If people abroad want to know about an anti-Negro incident in the South, the wire services have to tell them about it, even if it is harmful to American foreign policy.

The wire services disseminate news that USIA would rather see played down or suppressed. They also carry many speculative stories. Yet, for reasons of credibility, USIA must take account of these stories. The commercial services are not so concerned as USIA with possible errors, because there is not the implication of government support for what they say.

The IPS Wireless File is necessarily dependent on day-to-day events. This is described as living "on a hand-to-mouth basis," seizing on material most readily available on a given day. (This observation is made critically by those who feel that there should be more planning of output.)

VOA attempts to give a rounded news output; the Press Service does not. The Wireless File's primary emphasis should be on official news related to foreign policy, a government news service reporting on official events.

> We are not trying to beat the wire services with a bulletin lead at all. If a story breaks, the wire services will beat us with a bulletin undoubtedly, because we only move a few hours a day but we will get the full text of it there so that the editor can look at it and print it if he wants to, but more importantly—so when he writes his editorials he's got a full text and the American viewpoint.

Does USIA compete with the commercial wire services? There are two contradictory positions on this point:

1. USIA competes with the commercial press services. There is a disposition in both the press and broadcasting services to think of their news functions in this way, at least "in a sense." A radio service must have a public. It must be "listenable," dependable and prompt in its news, "so that it can compete with other news services." USIA is in competition with them in the sense that what it says must be consistent with what they do. Output must counteract what they have to do in order to sell papers, and supplement them where they cannot devote linage to a topic that is important from a USIA policy standpoint.
2. USIA is in no sense in competition with the wire services. It provides texts, backgrounds and interpretive material from the official U. S. position that the wire services do not offer because they are uneconomical to transmit. Straight news reportage is the Press Service's "least valuable medium." Output should advance the program's basic purposes. It should have some other purpose than straight information. "We don't cover the whole news front."

Coverage of domestic news can better be done through interpretive articles than by day-to-day news coverage. IPS has the task of building a context into which the foreign audience can put the fast news it receives.

> It's not necessary for us to do a day-to-day coverage of the news. To whatever extent we feel qualified to do it, we try to explain the deeper aspects of life in the United States. That to some extent tends to get you into a Sunday magazine rather than a daily newspaper type of reporting."

But, IPS must continue to provide day-to-day reporting of domestic news rather than interpretive treatment. "There are a great many areas that are not serviced by the commercial press services. By providing them with news they're more likely to accept our more loaded material.''

There are also differing conceptions as to whether stories and texts from the Wireless File are used directly by foreign editors, or whether they merely provide background that may be reflected in their editorials, in their news treatment of the United States, or in their personal influence.

XI

Tone

USIA's VARIETY OF MEDIA AND TARGETS makes it impossible to achieve consensus as to how "hard hitting" output should be. One school of thought contends that propaganda must reflect conviction, and therefore emotion, to be persuasive. But this doctrine is challenged by those who argue that both the audience and the specific subject matter may make a sober, factual tone more appropriate. The use of subtlety and abstraction, humor and satire, similarly defies generalization. A personal touch in news commentary can make propaganda seem more convincing. But it may be precisely the impersonal official viewpoint that the audience expects and wants. Propaganda should concentrate on a limited number of themes in order to achieve a cumulative effect.

THE DIVERSITY OF USIA's MEDIA AND AUDIENCES creates a wide range of opinions about the proper tone of output. Operators variously relate it to policy guidelines, the nature and attitude of the audience, the character of the material, or the writer's or producer's choice of treatment.

> We are inclined to start with the problem and the products we have to offer for it. I don't recall any incident in which we have debated whether to play the thing on an emotional level or a sober factual level. That has arisen naturally rather than out of any debate.

> Policy guidance may determine its [tone] to some extent. If it says, strictly, "We treat this factually," that's what we do. If there's no specific guidance on the subject, it's like a guy writing a piece for a magazine, he's going to write it in the way that's going to sell it first to the editor and then to the readers. Again, the audience determines it to some degree.

One basic debate pits facts against emotion. Other issues involve the use of subtlety and abstraction, humor and satire, a personal touch, and repetition.

EMOTIONALISM

Views range from a belief in the essentially emotional character of propaganda and attitude change to espousal of completely dispassionate reporting.

> Emotionalism indicates to a listener that you are not in full control of your faculties on this score, you're hep on it. Your zeal gets the better of you. It's generally conceded as bad. But emotionalism that shows that you feel strongly on something, that the listener also feels strongly on, is good. An appeal to emotionalism is good because you can get more by an appeal to emotionalism than by an appeal to reason.

Output should not be "blatant" or "hard-hitting." Invective, colored adjectives, and "horrific emotion" in drawings or photographs weaken credibility. This view has as its major tenet the premise that USIA, as an organ of the American government, should not indulge in exhortation. Namecalling serves no purpose, and offends opinion leaders.

> At the Voice, they say, "Malenkov was lying again today," instead of letting him have his say and then saying, "Comment on this subject points out that—." The Voice so often starts out making the propaganda in its news presentation. I think it's not effective at all. I think the other way is more effective. The one who thinks Malenkov is a liar does not need to be told so and the one who hopes to goodness he's not a liar is going to be put off by the way you say that. You can put it in the mouth of a commentator, but you must let Malenkov make his statement first. There are plenty of people who snort and say, "Our business is propaganda." I merely say it's not a good way. The way to persuade people is to inform them and in the information persuade them. Assume that the man you're trying to explain this to wants the freedom to make up his own mind.

Presenting facts is good enough. A matter-of-fact tone is far more convincing than displays of emotion.

> Somebody that you have found is calm and factual you will learn to believe. Somebody who gets excited and emotional about it, you don't have the same confidence in. I don't mean to preclude color and that sort of thing, but not this tear-jerking.

> The approach should be basically one of information. If you start exhorting and obviously trying to tell people what to think, your stuff will be classed immediately as propaganda.

> The audience is tired of being the audience for the U. S.-Communist debate. They say, "Shut up, cut it out, let me sleep." That's the way a lot of these local people feel about it. When you go away from that let's say they don't mind. What they would mind is any impression that we are telling them what to think.

It is not possible instantaneously to convert anyone from communism to a neutral position. Such a long, difficult task calls for reasons, not emotion. USIA's most forceful propaganda merely uses the Soviets' own words to expose the falsity of communism. Firsthand accounts of life in Communist-dominated countries should not vilify the Communists but simply present an objective account of the narrator's own experiences and reasons that impelled him to leave.

While an already favorable audience needs reasons and facts to support its predispositions, an audience that is not ready to accept a position as true must be approached very carefully, not presented with direct arguments that may only alienate it further. Besides, certain prejudices and stereotypes are immune to argument. If a person in the target audience happens "to be 'hep' on the Negro question," no amount of factual presentation would affect him.

Strong advocates for using emotion in output point out that facts do not speak for themselves. They must be put in perspective. Further, since no matter how much information a person has he will interpret it subjectively, strong emotional content is necessary to effect attitude change.

> It's pretty well established by years of psychological research that people are motivated 90 percent by emotion and 10 percent by rational logic.
>
> We can publish all the books in the world that have all the information in them, but to get people reading these books and get them to believe that, it must have the thrill of romance or the shocking facts of crime. Something more has to be added. Do we want to merely create doubts in these target audiences' minds on a purely logical basis as to the theoretical validity of communism—or are we trying to go farther? Are we trying to graduate them from a course so that when they come out they can pass an examination and say communism is terrible economics? Or are we trying to give people a feeling that this Iron Curtain business is terrible, just on an old-fashioned, old-lady-talking-over-the-fence basis? People abroad are no different than a bunch of neighbors in a community. They don't get together discussing economic theory abstractly like a bunch of students. Even when you get a bunch of fellows in a coffee shop discussing political issues, it's not more logical than a political discussion here. "So-and-so beat his wife; I wouldn't vote for him." These are the things that make the principal impression on your average vocal individual who is your principal audience.

Communication is emotional. Using media effectively requires dramatic, emotional techniques.

> I feel that we deal with words and pictures, things that are all man-made and therefore, basically emotional. The idea of separating out the material that has emotional impact and material that has factual impact has always seemed to me a little unrealistic. There's no such thing as pure factual impact. You're not going to send them anything that affects a man's thinking without affecting him emotionally.
>
> After all, the Communist menace is a religion to many millions of people, which means that it's an emotional thing. The Communists have used emotions tremendously.

Factual and emotional approaches are not necessarily incompatible. "You can combine facts and emotion." A calm, factual tone does not preclude color or drama. These precepts are offered:

- Where possible, news items should be combined to produce a cumulative emotional effect.
- Emotional epithets should be used, up to the limit that a given audience is willing to accept as "not too propagandistic."
- Full use should be made of existing hostilities.
- Voice and inflection should be expressive and on occasion strongly emotional.

Qualifications are put on using emotion. It is suitable in wartime but not in peacetime; it is permissible if the message is not attributed to USIA, or if the subject is altogether clear-cut and the objective is definite.

> Emotions cannot be sustained without having some specific points. We are talking thousands of miles away to a vast audience, millions of people. If we wanted an uprising against the local government, I presume we would be working on the means of doing it, but if we were working over the long pull to pull people away from communism or neutralism, it's got to be induced by reason. They're not going to fall down on their knees in the street and say, "I have been converted!"

Also, it may be necessary to frighten or threaten the audience. Thus, the U. S. warned the Italians that in the event of a Communist victory in their 1948 elections the McCarran Act would prevent them from visiting relatives. In any case, some subjects lend themselves to exhortation, others to information.

> You want to do the calm and factual when you're talking about the peace negotiations in Korea. You want to show the patience we had, the moderation in our proposals. On the other hand, when you talk about Communist atrocities you have the emotional.

The danger of getting excited and sounding "too propagandistic" should always be kept in mind.

> The purpose is to arouse an emotion in the listener without indulging in that emotion yourself, because you can do it better if you yourself are not carried away with the emotion. That's an argument for restraint in output, even where emotion is a good thing. There are some who argue that emotional tone is compelling because it shows the man speaking means what he says, he feels it deeply. But that has to be definitely restrained emotion. It's something that's not clear-cut and precise, probably one of the questions that won't ever be resolved.

A treatment that appears factual and objective to one audience may appear over-emotional to another. VOA announcers "sound like salesmen" compared to BBC announcers. But Latin American and Middle Eastern audiences may respond favorably to invective and emotional output.

Intellectuals may not necessarily respond rationally all the time: "Workers of the world unite! Is that something that intellectuals would go for? That would be worth another study. Perhaps we have been assuming all this time that it's best to reach the intellectuals on a rational basis. Perhaps we have overemphasized that."

Friends must be approached differently than enemies or neutrals. They should be approached emotionally, while an antipathetic audience should be presented with facts. "We use emotional films with a friendly audience and factual films with an audience that needs to be aroused."

SUBTLETY AND ABSTRACTION

Most USIA operators believe—at least in principle—that a subtle, unobtrusive propaganda point is much better than a direct one. "You don't win friends by hitting them over the head." A quotation from a speech or a newspaper is more effective than a direct propaganda statement. The audience should be permitted to draw the necessary parallels and implications from the message. A point may be made indirectly but effectively through a parable or a book or film plot. For example, showing pictures of Negroes and whites together, without social labels, permits the audience to draw its own conclusions about tolerance and equality in the U. S. Communism should not be attacked frontally. In presenting a picture of America, its political advantages should be shown only unobtrusively.

Subtlety flatters the sophisticated audience. Audiences are intelligent enough to relate American policies to their own situations without having them spelled out. Abstract themes may be effective even in the Middle East. An anti-Communist message is implicit in the folk saying that it is better to light one candle than to cry against the darkness.

But subtlety is unsuitable for some audiences and for some media, such as radio, in underdeveloped countries or in strongly anti-Communist countries like Thailand or Taiwan.

> You can say some things about Russia in this country that you can't say in Western Europe or in India. You have got to rely on a more subtle approach or you lose your audience altogether. These things are not easily described.

> Listenership should be cultivated by presenting political material in a vital and pungent way, rather than by trying to introduce subtle, political implications into material that ostensibly has primarily an entertainment function. Our primary target is the politically conscious minority in every country, and such listeners will respect us more if we lay our cards on the table instead of trying to be subtle. They want depth and solidity, not indirection.

It can be overdone. In films, an indirect attack on communism may be misinterpreted. "Implications should be always clear and usually explicit. The degree of explicitness necessary to achieve clarity depends on the intellectual level of the audience."

Where definite action is possible, it should be called for. (In showing a film to illiterate villagers in India there should be a specific act, such as acceptance of the idea of a village development plan, to give a point and direction to the general message.) Abstractions frighten people. It is axiomatic that "you cannot possibly make propaganda with generalities. You must have specifics"—specific daily events and individual human experiences and interests—without losing touch with broad, important issues.

HUMOR AND SATIRE

Humor is regarded as an important propaganda ingredient, a way to make a point more readily than by reasoning, but one that has been insufficiently utilized. It is particularly suitable for dealing with certain national groups (Italians, Persians, Latin Americans). Anything that makes people laugh at communism is valuable. Ridicule reduces its stature.

> We literally take everything they do and everything they believe and just make them look like a bunch of bumbling idiots. . . . We carry out to the ultimate degree their doctrinal principles and just show that they lead to nothing but sheer stupidity.

Satire is far more effective propaganda than official speeches and statements. There is nothing that cannot be satirized. Comic books are an effective medium in semiliterate areas. But caution must be employed. An unhappy subject or one that affects people in deadly earnest cannot be treated facetiously. Sarcasm, irony, and satire can be misunderstood and can backfire.

According to one school of thought, satire should be confined to nonattributed output, and it is not suitable for an official U. S. agency.

> In attributed material, I think anything put out under the imprint of the United States government ought to be calm, factual, and noncombative. It should be just a straight theme, because the facts stated straightly will do more for you than anything else.

THE PERSONAL TOUCH

How far can the operator go in projecting his own personality into output? This is especially important for commentators and column writers in the fast media. In favor of minimizing the personal touch, one opinion argues for anonymity and against building up personalities, particularly in the Iron Curtain areas. The other group believes that personalizing the message gives it interest and authority.

Listeners generally assume that what USIA says has an official connotation. Everything must be carefully weighed to make it sound authoritative, not personal or prejudiced.

> A newspaperman in Rangoon, a university professor in Karachi, a high-ranking minister in Saigon, when listening to the Voice of America, either in English or the vernacular, is listening to the United States government, and he is listening to state-

ments which represent the United States government. My colleagues don't know how significant it is what they do or don't do, and how overinterpreted are the things they say to their audiences.

The task of the commentator is to draw facts to their logical conclusions, avoiding any implication that his analysis is purely personal. The facts should speak for themselves. The writer must absorb policy and become its articulator, never implying, "This is what I think."

The opposing argument is that abstractions must be expressed in individual terms. Descriptions of life in America, for example, carry more conviction when expressed in terms of a commentator's personal life and experience. Even the commentator's voice sounds more convincing when he talks about his own life than when he discusses American life in the abstract. A firsthand account of a personal experience is worth any number of stories on institutions or organizational meetings. A sense of rapport between the listener and a radio announcer or commentator may considerably multiply the emotional impact of what is said. The tone of voice can carry a quality of conviction, even to persons who do not know the language.

Similarly, in print, a byline column interpreting the ongoing news is regarded by the audience as more authoritative and analytical than piecemeal dispatches rounding up information on the same subject.

CONCENTRATION ON THEMES

The program has often been criticized for spreading its efforts too widely and failing to adopt themes that can be used repeatedly. "We are covering the waterfront every day" in the number of themes used. If too many themes are used the audience becomes cynical and rejects them all. As in advertising, saturated coverage of a few points is better than "tackling everything that comes up in the papers."

> It made more sense to get one clear-cut and simple idea related to every poor slob on the upper reaches of the Amazon than to pepper the few government leaders who might be out of office in six months anyway with so many themes . . . that after a while they get a little cynical and start rejecting everything.

Estimates of how many themes are advisable range from one to seven. Only one theme should be stressed at a time, and this one idea should be hit over and over.

But others point out that if there is too much concentration on a few themes (like the "Atoms-for-Peace" proposal), others may be neglected. USIA cannot confine itself to "harping" on one big theme.

> A lot of people in USIA, operators who are probably literal-minded and easy to please, would never again touch Point Four, technical assistance, with a ten-foot pole because it has nothing to do with nuclear energy.

Operators generally accept repetition as one of the cardinal concepts of propaganda.

> Propaganda is as fully a matter of reminding the listener of what he already knows as of enlightening him with new facts; facts which are already known to pro-Western audiences should be often though briefly mentioned.

All media send out material that keeps important topics alive, and hence gives added support to a policy objective. An idea (even a key phrase like "Red atrocity") must be repeated many times, until finally it has an impact.

However, a theme cannot be played on indefinitely, without new developments to report. Output must have an effect that is cumulative rather than instantaneous, and that cannot be accomplished by a single message, film, or broadcast. Content should be presented with maximum consistency, continuity, and coherence in order to achieve a cumulative effect. The information program is designed to win people over by a slow, long process of repeated contacts and impacts.

> Generally you're just pushing them a little more toward a change. You're making them doubt something they believed before.

> When you pick up a magazine and read it, do you immediately change your ideas? However, if you're interested in a subject and want to learn more you're apt to make some effort to get this material and look at it, and because you have made the effort you will feel much more confident in the opinion that you're forming.

> It's almost impossible to say that one experience changed a person's mind or attitude. It can certainly help lead in the right direction. I think it's only one of a series of experiences that the audience has that will finally change their minds. Our information program is like the guy beating on the rock with the sledgehammer. Someday it's going to break. Take this sort of situation. Everybody is doing his best to influence public opinion, and I think we had done it at one point, in Egypt. Then out of the clear blue sky the British do something that makes everybody mad and then you're right back where you started from. But at the same time it's impossible to measure whether you went back one step or two forward. Eventually, if you're not confusing the audience and you're not inconsistent, eventually the sum total will be what you want.

XII

Using the Media

EACH OF THE FOUR MEDIA SERVICES that produce USIA's propaganda has distinctive capabilities and techniques that must be harmoniously orchestrated. This chapter examines working practices and assumptions characteristic of each medium. All four services face the necessity of offering "bait" with no programmatic purpose in order to lure audiences who can be exposed to content with an ideological cast. However, some operators favor an undiluted propaganda effort, lest the bait swallow the quarry. Ideally, the different media can be used in tandem, although fast and slow media are understood to have different functions.

The Press Service produces news and feature material suitable for local adaptation, but it must rely on operators in the field, and it may be just as important to have its articles read by influential editors as to have them reprinted. Publications' graphics must be designed to fit their specific targets and must use illustrations skillfully to enhance the text.

The Voice of America, as the only medium directly reaching audiences in the Soviet bloc, operates with an independence that irritates others in the Agency. But in many parts of the world the Voice's effectiveness depends on its ability to rebroadcast programs over local stations. Since the Broadcasting Service needs language skills, it relies on émigré personnel whose political outlooks must be reconciled with official assignments.

Motion pictures have a broad appeal, which weakens their utility in reaching specific target groups. Individual films have merit insofar as they become part of ongoing programs and stimulate direct personal contacts.

Operators within the Information Center Service similarly regard their USIS libraries as an instrument for winning friends on an individual basis. Each user of the library has his own purpose, and his contacts represent a continuing relationship that results in a more favorable opinion of the U. S. In selecting books for the libraries and for translation, USIA must trade off the advantages of serving a general reference function against its propaganda objectives. Similarly, it must weigh the theoretical merits and political dangers of circulating books that are critical of the U. S.

EVERY USIA MEDIUM at one time or another carries on activity that does not bear directly on program objectives but is considered to support long-run goals because it attracts an audience, thus making it possible to disseminate other output. Much of USIA's Americana is partially justified on this basis. But this leads to criticism. USIA lacks definite criteria as to how far afield from direct propaganda purposes it can go.

BAIT AND PROPAGANDA

Existing practice can be viewed from completely opposite viewpoints:

1. All output is tied to U. S. foreign policy. "Every item in the Wireless File has some purpose other than straight information or news reporting."
2. "There's virtually nothing that somebody cannot rationalize as helping to advance program objectives." Only the good judgment of experienced people can determine whether the rationalization is valid.

The second view is supported by the belief that "bait" is necessary—material that entertains, instructs, or interests the audience opens the doors to harder hitting messages. According to one estimate, less than 10 percent of USIA film output may be properly termed "propaganda." There is nothing about a propaganda film in itself that would make people want to sit through it.

Never in any film presentation do we present just one film. It's in the choice of a well-rounded program that this begins to be vital.

In a newsreel sequence, one story "with a hook in it" is a satisfactory proportion.

We quit being documentary and overconscious. We make it up like a sandwich, take a good international story to lead off with, then put in a slightly slanted story and a local story and a typical neat newsreel story. Then you put in another big international story, then maybe another of definite State Department interest. It might be nothing more than getting something into the lines.

In films, entertainment must come first; then, stronger content is gradually introduced.

We had a labor leader come up here on a grant about two years ago and when he came back down there he was fired with a great ambition to show as many hard-hitting films as he could get his hands on and show them to his union. We tried to discourage him from doing that and urged him to go slow and test his audience first. Through that testing he discovered that the message was getting across and gradually stronger films could be shown.

Nonpolitical films on Americana or technical subjects for showings to Communist or pro-Communist elements open the way for stronger propaganda films and are a means of developing contacts.

Let me give you a concrete example. At Cairo University the engineering faculty and medical faculty were reported to be intensively infiltrated by the Communists. A great number of the professors were either sympathetic or actively pro-Communist. These groups were sufficiently anti-American that they would not come to the library for information nor would they voluntarily read our output. However, when we had a film about a new surgical technique developed by a doctor in the United States or new cancer procedures, or in the engineering school where we had a film on the application of a new engineering principle to industry, those sympathetic professors who could get students to come and see at least one film about America—they would come to see a film.

Particularly where you get a group that's antipathetic, where you can show them a film about a subject on which they have a professional interest they're going to have a basis for judging whether it's true or not. . . . In our program our effort is with that particular group to make them feel that we have something aside from politics that is sufficiently valuable and desirable to come and get more of it. In these films about some scientific subject they see that these things are better than any information that they have gotten from any other source in their professional specialty. Because they're not looking for propaganda in that kind of film, they absorb the impression without being aware of it.

These showings in addition to the first task of getting us an audience have an additional effect of modifying their attitude. The principal thing you do there is arouse their desire for more information of a professional nature. They are interested in politics but they are still students and they want to become competent doctors or engineers. They start coming to the USIS library.

In radio, entertainment is "sugar-coating on the pill." No one will listen to more than fifteen minutes of political commentary. VOA's projection of American foreign policy "is largely lost on the air." Output (for example, to the Middle East) is comparable to a commercially sponsored program on the U. S. radio.

Five minutes of propaganda with two hours of sugar-coating. Music is the vehicle rather than the end in itself. We wouldn't have more than five minutes of propaganda in one hour. It's like a commercially sponsored program here. Our commercial is our political commentary.

A program must attract an audience to get across its message and present what it has to say acceptably and interestingly. An entertainment format can carry a message more effectively than direct political commentary. Political content may be introduced covertly into all programs—dramatic shows, programs dealing with stamps or "pen pals," and even musical programs.

> To some extent you have to have some programs that are not for the salvation of the listener, because he gets tired of having his soul saved. You can devise programs that are going to have a kind of secondary effect on his soul without his knowing what is going on, like an orchestra concert.

Output that is "all message" will be considered straight propaganda. It is of no value to introduce propaganda into a radio program designed for relaxation or entertainment. Since much of the Free World is oversensitized toward radio propaganda, a program with a political aspect that is not obvious gets a good reaction. ("How wonderful. A fifteen-minute program without propaganda!")

But news itself can be seen as bait for VOA listeners. Some operators regard objective news reports as the main attraction for the audience, and believe that they should have an important share of air time. Moreover, most foreign policy aspects can be brought out through interpretation as news develops.

Radio output requires a certain amount of human interest material for "listening value." This is stated in the form of a criticism.

> Everything is handled with a heavy hand where it should be light. They give the heavy-handed approach because they are heavy-handed people. People listen for news first and entertainment second. In the course of it you would give them your message. There is not anybody there who is concerned with listenability.

The operator wants a well-rounded program with lively and varied shows. An intellectual listener may be interested in a controversial program simply because he appreciates the talent that goes into it.

Output would be deadly dull unless there were variations in style. Wherever possible, programs should try to avoid too slow an announcing tempo, the monotonous effect of having one voice talking for fifteen minutes or more. The dialogue form is a good way of creating this change of pace. Dramatic shows are valuable because they lend variety. Dramatic sketches can convey a propaganda point that cannot be stated directly and bluntly.

As with radio and film, a number of library program activities are said to have primary importance as bait for materials that carry the real "bite."

> A clever PAO can use this language class as bait to bring people into an information center, and then he can make regular film patrons of them for the USIA films and then they hear lectures, they use the library.

> I think we should be downtown so we would get the literate man in the street. If we had a glass window with flowers around and a pretty, inviting place they might wander in. Maybe the first day they wouldn't read anything but *McCall's* magazine, but eventually maybe they would read something we would want them to read.

Popular fiction is used in presentations as a prelude to more serious books. A book presentation may serve no immediate program value, but achieve goodwill for an ultimate program purpose.

In the presentation program we had one request for a subscription for *Esquire* magazine. When it was made clear that this was to go to the Maharaja of something or other who owned the building in which our center was located, it made sense.

In supplying economic, agricultural, scientific, political, and social information about the U. S., USIA performs a greatly appreciated service.

We get requests from the field for material of a technical nature. They want straightforward accounts of developments in fields of medicine that are important for Asia. They want it in simple language and they want to know if it's available in five years. In the whole Far East there's a tremendous amount of curiosity about these things. We can point out that this has a social implication, that there is a considerable amount of effort in the United States devoted to improving the welfare of the people.

"One-shot" requests from the field, originating with local editors whose goodwill the public affairs officers want to cultivate, are often of marginal propaganda value.

We had one from Singapore. We had a request for an article and information on motorboating in the United States, which is apparently a hobby for some people in that country. It probably would be of considerable interest. It would probably get a good spread. We could not take one man off an anti-Communist piece or a UN piece to do an article on motor boats, but the editor of that paper might be much more ready a week or two from now to run an anti-Communist piece if we give him a thing on motorboats at this point.

Say our post in Athens wants to do a feature story on bicycling in the United States. Then they'll say, this editor has been a tough nut to crack and though this is of marginal value propaganda-wise, it's of benefit to give him this and then get something else in there some other time.

People acquire information indirectly. First they read the books that are important to them, and then they read books of importance to the program. Audiences may be reached through their avocational interests. Even persons who use the library for purely professional purposes—to consult technical works—acquire information that reflects favorably upon the United States.

This medical student who has gotten information that is useful to him professionally, who has gotten his information from an American library in his country, who has been reading American books—he has not only gotten his medical facts from an American. You can assume that if he got them from the information center it's easier for him to get it in this way than in some other way. That reflects favorably on this country. There definitely is this informational exchange—free information, full information available from American sources, quite apart from the specific information that they get.

THE CASE AGAINST BAIT

Those who believe that all output should advance a program objective point out that bait is not always valuable.

Entertainment that does not also carry a political message should be reduced to that minimum which is demonstrably necessary in order to get listeners. Even a moderate loss of listenership should be accepted if it is necessary to make the best political use of our time with those who do listen.

"Every particle" of output must be projected to some propagandistic end. This reportedly "general feeling" in VOA is reflected in the position that even output on specialized technical subjects should be politically angled. A discussion of fertilizers on an agricultural program beamed to the Iron Curtain must point out that certain fertilizer problems do not exist in a free economy.

According to one critical opinion, VOA is no longer concerned with building an audience. Policy has swung away from emphasizing audience-building output to straight news and official statements and de-emphasizing entertainment. Entertainment is not VOA's job; VOA has a responsibility to its government as well as to listeners.

> You know the problem of entertaining or not entertaining. I agree that a good program must have an appeal but from there to say that a program has only appeal if it's entertaining for the majority of the audience—you wouldn't say that a government radio should put entertainment programs on the air because the majority of the audience wants to be entertained. It's legitimate for a private station. For an agency like the Voice, I feel that the program should have listener appeal, but this is very different.

An activity cannot be justified because it makes good "bait" for other activities. If output merely pleases but conveys no message, it is wasted. ("What the hell good does it do to show the prime minister a Lionel train running around the track with the lights flashing?")

In dealing with publications overseas, it is not always necessary to meet editors' requests. PAO's exaggerate the value of contacts with local editors made by meeting requests that often have nothing to do with program objectives.

> We hear the argument all the time that IPS spends a terrific amount of time doing articles on request from PAO's overseas in response to requests from local editors, and 80 percent of the subject matter has no first-hand connection with our policy objectives. Are we justified in having IPS spend its time and money on producing this on the ground that the PAO overseas had made a contact and established rapport with an editor who can do him a lot of good in getting through other messages and so on? I think they have probably exaggerated it a good deal. I think there is just enough truth in that concept to make it irritating. It's like the pearl in the oyster. I have a very radical solution, to let the Library of Congress do it on a contract basis and have the post pay them for it out of their program funds. They would take a little sharper and more business-like view of it. They probably exaggerate the contacts that are made. It's easy for the local PAO to pass on a request.

One observer notes that media with a large basic salary overhead are most likely to produce output of marginal program interest:

> In your Wireless File and in your feature stories, in which your principal cost is personal services here, which we pay for whether a man is writing a story or not, there

you have a tendency to bring in more of your peripheral objectives. Your Wireless File concentrates on your major objectives but it also gets into the peripheral things. In pamphlets you have got to concentrate on the major things. You're using your pamphlets to get a maximum impact on a particular subject and on a particular population.

Information centers will not lose many clients by discontinuing technical books. Besides, the audience may swallow the "bait" without touching the "hook."

> The people who are interested in a welding manual are not those who are going to advance your program. Are you going to make them more convinced about democracy or the American way of life? I don't think we have any proof that we are. The technical student, if the books on technical things that he has been in the habit of using are not there, will be disappointed, true. If the doctors suddenly find that the medical journals are no longer there, they're going to come to look at the books in the other fields. But we have never been able to prove that the people who come in for books in specialized fields also take out books on dynamic democracy. I fear that they only took out the medical book.

If library staffs must devote time to "unimportant" visitors who seek technological information, they have "less time to spend on the important people." If technical material is removed from the libraries, it may be an impetus for the locals to improve their own libraries.

It is better to reorient the libraries by eliminating all scientific works, except basic reference books and those showing the social aspects of science, than to cut down on the number of libraries.

PAID VS. FREE OUTPUT

Another issue is whether a token price should be charged for USIA output, particularly publications and films. Handing out something valuable for free reduces its value. If pamphlets or publications are placed on a table in a public place, everyone will take one and discard it. If they are made available on request, only those really interested will get them. In some cases, sample copies can be sent out with an inquiry form. This places the burden upon the audience to acknowledge its interest.

> It would be nice to get some return from them. They would be more apt to use it than something they just got as a handout.

> The fact that our books are being bought by somebody we hope will have greater impact on them than if they have read it free of charge in a pamphlet handout. We must just assume that people who keep on buying books have an interest in the subject that the book deals with.

Free distribution has value. It builds goodwill if films are circulated free of charge in a country where no other organization does this. Whether or not more value is attached to something that is paid for depends entirely on local attitudes. A charge automatically limits distribution. (This may be desirable or undesirable, depending on what view is taken on the subject of selective targeting.)

SELECTION OF MEDIA

It is perhaps inevitable that operators in the different media services do not agree on how individual media can best be used or what their capabilities and limitations are.

All media are valuable. USIA can use all of them in every country because each one can contribute something, and all should be coordinated. USIA should organize its campaigns as the Russians do; that is, someone should be assigned to follow through with all media to implement basic themes. It is desirable to hit the same audience through a number of media. But the problems of coordination are great: "It's like trying to put out a daily newspaper with the same basic format in every country in the world."

Each medium supplements the others. Radio complements motion pictures.

The centers serve as a repository of more detailed information to supplement the operations of other media. Anyone who has heard something on the radio or read it in the newspaper can go to the center for further information on the same subject.

Leaflets given out at film showings or exhibits can address themselves to specific points that complement the presentation of the broader issues. They will be passed along and provide a permanent reminder of the themes.

So often with a film, people go in and look at it and enjoy it and they don't think about it very much. That sort of ends. If you give them a leaflet maybe they will show it to Joe next door and he will want to see it, too. It extends your audience and therefore extends the carrying of the message that your film has. It opens up new outlets for your material. More people are going to understand something you're going to tell them. They will talk to other people and you get a continuing chain of information.

Media should be selected to reach the audience. Where illiteracy is high, more people can be reached through film and radio than publications. But films must be used where radio does not penetrate. (USIA radio and films are not intended for illiterates.) Leaflets and posters are a way of reaching the masses.

The media suited to contact hostile and neutralist targets are local radio, leaflets, and theatrical film showings. They can reach an audience already assembled for another purpose. Pamphlets are useful where films cannot penetrate, particularly among Communists.

A specific target audience cannot always be reached through a specific medium. It is impossible to break down specific targets by the media used to reach them. A combination must be used to reach specific key groups, varying from country to country. For a broad target, it is better to reach many different people with one medium than to reach a few many times through different media.

USIA reaches the same audiences with newspapers as with radio. The five percent who read newspapers may be identical with those who read magazines. When two or three media can be used in an area, a mass medium should be used to reinforce the more selective media to insure that when a message gets down to the masses people are already generally familiar with it and are receptive.

The fast media, radio and press, lend themselves best to discussing news and foreign policy objectives, particularly when immediate effects are desired. Slow media (motion pictures, libraries, exhibits, private enterprise cooperation, picture stories and pamphlets) are for subjects requiring long-range exposition, such as Americana and fighting communism.

> Working with books and publications is not as clear-cut and specific as working with a radio program that hammers away on one topic.

Fast and slow media complement each other. Also, radio and press can be used together "like a jab and a bodyblow"—one "fast and official," the other slower, but "down in black and white."

Do the mass media have any value? The mass media are seen both favorably, as the most effective means of pulling over people on the Communist fringe, and unfavorably, as appealing only to "people who are already convinced." They "bounce off" the population and cost too much money. The individual approach (through personal contact) is far superior. The merit of the book program is that it consists of individual contacts.

USIA overemphasizes the importance of the media because of the way in which it is set up.

> There is no program separate and apart from what you do with media. Let me use an analogy with the public school system in the United States. You have an educational program. You have a curriculum, students you are trying to reach. You have the nucleus of the program, but you don't have textbooks to run an educational program. You can run a school without textbooks or films or blackboards. The essential ingredient is instructors and pupils. What this program gets around to is a dissemination of texts and films without a program at the core. In other words, it is what I call a media-centered activity rather than a people-centered activity.

A mass media program is effective only to the degree that mass media channels in the target country are comparable to those in the United States. In Asia USIA can show motion pictures and give away pamphlets "till Kingdom come," but it will accomplish nothing because of the size of the populations it must reach.

IPS: PRESS

The International Press and Publications Service (IPS), unlike the other media operations, does not provide a finished product to disseminate directly to an audience. It combines under one roof two distinct types of services: tactical, fast, news-oriented output such as the Wireless Bulletin (or "File") that reaches the field five days a week [1] and general services or "slow" output—features, articles for reproduction and translation, cartoons, picture stories, pamphlets, leaflets, and books. When Press Service operators compare their output with that of other media, they point first to its versatility.

> A press operation is the only one that is for my money a truly mass medium operation. Everybody looks at newspapers or looks at posters and is most vulnerable to that type of approach—more so than they would be to getting in a library, for example, or stopping to go to a film showing or listening to a radio, if they do have a radio.

> In press alone you can reach from some high cultural level to comic books for kids that reach the lowest level. Of course the guy has to read.

Moreover, print is the cheapest way to get a message to an audience. It can be read and reread with more lasting impact than any other medium. Therefore, IPS is more conservative than VOA in handling news. Writing for publication demands a tighter style and more positive statements than radio writing. "There's a hell of a lot of difference between spouting something off on the air where it's gone and having it down in black and white."

The very fact that IPS output must be adapted and placed before it reaches the ultimate audience means that the operator is often unaware of the ultimate use and form of his product in local publications. He rarely sees his press clippings. Because IPS must rely on the field to adapt and push its product, there is a tendency to regard the public affairs or press officer in the field rather than the ultimate reader as the customer who must be "sold."

Output is not directly translated in the field. It is actually rewritten by local newspapermen, or used as source material for original stories prepared in local style. It is not sent out as a finished product. The emphasis on "beautiful style" in writing arouses complaints in IPS. Copy is repeatedly edited and rewritten for style in spite of the fact that it must be rewritten in the field.

Contacts with the press in target countries are necessary to get editors to use USIA output. The success of press activities depends largely on personal relations with editors and knowledge of their views. Attempts to place articles through the mail are worthless unless there is prior personal contact.

> Your cultivation is a combination of simple personal tactics of public relations, spending endless time with them, listening to their griefs often about the government, but not committing yourself officially; drinking with them, hunting with them.

Therefore, USIA should spend less time turning out material and place more effort on personal contacts with editors, particularly where the press is

---

[1] One day's Wireless File, of ten single-spaced legal-size pages, was made up of the following items: "Dulles, Humphrey Urge Extension of Trade Act," a commentary, "Behind the Curtain," "UN Names Pakistan as Neutral," "WHO Reports Drop in Tuberculosis Mortality," "U. S. Governors Meet in Washington," "Dulles Pays Tribute to U. S. Military Personnel," and "UN Watch Committee for Laos Proposed." There was also a page of "Newsbriefs" and a page logging regional wireless files.

censored. The personal friendship of an editor does more good for the program than placing articles.

> The third most influential paper repeatedly took the line that Greece had suffered so much that, "The Americans had to do something for us. We are lost without the Americans." This, after three years of the Marshall Plan! This was directly opposed to one of our program objectives, which was to build up a sense of self-reliance in Greece. We met with that editor and without referring to his editorials discussed the whole concept of one nation helping another and of how one nation makes progress, economically. It took place over ten meetings. He was a reasonable guy, and we had some very stimulating discussions on the whole subject, the crux of which was "God helps those that help themselves." About two weeks afterward, he wrote his first editorial about how "We Greeks have to get together and roll up our sleeves. American aid is a catalytic agent." We felt that we had influenced that man. We didn't consider our press operation merely placing material. We try to generate editorials and we try to know the editors and to chat with them on subjects that were relevant to our program objectives.

A press operation must be carried on in the planned, systematic fashion of domestic public relations.

> We have tried to give the Greeks a sense of military security, in NATO. We made arrangements with the American Navy to put on a guest day for various northern Greek newspaper editors. We sent automobiles to the six top newspaper editors in northern Greece and brought them to Salonica, paid for their hotel rooms, and took them to the ship for two days of operations. The Navy cooperated perfectly. We gave them press releases in Greek, interviews with Greek-Americans aboard the ships. They were of course most impressed by the "city in itself" aspects of the big carrier, press conferences with the admiral. Each individual editor had his picture taken with the admiral. They also observed, though they didn't think it was intentional, Greek orphans coming aboard for little parties, Greek visitors, the fact that Negro and white seamen were working side by side on board the ship. When they left the ship they were presented with every photograph that had been taken of them, the best of which had been made into a plate adapted to the individual newspapers. Of course when a Greek editor goes back to his own town after an experience like that he's going to write about American armed might, about the American care of the individual sailor on the ship, the terrific mixture of nationalities and races on the ship, Negroes operating electronic devices. One of the editors who was lukewarm toward the United States when I left was strongly pro-American, the other one was more plus than he was minus.

> It's well known in Rangoon that the editor of the leading Burmese paper is a close friend of the Prime Minister. That gives additional authority to what he says in the paper; to the extent that we can cultivate his friendship we are getting across more effectively than having ten stories in his paper.

IPS: PUBLICATIONS

IPS products should be given the most indigenous possible look to achieve credibility. Their style, format, and printing stock should, as far as possible, resemble the local product—particularly where they compete with Communist publications that masquerade under the format and attribution of local groups.

> The importance of looking indigenous is the importance of being indigenous as far as possible. I don't give a damn about a U. S. message. If by looking like a U. S. publication you're attracting attention to it, you're not accomplishing what you want to, because the United States message is going to be rejected.

> We have greater credibility if our publications resemble in printing, style, and format local publications. The comic books we have turned out on very poor newsprint have in general matched the quality of the opposition's output and the comment I have heard is that they are more effective that way.

"Prestige pieces" which carry U. S. attribution should be on slick paper and of a high production quality, particularly if they are intended for presentation. For this reason most Americana should be "slick." (Communist output is of high production quality in areas where indigenous publications are crude and printed on rough stock.)

Local publications may be subsidized to give an indigenous look to USIA output, although subsidy entails the danger of a loss of credibility.

> There are very few people who would care to engage in anti-Communist propaganda, and you have to open up some opportunities for them, and profit. In our case it was not outright subsidy but legitimate job printing contracts. We didn't pay them for printing anti-Communist output. But their profit from the open stuff was good enough to open the way to some of the others. This we felt was the best method for not exposing ourselves to the sub-editors and printers who would eventually learn that you were paying for the hard line output.

In some areas, indigenous publications are more effective, USIS publications more practical.

> From a propaganda viewpoint, your program is more effective if it's placed in indigenous publications such as magazines and newspapers in the local language. However, in the Far East you don't have sufficient such publications to do the job. Your newspaper circulations will run 2,000 to 8,000. Your magazines are fly-by-night affairs with circulations of maybe 10,000. If you're going to get a continuing program with publications that will build up solid reader habits and following, you have got to subsidize some magazine in order to make it work. The only alternative is to put out your own publications attributed to USIS. Granted that your local publications are more effective, they're also more expensive and it's more difficult to do that way.

> Do the advantages of using local publications outweigh starting USIS publications? The cost and effort is so much greater. I think we need repeated impact in order to make any impression. Therefore I would insist on my PAO's getting first crack at all stories. On the local publications, I would subsidize them however I could. I have found that USIS publications are essential to carry the material that we cannot get printed locally because it's too anti-Communist or what have you.

> Secondly, our own publications are a form of insurance. Because the censorship

laws change almost monthly your flow of materials may be cut off by a sudden censorship decision. I would like to see at least one publication in each country that would be attributed to us so it could get printed, because any country which cut out "Free World" would be subject to retaliatory measures by the American government. We would cut out their propaganda over here. That's true right now in Indonesia. They won't let us bring "Free World" into Indonesia from Manila. If they do they would have to give the Russians equal privileges. However, we bring in raw material stories and publish our own magazine called "American Miscellany." Meanwhile, the Russians are still barred.

The graphic element is accepted as an important ingredient in making printed output more effective. Graphics impose certain standards and rules derived from the principles of aesthetics rather than from the arts of persuasion. (By implication, the audience is more receptive if production is of high quality, governed by aesthetic rules.) Any printed piece should have a logical visual relationship from picture to picture and cover to cover.

Pictures heighten interest. A pamphlet that reproduces an official speech or statement will be far more successful with an illustrated cover and typographically varied format than if it is set up in plain type.

Pictures convey information more readily than print. "One picture is worth 10,000 words." But there are different views of the relation of pictures and text:

Editorial matter is dominant. It takes a strong picture to predominate over text. Pictures are never completely self-evident; they require an explanatory text. The only function of graphic treatment is to complement the editorial content. Visual treatment must play up editorial content and tone to best advantage. Ninety percent of the time the editorial content "automatically" determines the tone and level of the art work. Good illustrations vastly enhance the credibility and effectiveness of the text, but an effective text is still possible if no pictures are available.

Illustrations should carry their own message. Picture stories or exhibits should be planned in such a way that the pictures themselves tell the story, regardless of whether or not the captions are read.

The emphasis that pictures receive should be determined by the literacy of the audience. Material designed for mass appeal requires illustration. Low-education areas require the highest possible picture-to-text ratio and comic-book techniques. Material intended for an intellectual group requires no illustrations.

While photographs carry credibility, drawings create mood. "A drawing can be made out of whole cloth as well as a text" (although a photograph, too, can be retouched). When the subject of a piece is specific, photographs are better than a drawing. A drawing of something which cannot be documented by a photograph may be rejected by the reader: "An artist's concept. He's dreaming it up." Words can be more eloquent than a drawing. A text should not necessarily be illustrated in exactly the same tone in which it is written. Photographs may destroy credibility because of the very horror they depict, as in the case of the Katyn Forest massacre.[2]

> The reason we used drawings was, I felt, a good reason. There were photographs of the massacres which weren't especially good, but more important yet, pictures of this enormous mass grave, it was so big it was almost inconceivable. You just couldn't believe the thing existed. If you notice in the leaflet, we didn't show any drawings of any bodies. The main reason for doing that is we didn't want the drawing to look too propagandistic, we didn't want a horror story in drawings, we wanted the documentary evidence which would speak for itself and have the drawings lend the mood of the thing. They were very much incidental drawings.

The distinction between a photograph and a drawing may take the form of a distinction between straight presentation and caricature. It may be better to use a photograph of a Communist leader rather than to weaken an argument by levity in depicting him as a cartoon character.

Symbols are constant reminders of a propaganda point. However, they are difficult to popularize. It would be desirable to have an anti-Communist symbol (analogous to the Communist hammer and sickle) "that could be used all over the world, be used by different kinds of people, be chalked on sidewalks."

A symbol can link a known value (favorable or unfavorable) to a subject as yet unidentified. Communist symbols may be used in USIA output to dramatize the connection between the Communist movement and its fronts. (For example, hammer and sickle armbands identify the Huks, in films for the Philippines, as members of an alien organization.) It is hard to find universal symbols. The use of symbols may therefore limit the outlets for output. Different cultures have different symbols. (The Russian bear cannot be used in the Far East, where it is the symbol for Korea.)

IBS: RADIO

Because it beams its message into the camp of the adversary, talks directly to its audience, and deals daily with the developing news, the International Broadcasting Service is more self-consciously engaged in propaganda than the other media services. Its work is permeated by a strong sense of urgency.

The Voice of America has always had a high degree of autonomy, largely because its former physical separation from the rest of the Agency created an independent outlook. Its personnel are "of higher caliber," and radio, as USIA's only direct medium for reaching the audience, requires a higher degree of independence.

> There is a prevailing fiction that there is a great United States Information Agency which has a number of media. That is rubbish. The USIA has one medium and that

---

[2] Stalin decreed the slaughter of the captured Polish Officer Corps in 1941, as the Nazis revealed after their invasion of Byelorussia.

is radio. The others are not media, they are services. The Wire Service, which gets out a telegram which can be used or need not be used by a local PAO, but used as he sees fit. Volumes which are sent out, which may or may not be put on the shelves in the libraries. These are all service operations. The one medium which delivers the message to the customer is the Voice. This has always given undue weight to the strawbosses of the Voice, and the front office has never been able to domesticate this beast.

You have a very definite prejudice among a great many people in this organization that radio gets a big chunk of money and they never see what it is accomplishing. They overlook the fact that radio has one major target—the Soviet and its orbit.

The Voice has caught the popular imagination more than any other facet of USIA. This has posed problems for the Agency administration.

I think the biggest problem that was coming up all the time was the whole matter of the usefulness or non-usefulness of VOA operations. The very great difficulty of proving anything about the effects of a broadcast going off into space, except through the most fragmentary kind of information, on which you could build a tremendous structure, but which, from a cold scientific approach, was very insignificant. The people most directly identified with the Voice tell us it is the end-all—that their program was not only the only thing that was important but that it was achieving most miraculous things.

On the other hand, we were faced with a Congressional attitude of complete doubt that even a dime spent on the Voice meant anything. I wouldn't say that the group at the top had any absolute belief that the Voice was achieving the thing it believed it was doing and that we wished it were doing. Very often, I detected a feeling of the necessity of fighting for it, not because of confidence, but because they weren't sure it was wrong. To get information beyond the Iron Curtain the only method was the Voice, but they were doubtful about the utility of broadcasts outside the Iron Curtain. They were skeptical of the device of listener letters. A great deal had to be done on faith and hope. It was both a question of the distribution of Voice facilities and a question of its effectiveness.

The Voice was usually able to do better in Congress than any other operation. The people there have used their public relations resources very intelligently and they have also had something very good to dramatize. Even if they had been poor at publicity and public relations, people would have beaten a path to their door. Hungarians sitting here and putting on a Hungarian program! It was of intense interest to a great many people. This interlocked with the entertainment industry. It was not unusual for a commercial radio fellow to mention the Voice on his broadcast. I guess I'm saying it was a good public relations and advertising situation as opposed to the other media. It has a snowballing quality.

In the eyes of its critics, IBS has never properly submitted to the control of Agency management.

It was the frame of mind of all the top people at the Voice. If you sent a new man up there in six weeks he had that attitude too. Even when you very patiently explained the reasons behind a move—for instance asking for a particular kind of budget information because the Bureau of the Budget asked for it, they might refuse. They had no sense of responsibility to the parent organization. I think it was a pretty fundamental thing. They had a kind of myopia because of their physical location and the fact that they got their money pretty directly.

On the other hand, VOA operators tend to feel that field personnel generally are not very much interested in their operations.

1. VOA is more difficult for the posts to control than local broadcasts.
2. No one in the missions is responsible for promoting programming.
3. In dealing with local problems, the Public Affairs Officer may be able to put on his own radio programs quickly, and he is less likely to get immediate cooperation from a big "bureaucracy."
4. Few legations monitor VOA output.
5. Since they cannot see VOA listener mail, Public Affairs Officers are unaware of audience response.

> One thing that would convince the Public Affairs Officer that the Voice had value would be if the letters from listeners were addressed to him. If he could see these letters, he would begin to show an interest in that operation and see that it was a tool he could use and could direct with an occasional cable and that when he had some trouble spots, some guidance back here could quickly bring the Voice into his reach.

6. PAO's have the impression that no one listens to the Voice of America, because they don't listen to it themselves. A former PAO remarks that:

> They are entirely ignorant of what the Voice is doing or trying to do. The average Public Affairs Officer or Foreign Service Officer overseas frequently does not know the language of the country in which he is working well enough to tune in on the Voice and enjoy it. They might tune in on an English-language broadcast on occasion; but they have their extracurricular activities, official entirely, like cocktail parties and dinners. These preclude the possibility of listening to the programs, even if they did want to listen to them.
>
> The Voice is not a subject normally that comes up in conversation with foreign officials any more than you talk about programs here. You don't see the man in the street often enough to know whether he listens to it or not. So you get the opinion that nobody listens to the Voice of America. You don't listen to it yourself. People don't normally talk about radio or television programs. Because they don't want to admit they don't listen to it, they say that nobody listens to it, in order to make it appear that they're in the majority.

IBS operators are highly aware that USIA as a whole is oriented to the Free World, while VOA is oriented to the Communist world. The highest priority should be assigned to the heart of opposition to the U. S. Therefore, the Soviet Union is VOA's most vital target. The preponderance of broadcast time and the attention of VOA's Central Services [3] are directed to the Communist world, where VOA's importance to its audience is far greater than in the Free World.

---

[3] These produce the basic news, commentary, and feature scripts that can be translated and adapted by individual language "desks."

VOA is popularly (even within USIA) thought of as a shortwave radio operation, with no awareness of the medium-wave arrangements that represent a major part of its operations. Not all operators agree that medium-wave relays are valuable. A program carried on a foreign government relay cannot be as outspoken as one broadcast directly from the U. S.

> If your program is carried on the domestic local relay, you obviously can't be as outspoken as if you were talking direct to listeners without regard to the government. In France there are certain things you can't say if you expect to stay on their domestic radio. You can't criticize actions of their government and at the same time you have to have better quality programs in order to hold your place on a domestic network than if you're broadcasting to an area where outside news is at a premium and where it's somewhat dangerous even to listen.

A tough anti-Communist message from VOA would sound ludicrous coming over a local station, even if the facilities were available for it. This leads to an opinion that foreign-government offers of relays should be rejected, because VOA's freedom of speech would be hindered by them.

Local programming (prepared on the spot by USIA field personnel with the aid of recorded "packages" from New York) presents problems analogous to those of local relays. PAO's reportedly believe that locally originated programs are more effective than broadcasts from the U. S., particularly where U. S. broadcasts are not locally relayed, when the local radio program gets a larger audience and a better signal than short-wave. Local programming has greater cultural influence. It is the only means available to use music in broadcasts. However, the local product cannot be controlled, and in certain areas it is difficult to place packaged programs locally.

Central Services output represents a common denominator for IBS. It provides coordination and an approved policy line which various language desks can adapt to their purposes. It is used by understaffed desks as a major source of material. It supplements the original output of other language services.

Central Services writers must think in terms of the organization at large rather than in terms of any particular target country. They assume that when their scripts are used in full, they are used as they are. They do not see how their scripts are adapted; they do not normally know the languages used by the desks, certainly not by all the desks. Formal reports on desk usage of their output are considered virtually worthless; they do not reveal partial or delayed use, or adaptation of the original material.

The writer who speaks directly to his audience writes differently than one whose output must be rewritten or adapted by someone else. Language desk operators know more intimately than the Central Services writers how output is going over with the audience.

The Central Services operator should write as he pleases, without worrying whether or not the desks will use his output or how they may change it, since "it's casting pearls before swine anyway."

It is more interesting and enjoyable work to address people who are vitally concerned with VOA's output than to address a Free World audience with many sources of information and a less urgent interest in listening. "The more articulate and intelligent personalities" in VOA are on the side of the house that deals with the Soviet orbit. Their discussion sets the organizational climate. Policy problems stem from combining Free World and Iron Curtain operations within VOA.

> Chafing is perhaps equal on two sides. The Communist side, where I think the general impression is that guidance makes them less vigorous than they would like to be, and on the Free World side, where the prevailing feeling I think is that the atmosphere is set too much by the desks broadcasting to the Communist world, and that therefore the hard-hitting approach pervades the atmosphere of the place and makes the people broadcasting to Egypt or France more hard-hitting than they think they ought to be.

The difference between VOA's problems in the Communist and non-Communist worlds leads some operators to the conclusion that within a single organization the two operations are irreconcilable. Better, they should be separated, each specializing in an area and with a central core of personnel providing services for both. One would be closely coordinated with CIA and Radio Free Europe (for work behind the Iron Curtain). The other would be more closely coordinated with other USIA media (and devoted to a projection of the U. S.).

There is a dissenting view.

> Our main job is to impress the people behind the Iron Curtain that they are still part of that one world, the European community. If you were to separate out programming for the free and occupied worlds, they would lose that feeling because our writers would become specialized. A person broadcasting for years only to the Iron Curtain and never hearing about Free World problems loses his feeling for the over-all view. It is important that the people from the Iron Curtain desk participate in the policy meetings where problems of the Free World areas are also discussed.

Because VOA extensively uses foreign-born personnel, including aliens, some quarters tend to view it as an émigré organization. This is vigorously denied within VOA itself.

> I have talked enough with Washington people to know that they have the impression that most of our Iron Curtain people are of the émigré type, inclined to overestimate greatly the number of already fervently anti-Communists in their audience and to underestimate the advantages of the appearance of objectivity in propaganda.

One interpretation holds that operators on the Iron Curtain desks tend to see themselves "as the future prime ministers of liberated countries."

> Many of them having suffered from the Commies, it makes it very difficult for them to look at things reasonably. In many cases these people are ex-refugees, naturalized Americans, and it's perfectly understandable that they're more concerned with liberating their countries than they are with national policy.

Operators are "wild animals" who must be restrained; the morning policy meeting is the "zoo."

> The reason the desk heads and the desk people in the Voice object to policy is that many or most of them are naturalized Europeans who would have no self-respect if they didn't feel they were working for the liberation of their countries of origin. These people are therefore impatient with State Department policy and IOP guidances telling them that they have to go slowly and take it easy in what they say to the people of Eastern Europe.

A different accusation is leveled at operators from certain Middle Eastern countries:

> They have dedicated themselves to playing this part in the game of life. They think of themselves as American agents who are using America. I have only one American citizen. There's an old saying they have that any one of them is ready at any moment to sell his country, but none is ever ready to deliver it. They are devoted to this. They think that by being loyal, they are serving their own country.

VOA's reliance on émigrés reflects the importance generally attributed to language and area skills. A broadcasting organization can only function if it is manned by people who speak the language.

Division chiefs and even some desk chiefs do not speak their target country's language. Rank and file operators will only respect a chief who speaks their language. VOA cannot afford to have an executive responsible for output who does not himself speak the language. The management of the Voice has only a remote conception of what actually goes on the air.

Lack of language skills limits the ability to have balanced output. Output to the Far East, with the exception of that directed to China or Japan, uses very little Americana, solely because there are not enough trained personnel to produce it. Available linguists are busy translating political commentaries and other higher-priority material.

Heads of VOA language services must have considerable latitude and autonomy to make sure that their operations, as independent production units, are not turned into glorified translation services. There is also a belief that individual desks sometimes carry their autonomy too far, conducting activities that formal directives expressly forbid.

IMS: MOTION PICTURES [4]

To the operators who produce and distribute them, motion pictures are felt to be a medium with exceptionally great attractions. They have "more universal appeal than anything."

[4] In 1975, the Motion Picture Service covers television as well as films for direct showing to audiences. At the time of this study, the Agency had only begun to deal with television.

It makes no difference what we have to show them. They will come to see anything you have to show them. You will find this true almost anywhere except perhaps among intellectual groups where they are blasé about it. There's a fascination that films have for people. Even among the intellectuals there, they come to be critical.

Movies have the ability to get audiences and hold their attention. Seeing a movie is "like a prize." Films assemble a "captive audience." "You can do anything you want with them as long as you don't drive them away."

Movies are most easily adaptable for domestic use in the U. S. and can win favorable publicity for USIA. They effectively convey information and are accepted as authentic, showing people how to do things and how to improve their lot. They may be used to expound foreign policy with high credibility (unless the audience is so unsophisticated that it takes the theme literally, in which case the abstractions that a western audience would readily understand must be spelled out). They are the best substitute for word-of-mouth persuasion—and the purpose of USIA films is "attitude formation, not information."

Films have particular potential in creating a good climate of opinion— "planting seeds" among people who are on the borderline. Audiences learn indirectly about the positive values of life in the U. S. from observing films with no overt political content.

During the course of the showing of that film, they see Americans and American situations. There's background peripheral material in the film about America. Because of the fact that we are not saying, "Look at this, isn't this fine?" they receive some impression from it without stopping to consciously reject it, as is their creed.

Technical films serve a program purpose by showing foreign peoples how to overcome their problems and elevate their standard of living. Nonpolitical films are suitable for the mass audiences of Asia. Political films are best for selective target audiences.

Films can be shown to large masses of people at a single time, and can be understood by all types of people, including anti-Americans. They are especially suitable for unsophisticated audiences. Their impact can be increased by using techniques (such as pantomime or animation) that have special appeal to an illiterate audience. A crude animated style (that looks "like Grandma Moses' paintings") appeals to uneducated audiences, who feel it to be realistic. But it is also liked by the sophisticates.

Films may be used directly to reach a broad audience:

We didn't much use our films to reach public opinion molders. Our effort could be spent more effectively on a mass audience only. We did make an exception of technical films shown at factories for the benefit of plant managers and foremen. We had an excellent film on blind riveting. It's a marginal effort on our part but it's cost us no money. We lent it to them. It did, I suppose, show that American technical methods are good, but they know that anyway. Maybe some of it carries over into political fields. "If Americans are good at this they're probably good at other things." Actually I am doubtful about it. It's a possible argument. I personally feel that there is no necessary connection between the two. The effect on the plant management might be somewhat different. For one thing it did open up to us film showings in the plant after working hours and there we would show our propaganda films.

On the other hand, the very policy of reaching the widest possible audience is viewed as unwise.

I'm not a devotee of the film program because, though it's reaching large groups, it's not reaching target groups. Mobile units are getting to the hinterlands and reaching fellahin who may never have heard of the United States and may not be interested and who may have no political influence in Asia or Brazil.

But film production costs are high. Using this medium requires assurance that a broad audience is being reached. Ideally, there should be a separate program for each country. Since this is economically unfeasible, it is desirable for each film to serve the greatest possible number of countries. One way is to make a regional picture and dub in the local language. But lip synchronization, too, creates formidable costs. One theory is that the foreign audience prefers an American product to be authentically American, even in voicing, and therefore films with the original sound track are preferable to the dubbed-in versions. (It even helps them learn English.)

Films acquired from private sources depict the U. S. to foreign audiences, provided they are adapted for the information program. Whenever possible, the characters in a film should resemble those already familiar to the audience. Both friendly and hostile characters should be made as nearly as possible like people in the local community. When indigenous themes and characters are employed in a USIA film, the audience may be suspicious.

The question was raised as to what the justification would be of showing films on local folklore themes to a local audience when these films originated in the United States.

There are internal debates as to whether a locally produced film should be up to American standards or whether certain areas, such as Asia, require different standards, such as slower pace.

Another plus for the film program is its mobility. With mobile units in backward areas, it can achieve a continuously rotating audience. Of course, this is a one-shot affair, and it is problematic whether the average audience takes in the message. Which sets off another debate. The film program, in order to have a cumulative effect, must be regarded as a sustained activity. A single film can have little effect on its audience. Audiences must receive a continuous flow of output to retain their attention and good will. It is better to reach a limited number of important persons repeatedly than a larger number sporadically.

Films open up avenues of personal contact. They may not influence opinion with a selective target but are an entering wedge for personal contact and discussion.

If one of our field officers is having difficulty reaching a group of prominent industrial leaders, he will tell us he would like to have some films on iron foundries or police training, whatever the interest of that particular group is. You can see for yourself that this has nothing to do with the main objectives of our policy, but if he can get these films, he can get these men together for an evening and after he establishes rapport with them he can show them other films in which we do have a propaganda hook.

We asked them (PAO's) what motion pictures do for you. They say, "It's my way of getting entree to a hell of a lot of people that I want to talk to." He is not concerned whether the pictures he has say one damn thing that has anything to do with his objectives. It's an extremely useful device for getting a group of people together that he wants to get to. There's many an ambassador that has used his films just as a means of making contacts with public officials. He's not running a film program, but it's one of the little gimmicks that he uses to get them in and get them interested. It's a device by which you can involve indigenous groups and organizations in your own program.

It is necessary to show films to the mass to reach leaders who arrange the showing—teachers, officials, village headmen.

If the head of the UAW's equivalent in Turin asks the PAO for a film and it's thereupon shown to all the automobile workers, the value is in having the guy at the top as a friend. That has no more reflection on the value of the film program than if the guy happens to ask for a book for himself. The contact with the people who see the film is meaningless.

We like to have something on each program that the leaders will know is helpful to the village. So the benefits are twofold. The leader is grateful for this contribution we have made to his status, so we have a certain amount of value there in the kind of predisposition we want. When things come along that are unfavorable to us, there is less desire to believe them. Plus the fact that we have included in the program specific information he can acquire as a leader. It's not that we get no value from showings to the mass of the people—we do—but if we could get to their leaders without showing to them, I think we would do so.

Films are made more effective if followed up through small-group discussion before or after a showing, or with supplementary print materials that extend the train of discussion and thought. A local discussion leader will arouse more credibility and conviction than an American. The value of the discussion is further enhanced if group leaders receive some previous indoctrination.

ICS: USIS LIBRARIES

As the "hub" of the information program overseas, the USIS information centers are seen as a way of providing "a respectable front" and a storehouse of information. Audiences for other media, such as radio or film, can turn to a USIS library for further information on points that interest them.

Those who run the library program have a strong sense that it is unique, based on a nucleus of physical plants that must be maintained.

> I don't think it's widely enough understood [that] the information center is a completely different institution from any other USIA media. It's a physical setup; it has continuity. It's a tangible thing that you can see, understand, and come to. In all the sociological meaning of the word, "institution," they are institutions, as none of our other projects are. The other things can all be turned on and off. . . . You can't turn a book collection off and on or change the content from week to week. It's not an exhibit that people come to look at and then go away from. It's a permanent thing."

A library is particularly effective in communicating ideas because it is a repository to which audiences can go again and again and because a collection of books permits an individual approach. Each visitor can select his own reading matter.[5]

> For the same amount of money that goes into a film, you can stock a library with a great mass of things that will hit people as individuals. It's on the individual dignity of man that the strength of this government is founded—thinking of people as individuals rather than as a mass of 10,000 X's.

This advantage is reinforced by the conviction that information is conveyed more effectively when it is selected voluntarily by the audience itself. Anyone who makes an effort to get information is more confident of the opinion he forms than if the information is handed to him as a package. It is also held that the library program leaves a deeper impression than other media.

> With the fast media, you have a superficial impression, whereas with the exhibits, books, and personal contact, the librarian going out—[there is] a long-lasting, deepset impact.

> In the Free World, no one is going to listen to a squawking shortwave when he can turn to his own program. What can you say in fifteen minutes? No one takes programs to play back, whereas a library program provides a permanent repository.

Elsewhere in the Agency it is often held that the importance of information centers is exaggerated.

> Particularly in an area like the Far East, where communications are bad, no information center can possibly carry out an educational program. You have got to be out beating on doors, whether your program is trying to reach the leaders or the whole country.

---

[5] "A Greek employee of USIS who operates our library in the provincial town of Kovalla once made a listing for me of some of the questions he was asked during a typical day. A lawyer wanted to know about marriage and divorce rates in the U. S. A University student was supplied with names of early explorers and dates of explorations. A graduate of a commercial school and planning on studies in the U. S. was given information on all colleges in Indiana. An amateur fisherman planning to build a boat found interesting models in the book, *Boating is Fun.*" (Wilson P. Dizard, *The Strategy of Truth*, Washington, D.C.: Public Affairs Press, 1961, p. 143.)

There is probably closer agreement on objectives within ICS than in other parts of the program. Here the emphasis is on providing information about the United States, with the expectation that familiarity will lead to friendship. Both conviction and special interest make many ICS operators believe that the cultural approach is superior to hard-hitting anti-communism.

The library is a focal point from which impressions of the U. S. are made, particularly from the kind of service people get at the lending desk. Therefore, service to the patron is the major criterion of library achievement.

By making good books available to people who might not otherwise have access to them an American library broadens their cultural horizons and creates bonds of friendship.

Librarians feel strongly that the American library system is a major source of democratic strength and that its methods should be introduced into other countries. Introduction of U. S. library techniques, like the open bookshelf, or training local librarians in American methods, has a value in itself—strengthening local democratic institutions.

> We felt that the American library system with free access to information was a definite factor in a free society. If we could give them an engaging picture that would just start them thinking we thought we would fulfill our purpose. You can't change their whole outlook but you can certainly plant seeds.

> I think that the most important aspect of the *Amerika* houses is that here people can come and participate in activities without paying a fee, without the fear of being dominated. They can go to the magazine or newspaper racks and pick up a newspaper without being guided, participate in the lecture series, see exhibits, hear musical programs, learn that Americans are capable of hearing Bach, Beethoven, and—who is the other third "B"?—Brahms.

Part of the libraries' function is to teach foreigners how to set up their own libraries, since "the biggest thing that USIS can do abroad is long-range education."

The program may serve another useful purpose—help develop the communications system in an area like the Middle East—by giving local publishers greater familiarity with American publicity and book distribution techniques.

ICS personnel agree on the importance of American personnel in the libraries overseas. However, there is no clear agreement on how important the American librarians are in dealing with the audience. One view is that the main value of information centers is contact with Americans. Books and magazines are only props. The real task is influencing opinion through personal contact. An active program permits a library to pursue its function as an "educational institution." Library content is less important than how it is manipulated by trained and capable personnel.

An information center acquires value only insofar as the librarian can deal directly with the reader and move him along, from a romantic historical novel of little program value to a social history or other work with a message. Patronage for the library program must be actively sought.

After you have a certain number of books you try to operate a certain number of community enterprises. You try to establish relationships with the university system and the library system. You will have to renew your stock at a certain rate, unless you're going to fall back not only on your circulation and reference, but on your actual contacts, which are the basic reasons for your being there in the first place.

Requests for information should be encouraged and filled as far as budget permits. However, the librarian must not reduce himself to answering requests. "The average reader may just ask for fiction and the scholars will just ask for scholarly tomes."

ICS: BOOKS

A library, as a cross-section of the United States, should have books and periodicals dealing with many different subjects and representing many viewpoints. The greatest source of USIS credibility is the output of private American publishers.

I think that only through the output of the periodical and book publishers, the general literary output of this country, can you give a real picture of what goes on in this country. I don't think you can give it effectively any other way.

Our libraries have to be objective, but on the other hand the very definition of our libraries is that they're special purpose libraries. The best we can hope to do is to achieve and maintain the illusion of objectivity. Once that is broken down then credibility disappears. Without credibility you might as well close your door.

However, it is also noted that criteria of selection are subjective. There are no rigid, clearly stated, universally applicable rules.

Any book that's written reflects the ideas of the writer or the group of people that produced it. No matter how much they try for objectivity it's still going to be a personal project. The choosing of any book for any use or location is also a personal judgment.

Thus, the view is also expressed that Communist books or books of questionable taste have no place in the libraries.

To what extent shall books selected for a USIA library promote USIA objectives? One view is that since funds are limited, and information centers are intended to support the interests of the American people, they should not furnish recreational material. On the other hand, it is maintained that any contact with phases of American life, however slight and unrepresentative, is desirable to create a feeling of familiarity. Bridging these opposing stands is the view that a balance should be struck between books that serve a direct program purpose and those that give service to the user. One way to do this is to minimize the number of books with purely entertainment value.

It might be a good idea to create artificially a shortage of those books so that the audience would have to go to another book to do any reading. Since they were there it would be more than likely that they would, and wouldn't it be better to have more of the strong hard-hitting ones read? So that out of 100 books instead of having 90 popular and 10 hard-hitting, make it 50-50.

Books selected for the libraries represent "the cream of the crop" in terms of their quality. They are representative of U. S. output in terms of their range of subject matter:

> We feel nothing could be gained by sending the cheap, shoddy, and sensational type of material, things of poor literary merit, because we don't think they're representative or serve our objective. They're representative of the worst of our publishing output.

However, the "cheap, shoddy" type is often the kind of American publication that is most popular abroad and creates impressions that the program must counteract.

In selecting books for translation, a dilemma arises. The most useful books are apt to be the poorest sellers; the least useful ones for program purposes are those that sell the best. Books should not be selected for translation on the basis of their probable popularity but because they serve program objectives.

Books by U. S. authors are preferable because (1) reviews are available, (2) the books are accessible for screening, (3) they contain proportionately more subject matter related to the U. S., (4) procurement is more simple, and (5) there is a wide range of choice.

To what extent, if at all, should information centers contain American books dealing with other countries or by non-American authors? It can be argued that such works may have considerable program value. Works of foreign authors are more credible and effective than American works, since they appear to be disinterested.

Publications dealing with the target country should be included in USIS Libraries to show American interest. (A history of the Lee dynasty in an American library in Korea will do more for USIA aims than a book about the U. S., since readers are more interested in their own history.) The presence of any books by non-American authors or on non-U. S. subjects shows appreciation of foreign peoples.

> *The Adventures of Marco Polo* by an Irishman, *The Psychotherapy of Everyday Life* [*sic*] by Freud—that shows we have an appreciation for foreign peoples. *Coming of Age in Samoa* shows we are interested in the welfare of man—regardless of his color, race, or creed.

Pocket editions of world classics or of art books get across the idea that Americans are in the mainstream of artistic tradition and respect the cultural achievements and contributions of other nations: "The idea was to show that we did have serious books that were available at prices that people could afford."

An American encyclopedia of Islamic art translated into Arabic would create a favorable impression of American culture. (This is disputed on the grounds that the Arab audience is not "deceived" by such a production but looks upon it as propaganda.)

Selecting fiction is the most difficult because criteria of merit are hardest to define. There are at least three different assumptions about the role fiction plays: (1) to serve purely as "bait," to draw more people into the centers; (2) to display American cultural and literary achievement; and (3) to palatably convey to foreign readers information about the people, institutions, and history of the United States.

In any case, fiction should be either descriptive or "historical" as distinguished from "pure fiction" that serves only to entertain.

> *Of Mice and Men* would be the low-level type of fiction. *Grapes of Wrath* depicts a way of life of a segment of the American people during a peculiar social and economic period, but it probably very accurately reflects that period for that group of people. *Of Mice and Men* is a reflection of one idiot individual within a very special, not particularly American, scene at all—a scene just devised by the author to fit the story. He does not try to depict the actual. I would make some attempt to distinguish between historical fiction and pure fiction. If its only value is entertainment, we rule it out.

A problem arises with respect to bestsellers by new authors who are critically acclaimed in the United States—such as *The Naked and the Dead, From Here to Eternity* and *The Invisible Man*—but are critical of some phase of American life. There are several distinct positions on this matter:

1. Such works cannot be used within the program because they cannot be properly assessed by a foreign audience. They can lead to unfavorable impressions of America.

2. Critical novels of literary merit should be included to make the library reflect all facets of contemporary American culture. Prestige and credibility with foreign readers would be lost if books are eliminated because they portray some aspect of American life unsympathetically. Besides, the foreign reader is suspicious when well-known books are not available.

   > I have had that experience in India when Indians walked into my library and asked for Richard Wright's *Black Boy*. We had the book, and it was out at the time and they said, "Aha, you don't want to expose the real condition of the American Negroes."

3. An accurate book by a major author (Steinbeck or Hemingway) about an unappetizing aspect of American life should not be included if it is not particularly well written, but should be included if it is.

The atmosphere of anxiety created by the McCarthy investigations has caused titles that operators consider useful to be eliminated.

> We have drifted into a system where anything that's in the least controversial is pushed aside. You can't blame our people here. We have been beaten over the head with a dirty shovel for the last year and we are getting sensitive. . . . A great deal

of time at these meetings now is spent in discussing books that should never have been discussed at all, that should be a matter of individual judgment.

There is strong agreement in USIA that the "book-burning episode" undermined the program's credibility overseas and that in general "blacklisting techniques" are bad. Under present practice, a purely technical work by an author who is in any way suspect cannot be included. But an author cannot be considered acceptable simply because there is nothing unfavorable about him on file, since such information may develop at any time, even after he is dead.

We assumed that if no derogatory information could be found in the old State Department security files the author was OK. A wrong assumption. . . . It had never been possible in the history of this organization to do a periodic weeding out of the stuff that had accumulated from various sources. The result was that there was a significant amount of stuff in these collections that should never have been there at all. We found only 39 copies of books by known Communists. All the rest of the controversy was about people who had refused to testify under the Fifth Amendment. Of course at the time the books were bought there was no knowledge that they would refuse to testify. For example, suppose that in one of our posts abroad a technical work was needed, such as the work of a man like Einstein who would not testify before a committee if called upon and who would take refuge under the Fifth Amendment (because he has urged other people to do so, so there is every reason to assume that he would). Yet how could we not include the work of an Einstein in our technical library where this was a basic book?

The directives setting political criteria on authorship for a brief period completely stymied the book selection program and have continued to inhibit it even after being revised.

If you examine the technical literature on how you select books, you will find that in the normal set-up you can't answer the kinds of questions that the McCarthys are interested in. . . . Probably the biggest problem is adjusting to a pretty completely new concept of the factors that go into the selection of the book. The Department at the beginning of the hassle set up awfully rigid criteria as to political affiliations of authors in selection. It not only included Communists; it also included "et ceteras." For the first time we were faced with criteria over which we had no professional competence. . . . The political affiliation of an author, quite apart from what he said, was important.

According to a widely shared view, the fracas over book selection did more harm to the program than anything else. Having anti-administration books on library shelves would prove that USIS is democratic and that information centers are not "propaganda institutes."

XIII

In the Field

WHILE THE MEDIA SERVICES provide the essential uniform content of the Agency's worldwide program, it is the operators in the field who, throughout most of the world, carry the final responsibility of disseminating the product. While a strong argument is made for giving the field greater autonomy, many at headquarters voice doubts and warn of the dangers of "localitis." Personal contacts are at the heart of field operations, but their value for the Agency's mission is not universally accepted. The State Department's Exchange of Persons Program, which manages such contacts on a massive scale, encounters the same kind of praise and skepticism. In the field, USIA deals not only with individuals but also with governments. It faces delicate problems in countries with nondemocratic, dictatorial, and colonial regimes that tolerate local USIA operations and to which, in a number of cases, VOA also broadcasts directly from the U. S.

SUCCESSIVE ADMINISTRATIONS of the information program have coped with problems in the relationship between Washington and the field. These are expressed in debates over whether USIA is a media or an area program, to what extent the program should be tailored by country, and whether the same office can efficiently direct both policy and field operations.

> The dominant thinking had been a media kind of thinking, in terms of the best techniques of getting the American story into mass media channels, so that presumably it could be seen or heard by the largest number of people. This was mainly an emphasis upon technique; how do you do it. Starting from the American methods, adaptation in each country needed varying degrees of subtlety. And our information program, in its early days during and post World War II, was effective at all in the degree that we had mass-media channels and techniques in other countries in some degree comparable with what we have in the United States.

Our effort in Europe was most extensive as compared to other regions and was probably most effective because the blocks to communication, both cultural and technical, were least. But it soon became recognized that the problems were not confined to Europe or confined to where the techniques of communication were easily adaptable for us, and we first became aware of the problems from a propaganda point of view, with respect to Japan and Southeast Asia, India and parts of the Near East. And these concepts we began to respond to by getting a little more refined, and we began to think about how the effort ought to be represented in terms of distribution of resources.

Hitherto it had been a question mainly of producing for mass distribution, pamphlets, posters, radio programs—it was very largely a Washington-controlled apparatus responsive to what were interpreted to be the critical policy issues from Washington's point of view, designed to convey these issues in a favorable light for foreign countries. The material for foreign countries was therefore produced in great numbers in the Department or prepared in prototype form for reproduction abroad.

MEDIA OR AREA

The present USIA policy is to decentralize authority and to put the emphasis on area rather than media.[1] But media operators, in defending their budget before Congress, resisted the transfer of authority to the field. A program allocation board, set up to overcome this resistance, heard the budget recommendations but made its decision without media representation. Thus, the media-area conflict in essence remained unsolved.

> You couldn't be against the thing, because it was like being against motherhood. It took the form of nit-picking, agreeing in principle but objecting to details. . . . The thing was never modified. I would say that something typically bureaucratic happened. After voicing objections, the media went along pretty much as they have always gone.

The prevailing philosophy is that: "We don't ram anything down the throats of the field." Final decisions as to whether or not output is suitable for a given country must be left to the field (although area experts in Washington may have made the initial decision).

Policy lines should be set in Washington, but the field should be "given the ball to carry." The field is not obliged to follow Washington guidances. The media services should supply the field with raw material for adaptation to local conditions rather than with finished, prepackaged products. ICS can recommend a basic list of cleared books. Within this range, the field can use them if it wishes to, but is not required to do so. The field decides whether to release a given wire story or publication, and the method of placement or distribution. The Office of Policy clears material for content. The field should clear it for suitability.

[1] This policy stemmed from a report by a Congressional Committee headed by Congressman Jerry Voorhees.

The best operators are those who know what Washington is after and can be relied on to do things at times when Washington is not in a position to give orders. Those who always wait to take orders are not effective.

Meanwhile, the field has a number of specific grievances, some contradictory.

Washington doesn't give the field credit for having the intelligence to do locally what needs to be done.

While they give lip service to the field's doing things, they have a perfectly natural tendency to try to mastermind the detail. In particular, that means you can't put down broad objectives, you have got to deal with events. It also leads to the dangerous idea that you know how to exploit a given this or that. How do you exploit the ideas if you have not got competent people in the field?

Guidance is too detailed and restricts the PAO's effectiveness.

You can't look to the PAO as all-wise. He needs his guidance from the central machinery of the department or from USIA. He needs to be advised as to the general lines on which he should operate.

Too often they come to him in the form of innocuous generalities. Redrafted country papers, platitudes that were in many cases revolting. "The objective of the United States in Peru is to win as many friends as possible for the United States, to promote peace and good will."

The media are not responsive to field needs. Operators are arrogant about their products and do not take the field's ideas into consideration.

I think of all my field experience and trips to the field; the problem that always seemed to be the greatest was the heavy mass of material coming out to a very small staff that just couldn't handle it, and therefore there was a tremendous amount of waste.

Congressional investigators and others became more conscious of the frequently reported notes from the field that stuff coming out from Washington was just swamping them and was more than they could handle, and it was just piling up in their warehouses or had to be pulped and used for scratch paper. This was damaging to the reputation of the program.

Washington has an exaggerated view of the field's capacity for processing and adapting output.

I have the idea that some of these kits have not been used as widely as they should have and have lain on shelves because they have not been in finished form, because they have been bulky and have required too much work at that end.

The field is in the position of continuing many activities because the media continue to supply the raw materials.

If they keep sending material for that activity out to the post there is nothing that the post can do about it.

Two arguments are advanced for giving greater responsibility to the field:

1. Output can concentrate on specific targets.
2. The field is more realistically aware of and alert to audience sensibilities.

The PAO knows more about his country than anyone in Washington; being on the spot, he can evaluate the temper of the situation. Washington must trust his judgment.

Your opportunities for action keep coming up. It's a good deal different from the kind of centralized planning people like to think of, where a mastermind sits in Washington and reaches out to this vast harp he's got and plucks his string and somebody votes the right way in Lahore.

In fact, Washington is too far away to direct the field effectively. A policy man notes:

It has been felt to be wise to move responsibility to the field. Money and simple mechanics are an important part of it. How are you going to direct your field offices? You can't send them all telegrams every day. By the time they get guidance it's too late. So the field has to make policy on their own. We are always in the embarrassing position of sending them out a guidance saying, "Wednesday's speech by Gromyko should be dealt with so," and they get it the following Wednesday after they have already dealt with it. We had to wait for the texts, then we had to formulate a position.

Another man puts it this way:

The current position is, we cannot mastermind the field. They want a large body of guidance that will so indoctrinate them that they can deal with their own local and emergent problems. By and large the field runs its own show. That stultifies us. We don't know enough about what the field's problems are. You get a place like Bangkok saying it's primarily concerned with Siamese problems, and how are you going to get material to them? Telegraph costs are so damn high. If they get a problem, how are they going to get the party line? We can send a short telegram to a particular mission on a particular thing, but by and large if we try to deal with a larger segment we have to send something that's longer and more inclusive and your code clerks don't get at our stuff as quickly as they do at the State Department stuff.

But not everyone accepts field autonomy. Those who do not note that some of the arguments for autonomy may work in reverse.

1. People at the posts may suffer from "localitis" and be prone to sacrifice broad policy aims.

   Every once in a while the field is lax on things that we here feel are important. If you go in for complete field autonomy you end up with a fractional organization with a whole lot of little Information Services operating independently of each other.

   The feeling abroad is that the whole thing is deteriorating into a ladies' aid society with no responsibility for anything that happens. There is a danger of a completely decentralized program ending up in a completely chaotic condition.

2. Coordination may be lost when responsibility is shifted to field posts.
3. With authority decentralized, program objectives may be tampered with to fit the locality. The individual country plan may be written as though it were the chief target.

Localism. The guy in the field attached to the field, the guy in the media attached to the media, the guy in Bangkok becoming particularly concerned with couldn't he persuade the Bangkokians. For example, to persuade the people in Siam that the French were not doing a bad job in Indochina. He had to build credit with the local press and he wasn't going to risk it by espousing an unpopular cause. That meant that we tampered with our opinions to fit the locality. Desperation and division. And then the lack of control. What are the Siamese interested in, what are the Greeks interested in? The country plans are based on the idea of treating Greece as though it were the chief target; self-justification became the chief aim of the field reports.

4. Nor is the field man in a position to know what the Washington specialist who is exposed to political pressures knows. Washington sees the global picture, while the field man sees only his area. In fact, personnel in one country may be so obsessed with their own problems that their output may be offensive to other countries: "They can't see anything but trees. It is like saying that an ambassador should run his own show."

5. The PAO is too influenced by the local outlook.

A two-way indoctrination takes place when we send representatives abroad. Our representative abroad is one man among millions in a foreign country. Whether he likes it or not his attitudes are subject to opinions and to influence by the officials and the people whom he is living among. It sometimes happens that our operators abroad request media output that would be popular among the people they are living among rather than accepting an assignment from home to promulgate certain ideas. The heavy demand that we get from most of the areas for a relatively innocuous kind of Americana, as against the harder hitting type of thing, I think reflects that.

6. Field autonomy leads to loss of continuity when personnel change. Different PAO's who have not had the opportunity to pool their knowledge often must tackle the same problems again and again: "Sometimes a man will go out to the field and say, 'Can we have a story about the Arab-Americans?' We have to tell him we have done it fifty times."

7. If the PAO is replaced by someone with diametrically opposite views, the existing material may have to be changed drastically.

If you want an extreme example of what might happen when you decentralize out to the field, you ought to look at that German program. In one of their memoranda they asked for a film on a young American businessman. A script was written about some American mechanic who invented a new type of welding torch and had various problems getting it produced. He went to a sympathetic banker who was willing to finance him to a certain extent. He finally got married and lived happily ever after. We finally got this script written. Meantime, personnel had changed. The people who were there when we had sent the script over were not those who had been there originally. They said, "We can't use it here because German bankers do not lend money to young businessmen." We said, "Hell, that was the idea—to inculcate a new idea that we thought would be beneficial!" But the thing was dropped.

8. Emphasis on the field leads to an unbalanced program, because each PAO tends to follow his own bent.

Whether we like it or not, there has been too much judging of the field program for individual media according to whether people in the field appreciated their media and did things with them. We did say that we gave field people material and let them use it or not, according to whether they thought it would be useful, but people judge a program according to whether or not a medium is used.

9. Field autonomy is uneconomical. "USIA's budget cannot practicably be allocated in 88 different ways." If each Public Affairs Officer determines his own programming, the information program becomes more costly. It is much cheaper to produce material for mass distribution than for each country separately.

10. The budget may reflect real needs less than the fact that a man in one country is more aggressive than another somewhere else.

The man in the field sees all problems in terms of the area in which he is. He may think that Afghanistan is the crux of our foreign policy and those people in Washington don't realize this, because they just don't see what's going on. This can lead to an unbalanced program if the man in Afghanistan is a fighter and the man in India is not. Your money and effort may be channeled according to the efforts of the PAO rather than on the basis of a balanced appraisal.

11. A decentralized agency cannot prepare for new policy developments. USIA must have a world-wide program with set objectives planned in Washington. The field should not have the primary initiative.

There are certain decisions that the country mission should make. The worldwide objectives of the information program should be stated in Washington and should be monolithically ordered. Don't ask the missions to set objectives on their own, outside of the worldwide USIA objectives. The country mission should determine the tasks that should be performed and the means you use. I don't see how the objectives can vary from country to country.

12. Certain media output, such as motion pictures, must be prepared for across-the-board use. A media operator, producing for four different areas, cannot consider the local problems of an individual PAO.

13. Post activities should not be focused solely on the country of operations. There should be cross-fertilization of ideas and activities and a regional approach to an area. In Europe, common directives dictate that activities should be coordinated to avoid duplication. In fact, Europe should be treated as one unit, like the United States.

14. Just because the PAO is on the spot, he is not necessarily in the best position to judge what is going on. He may lack the ability or the time to evaluate the situation accurately: "Taking a man who's stupid in Washington and putting him into Bombay doesn't make him any brighter."

15. For the most part, field men are accustomed to carrying out orders from Washington. They were selected in the first place for a different type of responsibility than they have now and should not be expected to resolve political dilemmas that are beyond their scope.

The Public Affairs Officer overseas rules with an iron hand, but he is not God Almighty. He doesn't know everything at all times. The assumption is that he does because he is there, because they feel that since he's there he knows more about what's going on there than they do, he knows the temper of the situation, he's able to evaluate. In actuality they've never had any check on his ability to evaluate the situation, or on his ability to use the techniques of evaluating it. What formerly was a reportorial State Department function has now taken on a new sense. Instead of just saying, "These are what the papers say," they now say, "This is the state of opinion," and say exactly the same thing.

16. Washington personnel are of higher caliber. "In every case we have people who are far superior to the people in the field." They know more about political realities and the technical requirements of the media and are better able to foresee needs.
17. Any field operation tends to become self-perpetuating and stereotyped.
18. The field does not follow guidance. Washington is piqued by its tendency to use available facilities, even when they don't accord with policy plans.

While regionalization and area specialization have brought about a "two-way street feeling" between the field and the home office, a great many operators disagree. They claim that communication is not as good as it should be. Washington does not know enough about field problems, partly because of a tradition of secretiveness and uncommunicativeness in the foreign service. This is expressed in the phrases, "You pat me on the back and I'll pat you on the back"; "We don't want Washington to know we can't handle things by ourselves."

Since field experience filters in over a period of years, there is a time lag before Washington acts. Yet, field guidance is needed to avoid wasted effort. If media operators get insufficient information from field reports they may have inadequate knowledge of how to put products to use. A media unit that may be knowledgeable enough to sense that a story can be used in more than one post may not always know specifically where it can be placed or how it can be used. Thus, regular, detailed reporting of field use of centrally produced output is needed both for Washington and for the regional service centers.

Field men do not have the time to keep Washington fully informed of what they do. Trips to the field by Washington personnel are extremely valuable in improving communications flow. A man sent to the field can settle in a few hours of conversation issues that could never be resolved by correspondence. Yet, administrators do not sufficiently appreciate the need for frequent field trips, and tend to look upon them as junkets.

Interviewing returned field personnel is regarded as an important means of communication between Washington and the field. It is desirable to bring personnel back from the field to learn about their problems and get their suggestions to operators. (Debriefing is conducted by each of the media separately.)

In the eyes of some returned field personnel, debriefing is uncoordinated and unrewarding. The "debriefers" try to sell their part of the program. Three returned PAO's comment:

Each one thinks that his is the all-embracing thing, and he wants you to stress that 99 percent, and one percent the other. The view of the man in the motion picture program is that you should cut out everything but the motion picture program.

You're the first person in this debriefing process who has bothered to listen to me. Most of these sessions last only ten or fifteen minutes and then they're only concerned with telling you about their output. I was up at IMS yesterday, and the debriefing consisted of getting a two-hour lecture, with charts, on how to detect a Communist. The fellow in IPS wanted to show me how they got the Wireless File out.

Here no one was interested in finding out anything I had to say. My experience here was that each one was interested in furthering their own part of the program and each was seeking evidence to show that it was the effective media. The general impression I got during that week of debriefing was lack of coordination. They all seemed to be pulling at different directions.

INTERPERSONAL CONTACTS

The value of interpersonal contact in overseas operations is axiomatic. The most effective way to influence people is word-of-mouth. It can accomplish a great deal for a little money.

A person is more apt to believe another person. There is a certain warmth of relationship, a certain credibility that you get, more than for a printed piece of material.

It might even mean getting drunk with them. I have done it many times. I have sat with labor groups till six or seven in the morning. What I said didn't make any sense. It isn't what you said then. It's the confidence you gained. When you get home you can do a hell of a lot more because you have the prestige, the backing. Our people in Europe, when they get some of these friends, anything that we want to do we let them do because that's a powerful weapon when you are dealing with that group.

I would greatly strengthen the so-called indigenous activities—those that are given a local basis within the countries in which we are working. I would strengthen the use of the device of the man who goes into a town and gets to know the people and becomes the accepted source of knowledge about the United States and becomes identified as a friend. Preferably the fellow who could sit in a particular town or county for three or four years.

The success of Communist tactics proves the effectiveness of large-scale personal contacts on the local level. But USIA has not stressed personal contact enough.

I think it's very important to reach the leaders, but I think our message goes deeper into them if we get down close. The success of some of these Communist infiltrations suggests that this is so, and they carry this to the point of becoming one with the population. I think if we miss it, one of these days we will be very sorry.

We are relying too much on mass media and not enough on the individual approach.

There has been inadequate recognition of it at the highest levels of the information program. I suppose another reason is that when we started out in this thing—before the Smith-Mundt Act—we were awful media-minded. Our national preoccupation with mass media as a way of conducting our affairs with each other.

Contact has advantages both ways. Further contact with people in target countries helps operators more effectively communicate through the mass media.

The business of getting close to average run-of-the-mill people and getting a feeling for the land and the people and the circumstances makes it far more possible to get somewhere with our propaganda. I think that applies in any country. The very fact that it does call for adjusting yourself to local realities means that it will vary a great deal from place to place. Your method in dealing with a Frenchman is going to be a lot different than dealing with an Indian or a Spaniard.

It all gets down to the fact that if you understand your audience all the way you're much more able to reach that audience. You're more inclined to listen to the guy who's gone to the same school with you and rides on the same trolley car than to someone who is away off in some remote place. Establishing that community of feeling and principles is so often important.

I think we should keep our minds open to the opportunity of learning something from these foreign peoples—not just adding to our moral and cultural stature, but in the technical sense that in a face-to-face situation you're more likely to learn more profoundly what it is that's troubling these people and why they have not been more actively accepting your foreign policy message.

When they have personalities coming to their homes for tea or dinner, and they want them to talk about certain things, you show a film that sets off a discussion period.

Contact requires planning and special techniques. It should be systematically maintained through card files broken down by professional categories or interests. Field personnel must deliberately capitalize for business purposes on their personal and social contacts. Often this requires that the PAO be of material service to his contacts, and sometimes this creates problems for him. The PAO's religious affiliations may be used for contacts with church leaders.

Crucial to the value of personal contact, however, is the caliber of field personnel. Spontaneous acts of personal kindness and friendship by the "right" USIS personnel may be worth many times the equivalent effort expended on formal and official media for selling ideas.

One week a well-known Korean painter who's always in rags was leaving on the train, which was 40 minutes off. A newspaper writer was very much impressed by the fact that X waited for 40 minutes for the train from Pusan to come in so he could see this painter off. A friend of his, a writer, came to see him and was offered a Lucky Strike cigarette. He was asked, "What are you doing with American cigarettes?" He was told Mr. X had given it to him for his comfort. This writer had been very critical of America and he wrote an article in the newspaper saying that he had been critical, but he told of his experiences and how impressed he was. He said, "We see so many Army people here in Taegu; we just see the cars going by, and it's good to show how Americans really are.'' His waiting for 40 minutes at the train seeing off that man was worth many times that amount of time at a center for selling our ideas. It's the strong personal relationships we have and our ability to talk informally in our homes.

Subtlety is required, however. Slow, careful groundwork must precede any practical results. Local opinion leaders (and other key targets) can be influenced easily if the PAO has sufficient personal contacts with them, even without design. They are flattered by the personal touch. The message "goes deeper into them.''

The Americans were working with the top government leaders. To the extent that they worked with you, they would come to your homes for receptions, they would be seen by higher leaders and their status would be enhanced a bit and they would come along for that reason.

When you're dealing with a labor leader who speaks English then your best method is just conversation. You wouldn't give him a pamphlet but you would sit down and have a bull session all night long. You might accomplish a great deal. I had a badminton court in my house and youth organizations used to come over and play, and I found that after a couple of games, sitting on the lawn and talking to the youth leader was just about the best opportunity conceivable. All we can do in a place personally is to try to get to know people who have the ability through their positions to reach a vast audience . . . I was very active—and this was not assigned, it was done—in youth activities. It kind of grew. The personal friends I made turned out to be youth leaders. I wasn't told to get into the youth movement. At the beginning I was told to see about forming some kind of organization to keep those who had been in America in touch with America and mainly through my youth contacts I succeeded in forming a society which has been doing very well.

With government leaders, personal contact is a particularly important medium of persuasion, since they are often too busy for the mass media. But good personal relationships are essential in promoting use of the media, too. Editors are more apt to use material if they know the PAO. A motion picture showing is more effective if the audience knows that an American is giving up an evening to bring them some films.

Social events should be held at the PAO's home, wherever possible, although each field post needs a place in which to hold gatherings, parties, and discussion groups.

The government makes such a mistake in not allowing more funds for entertainment. Getting people to come into your home and argue things back and forth. Our people do this all the time. You get intellectuals together arguing on a rational basis. They don't necessarily agree with us, but we convince a lot of them.

A minority believes personal contact has its limitations. It is not propaganda, and it is unlikely that opinion leaders, particularly in Western Europe, can be influenced this way. The PAO may know a man closely for several years and make earnest efforts to influence him but not change his thinking one iota.

The very people who are most important to reach may be the hardest to contact. Personal contact is difficult if various ethnic elements in a community do not get along. The typical PAO associates with locals who are friendly to the U. S. and to American ideals. Moreover, personal contact with locals may be discouraged by a suspicious government.

> It's possibly true that in a country that's just been set up as a new nation and has a new ruling group, particularly if it's set up with a fairly strong power group at the top, there may be worrying and suspicion about having these people scattered around and getting directly to the people. It's more a matter of whether a regime is secure or insecure itself than it is a matter of locality or general history.

Personal contact is not enough. It cannot cover all the people who have to be reached. (This is disputed. Despite the limited number of personal contacts that are possible, they have an important over-all effect—like pebbles dropped into a pond, the ripples spread out.)

Contacts with individual Americans are considered an important part of U. S. impact on foreign peoples. Any news story that makes an individual American "look bad" hurts the U. S.

Letter writing is an important means of interpersonal contact between Americans and foreign peoples. USIA should (and does) stimulate and organize such correspondence.

American tourists potentially do much good or much harm in creating impressions. (In one view, the reactions of Western Europeans to American tourists are by and large favorable and represent no great loss and no great gain for American influence.) "The average American does not want to be told how to behave by his government." Therefore suggestions on how he should act abroad or what he should write to overseas relatives or friends should come from private agencies. USIA's problems rise in countries where American troops are stationed, since they give the local public a "distorted picture of how Americans behave."

The presence of Americans may influence program content overseas. Selection of materials for USIS libraries may depend upon requests from American troops who use them. PAO's must maintain friendly relations with American journalists stationed in the country, as well as with the local press.

EXCHANGE OF PERSONS

Although the Exchange of Persons Program is no longer part of the Information Agency,[2] it remains a closely related activity which USIA personnel think of as part of their work, on the premise that familiarity makes for friendliness. The most useful way to convince people overseas is to bring them to the

---

[2] It has remained in the Department of State since the establishment of USIA as an independent agency.

United States to see things for themselves. If USIA brought 42,000,000 Frenchmen to the U. S., 41,000,000 would go back favorably impressed and would stay that way.

The Exchange of Persons Program not only builds friendship for the U. S., but democratic institutions in the country concerned as well. A newspaper editor or radio man who comes to the U. S. as an exchangee returns with a better knowledge of his own profession. But the Exchange of Persons Program is also criticized as not sufficiently selective (it should center on the select few who can disseminate their message to a wide audience) and as uncoordinated with private effort.

A three-week visit to the U. S. can have little effect on anti-American predispositions held by a sophisticated European or Asian (whose views of the U. S. are the product of a lifetime of reading and reflection). In some cases, the program has a boomerang effect. Often when a man goes back to his own country he is frustrated by the lack of opportunity to apply his newly-found knowledge. Exchangees become "completely Americanized." On returning they give the impression that they have been "bought."

Another problem arises in dealing with minority or underprivileged groups (for example, native Taiwanese) in countries where USIA must work through the local government. In some countries, the Exchange Program selects the wrong people. Public officials in the Middle East and Southeast Asia often try to get friends or relatives to America on scholarships. Since the Exchange Program in many instances does not pay transportation costs, it tends to exclude persons who are not wealthy; and as a result, the exchangees are not a representative group.

It is a waste of money to send people to America who are already friends of the United States. People who have not made up their minds are the best grantees. (This is disputed. It is important to bring over as many people as possible, including those already friendly.)

RELATIONS WITH FOREIGN GOVERNMENTS

USIA deals not only with individuals through personal contacts, and with media audiences, but also with governments. Some of its principal problems in the field arise out of its dealings with governments and the handling of output in which governments have an interest.

USIA must avoid the appearance of interfering in the internal politics of any country. It must stay out of local elections, at least openly.

There is another point of view on this. USIA is essentially trying to influence votes, particularly in Western Europe. To win people away from communism in a country where the Communists are a legal party essentially implies interference in internal politics. USIA cannot stay out of local elections, although it may attempt to disguise its role.

In the Philippine elections, any inference that the United States was interfering in that election would have been disastrous. The fact remains that hundreds of thousands of pamphlets were produced on clean, free elections and they were done in the native terms with the wholehearted but covert assistance of USIS, which never showed its hand.

USIA activity is often dependent on relations with the government in power. It is impossible to preach against a totalitarian government in its own country. The attitudes of the local government must be taken into consideration in determining program content—at least insofar as subject matter must not be offensive to it. This may be carried to extremes of sensitivity. A newsreel sequence on an Indian Army benefit cricket match was eliminated on the grounds that it might be interpreted that the Indian Army does not pay its troops enough.

Down in Venezuela the government has been having a lot of trouble with labor. We had a film that was pretty much pro-labor. Since we were guests in that country, since we were supporting the government, it would have been a pretty bad choice of film.

Government control may also make it difficult or impossible to use nonofficial U. S. attribution. Where film output is subject to censorship, the leading officials or personalities of the country may be shown in a film sequence as a safeguard against the censor. (It remains an unanswered question as to whether, in preparing across-the-board output [films] for wide distribution in Southeast Asia, it is better to present the strongest case, running the risk of censorship in a major country like India, or to weaken the story and pass the most rigorous censorship.)

Some USIA activities may be conducted more easily in a dictatorship than in a democracy. Cultural, educational, and scientific affairs are more centrally controlled and organized than in democratic countries; and if contact is made with the central authority, dissemination is easy. (In Portugal, an article cleared by the censor will be automatically carried by the entire press.)

DEALING WITH NONDEMOCRATIC GOVERNMENTS

USIA at times finds two of its objectives are in conflict: promoting worldwide democracy; and the stability of non-Communist countries. The operator in the field often faces the recognition that democracy and stability are irreconcilable. (Stability is promoted by the very process of operating an information program, coupled with military or technical aid.) There are two ways of describing this type of situation.

1. The USIA cannot oppose unpopular governments that are committed against the Communists.
2. "Corrupt and despotic" governments may be supported by the U. S. for po-

litical reasons. Direct or indirect association with these governments confirms local opinion that America is imperialistic or reactionary.

By preaching freedom and democracy, USIA makes people dissatisfied with undemocratic governments.

What the hell should your target group be in a country like Syria or Iraq? They're essentially despotic, corrupt governments and we support them for political and strategic reasons. They're anti-Communist and we find it expedient not to antagonize these governments. Yet these governments represent to large numbers of their people symbols of oppression, corruption and exploitation, and when we either directly or indirectly associate ourselves with these governments at the same time that we say to them through USIS that America stands for freedom and civil liberties and social and economic rights for all, they don't know what to think.

On the one hand they've put us in the same camp with the government and their opinions about American imperialism become confirmed, and yet with all this freedom-and-democracy propaganda that we feed them they become more dissatisfied with their governments. It's to our short-run interests to keep that government in power. If the government were overthrown today there would be a vacuum into which the Communists would rush. You could say that the targets should be the government but what do you say to them? If you give them an undiluted full dose of what we shoot into the arms of a lot of other foreigners in a lot of other countries you will make them resentful, because you thereby raise the resentment of their own people. People themselves can see the contrast and ask, "Why do you support that government?"

One answer that has been suggested, which I think makes sense, is to discreetly and indirectly and within limitations to encourage in all possible activities—and that won't be much—build up a group of potential leaders, at the same time giving the least possible offense to the ruling group or the incumbent government, assuming at the same time that this corrupt incumbent government is going to topple anyway, and someday be able to give the country a slightly more democratic and progressive leadership. To do that without giving offense to the ruling group is a hell of a job but it's being attempted in a number of countries and I think it's the most important thing we can do.

How far can USIA afford to go in propagandizing for social changes in a country where its chief target is labor and its chief indigenous supporters are undemocratic? It is difficult to convince an impoverished worker that he would not be better off under communism, unless he is encouraged to try to change his present social and economic system.

USIA must avoid identifying itself with unpopular elements, but in advocating reforms it runs the risk of inciting the masses against its closest local allies:

On the policy level, what were we trying to do in Italy by reaching a mass audience? Obviously we were trying to influence votes, which means interference in internal politics in a situation where the parties we are trying to help out are pretty much identified with reactionary elements. We have been trying to influence the government to institute planned reform, fiscal reform, and the government has dragged its heels. It seems to me we are risking the decision of inciting the masses against parties we are trying to help, since it's very difficult to have any influence on the labor audience in Northern Italy unless you believe in certain social reforms.

There's a question of how far we can afford to go and how far we want to go in propagandizing for social changes in a country of that kind. The situation arises when you try to convince a guy that he couldn't be better off under communism, that he's better off under democracy where he can make his desires felt and get these reforms. In fact he isn't getting these reforms. So what do you do? Do you reform the government, use diplomatic pressure on them? Encourage the workers to press their demands, or sit back and not do anything? I don't know the answers. I think we have been skirting a dangerous shore and haven't really come to any conclusions.

There is another question. How far can we dare urge socialism, say in a country like Italy? Whether it's possible for us on a policy level here to distinguish between what we want in the United States and what would be best for a foreign country. If the Social Democrats could get their program through in Italy, the Italians would be better off, and that brings us up to a high policy problem of whether or not we can support socialism or of how we do it without getting our funds cut off or being investigated.

BROADCASTING TO FRIENDLY DICTATORSHIPS

The Voice of America has far greater freedom from local government influence than the media that must carry on locally. It can say things in broadcasting even to undemocratic but friendly countries (Spain and Yugoslavia) that cannot be said on the spot.

This raises a question. Is it better to say critical things in a broadcast at the risk of incurring restrictions on local information activities, or to soft-pedal broadcast output in order to maintain local operations with minimum interference?

There are several answers:

1. VOA should back dissident democratic voices in its broadcasts to totalitarian countries. USIA faces the challenge of promoting democracy and of intruding itself in the local ferment of political ideas.
2. Such comment may be suitable in broadcasts to other countries, but not to the one involved.
3. Such an issue should be ignored altogether in VOA output, because it may stir up restrictions on USIS operations.

These positions are revealed in the following two quotations:

The tendency has been strong, particularly in recent USIA experience, to give the field posts a very powerful voice in deciding the limits of radio which is not controlled by local operating conditions, the limits within which the radio operation should move in order to keep from embarrassing the local operation. If you want my personal impression, I think this has a built-in bias in this method of approach that is somewhat questionable.

I have been in an embassy in a Communist country and I know the pressures on it. It tends to make your short-run considerations completely dominate any decisions. In Yugoslavia obviously our long-run goals have certain contradictions with the short-run ones. In the long run we would like to see a democratic Yugoslavia. They're subject on an operational level to all the pressures that the short-run considerations generate. A radio operation is not.

Let's take the Djilas case.[3] It obviously has generated a ferment on Djilas' ideas. The question arises of how much should we intrude ourselves into this ferment of political ideas? How much should we explain the guts of democracy? To the extent that we do this, and it has an impact, the USIS operation in Belgrade and Zagreb may find its own operations restricted. My point is that restriction of operations within Yugoslavia should not be an absolute determinant of whether to pursue a given course or not on the Voice. If I'm a person who is going to have my local activity restricted, there is what I described as a built-in bias in favor of dampening down the radio operations. This has its analogies in all of these countries.

We had a script on the Djilas case, when Djilas was removed by Tito. The first thing that happened was that it was vetoed, in Washington. I refused to accept the veto and appealed. I called up, going outside of channels. The policy man said, "The United States Government cannot underwrite this view even though it might be perfectly good for you to say it." I said, "What is the view? That we are for a multi-party system?" I said, "Why doesn't the United States government underwrite the multi-party system?" After consulting with his colleagues, he finally approved it for all desks but Yugoslavia. I said, "I still appeal, cable it to the Mission to see whether it's OK." They cabled it to Yugoslavia and Belgrade replied that "This is just what we needed." But the Yugoslav desk on the Voice still didn't use it even after that approval came through. It had already been approved by policy, it had been approved by the Mission, but still they didn't use it. This will give you an idea of how things can work out in practice.

COLONIAL PROBLEMS

In colonial areas, operators, in principle, would agree that USIA should talk outspokenly about independence—provided the colonial power does not mind.[4] In practice, the Agency is often discouraged from dealing with the native population.

I don't think we have come out very openly in discussing colonialism. It's just like racial segregation in this country. These things are continuing problems. Colonialism has been in that area for centuries. Certain attitudes have grown up in that area. It's there. Our policy is that it should be abolished by evolutionary processes and not by revolutionary ones. We can't get anything in the papers over there, unless they're expressed by very high officials, the President and Secretary, on the subject of colonialism, unless it happens to jibe with their own views or their own preju-

---

[3] Milovan Djilas, a close associate of Josif Broz Tito in Yugoslavia, broke with him in 1954 over the issue of democratization and was imprisoned.

[4] At that time, Egypt, Libya, Ethiopia, Liberia, and South Africa were the only independent countries in Africa.

dices. Now, how far do we go along in coddling or conforming to their prejudices and sensitivities? I find myself, when we discuss these subjects, putting it in the form of questions. I think evolution not revolution sums it up. There have got to be positive actions, not just words.

A discussion at a planning session brings into focus both the problem and the way in which it is often handled. The following dialogue occurs:

What is the reaction of the Vietnamese on a statement about freedom from communism without saying anything about freedom from the French?

All this prime minister has done that's to the good is fighting communism. We don't dare come out and say, "Throw the bums out." Of course, the emphasis we put on the growing army plugs the independence movement to a certain extent.

How about ending it, "in their fight for liberty?" The French wouldn't like that, would they?

What's wrong with, "Hopes of their people for a free world?"

VOA cannot be critical of French colonialism directly even in broadcasts in Asia, but must be critical by indirection, pointing to American and British actions to liberate formerly subject peoples. It must demonstrate that traditional Western colonialism is a dead issue and that the real threat comes from the new imperialism of the Communists.

This outlook is not universally accepted. VOA cannot use themes relating to American stands in the past for self-determination of nations or the right of people to rule themselves. Arabic-language broadcasts cannot comment on North African developments in such a way as to recall American support for native independence movements, because this may be offensive to the French.

If trouble flares up in Morocco what are you going to do? There's a "soundproof division of the world" theory, that says you should beat the French over the heads in the Arab world and side with the French in France. They'll very speedily catch you if you try double dealing. You have the delicate task of trying to tell the Arab commentators in the Voice of America how they should talk to their oppressed brothers in Morocco. What I contend I always try to do is make operators aware just how complex this whole thing is, of how dangerous it would be if they preached the Declaration of Independence to the Arab world or conversely took the French point of view, but on the other hand you have got to take a position, so you try to present an accurate version of the French side and of the Arab side, occasionally deploring that the issue had to arise, and try to weasel your way out of the problem.

XIV

Personnel

WHAT MAKES A GOOD PROPAGANDIST? A government organization as large as USIA requires strong administrative and managerial skills as well as the varied talents of its operators. Technical proficiency, political astuteness, area and language skills are all required; and in the field the art of human relations is especially important. USIA faces the ancient dilemma of any diplomatic corps: should its people be encouraged to become highly specialized in the affairs of another country at the risk of "going native?" How can the local employees (who make up half of the Agency's personnel roster) best be used? There are some sharp self-criticisms of the Agency's personnel practices, quality, and morale.

IT IS AN ACCEPTED FACT within the Agency that a propaganda organization's strength cannot be judged separately from the quality of its personnel. Getting "the right people," often called USIA's major problem, is a particularly acute one in the field.

> You can't do good propaganda with an organization that ain't worth a hoot in hell and vice versa. It must have the enthusiasm of the people who, once they are fired up, are capable of doing something . . . You don't need boxes, you don't need an organization chart and all the management people to make sure paper flows, because these deficiencies don't mean a hoot in hell if the people you have got are first rate. You only need this sort of efficiency procedure to make up for the deficiency in capability of the people.

THE ART AND ADMINISTRATION OF PROPAGANDA

Propaganda is an art requiring special talent. It is not mechanical, scientific work. Influencing attitudes requires experience, area knowledge, and instinc-

195

tive "judgment of what is the best argument for the audience." No manual can guide the propagandist. He must have "a good mind, genius, sensitivity, and knowledge of how that audience thinks and reacts."

Decisions about using material are intensely personal—"more intuitive reactions than conscious thought processes." The operator's mind automatically and subjectively weighs a great deal of technical and area experience. He must think "as an editorialist," as an argumentative person who is anxious to prove his point.

> In the back of my mind, I'm influenced by what I know, by official U. S. policy. And then I have my own personal views. You can't keep yourself out of something like this. We are dealers in ideas. You can't help it. The human element, personnel, is the key to the whole operation.

But those who think that propaganda is an art often describe it as essentially irreconcilable with a government organization's demands.

> Propaganda is primarily an art, and I don't know quite how you pick up the artists for that type of job. A McCormick or a Patterson of the *Daily News* are artists; they have instinctive feelings for what they want. They have a sense. Goebbels had a sense for what the German people wanted. Planning in a government agency practically makes it impossible to get that kind of artist on board.
>
> I don't think that in the normal bureaucratic situation the chances of getting such a person are good, not only because of the pay. It demands a certain flexibility that you don't get in a bureaucracy. You can do research to give you a better knowledge of what you want to do. But there's a point where all that ceases and all your contact with your audience is set up by individual direction. I think that's art, it's no longer science.

Agency leadership has been essentially managerial. ("They think that if things flow properly, we're doing a good job.") Top management has not been able to break loose from personnel, administrative, and liaison problems.

The "narrow, management-oriented approach" is explained by the need to maintain continuity during shifts in the upper echelons. A new director or top official, looking for someone on whom to rely, usually selects administrative personnel.

> Your managerial people are never suspect. They maintain the continuity, so they keep shifting over and over again from the substantive basis. During these interregnum periods the management people take over.

The danger in having a management-minded administration rather than a program-minded one is that it assumes its function is to spend dollars rather than to contemplate what program content should be.

> I have the feeling that the further up the echelons you go, the more the conditions you try to reach and the operations you conduct tend to lose reality and become manipulating symbols that all too frequently have no bearing on real problems. . . .
> You not only plan that way but the sweeping judgments about the organization have

that same lack of reality. Nobody can tell you what is happening. The director doesn't know on any given day what's being said today, last month, last year or anything else. Nor does he have any way of finding out.

Opinion is divided on the kinds of talent required in the top jobs of USIA. One view is that the only function of the program administrator is to provide good management. Top executives must know the public relations field and selling and be sensitive to "what gets people with what." Top officials must make a good impression on Congressional leaders. Administrative experience as a university president or business executive makes a person ideally suited for a top position in the information program.

The dissenting view is that business executives who take top jobs are not accustomed to handling the procedures of a government agency and are fish out of water. Understanding world political issues is of key importance. Top positions should be held by people like foreign service officers with a primarily political outlook.

Strong direction is necessary. Yet, the Agency suffers from "administrative confusion." Too many units make decisions. Actual responsibility is not centered anywhere.

A lack of any central line of thought has meant that no dominating idea can ever shape the organization. The people in it become more and more centrifugal because of the lack of leadership from the top. The channels tend to clog. The field is left to the field. Policy is left to policy. There was no strong infusion of central ideas that could create an organizational machinery. As the personnel at the top had to meet personal and Congressional charges, they have never developed a working body of doctrine nor have they been able to do their work properly. There has been a disregard for content. The administrative confusion that is presumably endemic in governmental agencies was compounded.

Administrative personnel essentially have "no understanding" of or sympathy with output and objectives. They are charged with being prejudiced against foreign-born operators and having a "provincial" outlook. Most "fights" in the Agency have been in the administrative sphere, arising when operating officials obtain responsibilities without administrative authority.

The usual battle between line and administrative personnel is exaggerated in the case of USIA. Administrative personnel reportedly want a larger share of responsibility than operators wish to give them.

At the heart of it was the administrative people's feeling that it was their prerogative, being responsible for the budgeting function, to take a responsibility in determining budget and interpreting that back, a feeling that the program should be expressed in monetary terms.

Questions came up: Who should prepare the prospectus; who should work out field requirements with the media services? The administration people claimed a large share of that responsibility, and there was a good deal of controversy. Perhaps even more serious were differences regarding who was responsible for selection, assignment, reassignment, and evaluation of personnel. The initial concept was that the personnel function was purely a service function, processing papers.

WHAT MAKES A GOOD OPERATOR?

The traits an ideal operator should possess are acknowledged widely to include a combination of "a diplomat's caution with the propagandist's enthusiasm," some feeling of dedication or at least of admiration for public service, a willingness to assume responsibility, capacity for hard work, "a sense of responsibility to the taxpayers," and "a little greater ability than personnel in private industry have to see beyond the immediate."

The ideal operator should have a strong belief in democracy, U. S. foreign policy, the information program, and the need to fight communism. Moreover, he should be interested in and informed about foreign policy and have "political awareness and understanding." Emotional stability is extremely important, particularly for overseas service; and he must be able to get along with people and not be a "climber." ("We don't want him stepping on other people's backs to get ahead.")

Despite the implication that the job requires a universal man, it may be possible to "fit square pegs in round holes." A man who is not philosophical, thorough, thoughtful, or well read on the deeper books may be interested in administrative or social things. In fact, a "warm body" may be adequate.

> The personnel office may say, "Is it more important to get an average or a mediocre guy there now and have him transferred later?" I have had to cancel the departures of people one day before departure time even after they have sent their belongings off. Sometimes you can afford to wait six or nine months rather than take your chances on a guy who can go next week. It may be that you will say, "We need a warm body who at least will protect the security of the office, see that equipment is not stolen." That's not strictly a personnel decision. It's a matter of how important the program is in that country and how important that man's contribution is to it.

A fundamental issue within the Agency is whether the mission is primarily a technical one, calling for universal skills to be applied anywhere, or basically a political one, involving understanding of foreign peoples and their cultures.

> I'm sure we have made mistakes in recruiting personnel and appraising personnel, because we have not operated on any firm assumptions as to the kinds of people we wanted—generalists or people with media skills. It would be a great help if the Agency specified what types of people it was looking for. Do you want a high-powered public relations man or a general foreign service type?

Advocates of technical supremacy maintain that skills of persuasion are transferable from the domestic to the international field. There is no essential difference between domestic public relations activity and USIA operations. It makes no difference whether an operator is writing an ad for soap, a movie script for "Sadie Smith in New Orleans," or a message for a foreign audience. A top officer of a large advertising agency or public relations firm is an ideal propaganda program executive.

> This is the business of international public relations, and we know on what basis national public relations function. Now we are going into the international public relations function. There's no difference whatever. We are trying to sell America to the world, and we should start preparing for public relations on an international basis because it's something for the future. Just as we have Chambers of Commerce for each state and Florida advertises itself to New York, in the same way international information will be more and more important.

This view is sharply disputed by those who maintain that international information activity is different from domestic communications work and that "salesmen" and advertising men cannot "create a world of opinion," which is USIA's job.

> We have brought in people whose techniques of persuasion were learned in the market place and who thought we had to justify our existence as a sales agency.

Men with good domestic experience are not always successful in USIA because they lack political or area understanding. In fact, they may make outrageous mistakes. "You cannot take a newspaperman from Podunk and necessarily expect him to adapt to the Asian culture."

> We have had many cases where excellent people from domestic agencies have not worked out because they did not have political savvy. The experience of translating policy into the appearance of objective reporting is something they have never been faced with and cannot handle.

From this debate on the importance of political and technical aspects of the job emerges a divergence on how important area and media skills are for operators. Ideally, they should have both (as well as "some knowledge of psychology"). And it does not matter whether a man is a media or area specialist as long as he can instinctively understand how to communicate with people and persuade them. However, there are expectations that within the media services persons working on specific area materials should be familiar with the area, and that "area people" who think in terms of regions are distinguishable from "functional people" producing across-the-board output.

Those who emphasize media skills believe that a good propaganda operator, like a good doctor, should be able to operate anywhere. He is a specialist, not just "a hired hand." USIS librarians also must be professionals, as the techniques of library science are important to smooth program functioning. The basic requisite for a writer is to handle words well. Publications technicians should get top positions in the field, since the problem facing them is often to work with local publications and locally produced materials. Public Affairs Officers may have adequate editorial or writing backgrounds but not know much about the mechanical and business sides of publishing.

Others maintain that media skills are overemphasized. If too much importance is placed on "how to get a story into the mass media channel," insufficient emphasis may be placed on planning and adapting output for the target audience. Existing media skills may be too sharply specialized for practical purposes, especially in the field where operators must combine a number of related skills.

Unfortunately, the central desk is not composed of people who have regional or functional experience. They're essentially newsmen. Whereas I can look at a piece of copy and decide whether it is useful for my area, they aren't able to do so.

Training in the American journalistic tradition may be a handicap in preparing overseas material. Area experience and knowledge are most important.

The fact of the matter is that most of the people writing the news for this program are trained in the American journalistic tradition. They are newspaper reporters in a different sense from which the European journalist is regarded. I don't believe that the only permissible style and technique and approach is the American approach. You should be influenced by the style of the country where you publish.

We can teach a Burmese radio in six months, but we can't teach a radio man Burmese in six months.

I think media skills are really secondary. I think the necessary media skills for that kind of thing can be imparted in a training program run by the Agency.

USIA's great need is for regional specialists. The area expert is "ideal," to the degree that he must know "the psychology of the people of the country." A person who has never been outside the U. S., sitting at a desk in Washington, is not in a position to address material to a foreign audience. Theoretical or academic knowledge of an area is not enough. It's necessary to be familiar with flesh-and-blood realities.

If I were given the choice between a good technician and someone with field experience, I wouldn't hesitate to choose the field man. There's no substitute in the world for smelling the Far East.

Somebody with a Czech background actually knows how to write about America much better, because he can make better comparisons and parallels with Czech life, and not just straight explanations of what America is. This week we are going to tell them something about the 90th Infantry Division, stationed in Texas. That was the first division to enter Czechoslovak soil in 1945. This is a good opportunity to remind the Czechs that they were not only liberated by the Soviet army but by the American Army as well. Naturally you cannot make comparisons between an American division and a Czech division. What I had in mind was that we would tell them about Texas.

We wouldn't speak like Texans on Texas, but we would tell them that the size of Texas is the size of France and Czechoslovakia together. that the 90th Division is stationed in an area that is reminiscent of a particular region in Moravia. This is very difficult to expect from an American writer.

USIA makes insufficient use of its area experts, despite their acknowledged importance. Whether or not they have actually had field experience in the area, they should have more say in formulating policy for it.

> Although we picked up people with area experience, they were not an all-star aggregation, and the media people would say, "What kind of area experience do you have? Your area expert has never been in Iran and here's Joe Jones on our desk who has been for years in Iran. You don't have any monopoly of field knowledge." This was the leading charge—lack of real area experience and failing to realize that we had no monopoly of area expertness. The real question was not, "Was your John Jones better than our Bill Smith?" but one of responsibility. You may have had a guy who has never been to India, but if you give him the responsibility for it, he becomes your area expert. It may be desirable to get a guy with 50 years experience but that's not always possible.

On the other hand, the operator needs more than area experience. He must communicate the American viewpoint. Personality is also important. And some PAO's do a good job because they have "a disciplined approach," without necessarily having all the answers.

> I think an area expert who has an intimate knowledge of the language and culture of the whole society and who adds to them certain kinds of approaches to analyzing the situation is ideal. But the area expert feels he does not have to do this, because to say that an area expert has to go out and find out certain things about the country implies that he's really not an expert, if there's something he doesn't know.

To present the area expert in proper perspective, other operators point out that without knowing media he cannot be effective. Having field experience doesn't necessarily qualify him as an area expert.

> The scholars of Egypt sat on their behinds for thousands of years and it took a Frenchman to tell them where the pyramids and the sphinx were. Just because a man is sitting in a place doesn't mean that he is an expert.

> Anybody who had spent six months in Shanghai was an old China hand.

Further, his expertise may be inapplicable or outdated. This is particularly troublesome in Eastern Europe, where USIA has necessarily relied on émigrés whose expertise declines steadily over time, as they become more remote from their area.

> A deliberate attempt was made to get people with what is called field experience in the planning operation. What happens is that there is not a great transfer. It's a different type of job and you lose your real contact with the field, the sense of immediacy; and while you lose it in actuality, you nevertheless continue to use it as a basis for your expertise. You still make sweeping judgments as though it were still immediate. You see this not only in the information program. The people who are Russian experts, who left Russia after the revolution, speak a different language but they refuse to admit they're no longer Russian experts.

Moreover, it's impossible to be an infallible expert on a country as vast as India. Experience in an area may actually aggravate the tendency to hold on to preconceived ideas that interfere with objectivity and accomplishing a mission.

> One of the assumptions of the organization is that the guy who has lived in the area and knows the language is a desirable person for that country. It ain't necessarily so, because he mixes in his own prejudices and his sense of what's important, that may get in the way of his doing a much more objective job. In many cases he may mistake the social elite for the political elite. This applies not only to the information program, but it's one of the faults of the Foreign Service.

> There is a danger of the regional people being so immersed in their areas that they lose touch with the broad picture. If your regional people really know the area—if he has a balanced view of what America's aims are he can make a distinction between his regional interests and the worldwide interests.

Those who stress that language skills are important in selecting people for overseas assignments stress particularly that if the PAO does not know the language, anything he does in a country is bound to be superficial. Émigrés and foreign nationals among USIA operators (at home and abroad) will only respect a chief who speaks their language. (Actually, however, a number of desk and division chiefs do not know the local language. This gives ammunition to those who maintain not only that language skills aren't necessary but that a field man who cannot communicate can actually get along better.)

> I have never found language to be a barrier, because I've always been able to find people I can trust who do speak English and are technically qualified. In many cases it is better that I don't understand the language because I don't get bogged down in detail. That language provision is terrifically overrated, particularly in the Far East.

FIELD PERSONNEL

A special set of criteria apply to field operators. Field assignment requires a different type of ability from that of the mass communications expert.

1. The field operator should have a "metropolitan" rather than a "provincial" outlook, and be free of prejudice.

> Certainly a man who exhibits any biases against the local peoples is not a good representative of his country in any foreign place. Negro biases or Indian biases specifically. You wouldn't send a man who hates Chinese into China.

2. He should be "a good, representative American."

> He's got to speak not with a foreign accent. I would like to think of him as clean-shaven. We like him to be open-minded. We hope he will be friendly. We are not talking about the typical American, but about a good, representative American.

3. He must be able to "get himself across personally" and get along with people "high and low." He should be easily accessible to all comers.

It is very basic that we have people who can carry on personal contacts with the type of cordiality that elicits the kind of cordiality we want to elicit.

Personal contact is critically important in the field. It requires imagination and empathy. A Public Affairs Officer spends his first year "just selling himself." Once he is accepted as a human being, it is easier for him to get his ideas across. He must be gregarious and extroverted.

I think that what we are doing with the USIA program is a sales job. We are selling ideas about America. I know that one thing that's basic to any sales job is to sell yourself to the client. Our salesmen overseas are the USIA personnel.

4. He must be able to deal with foreign officials and dignitaries, be active in the social activities of the diplomatic set, make contact with local officials. He should be able (particularly in formerly colonial areas) to gain the confidence of local leaders and advise them not only on American ideas but on their own problems. His accomplishments may be gauged in terms of how much he can influence newspaper editors, even if they do not directly publish material.

5. He must be versatile. He is often required to conduct activities that he is not officially supposed to be doing.

There is no generally accepted definition of what Cultural Affairs Officers overseas are supposed to be doing.

A variety of skills are called for. Librarians are a combination of receptionist, tourguide, and lending librarian.

6. A man who deals with indigenous media must himself be a capable practitioner, admired as a colleague by local editors and broadcasters, not merely a "bureaucrat."

7. He should be willing to find out about the customs and traditions of the country and to abide by them; to be exemplary in his personal life and to live modestly (although he must entertain generously).

Certainly it does our organization harm if anyone gets arrested for drunken driving. Certainly our enemies would build that up.

Another thing I think Americans should do overseas is live on the same scale as they live on at home, in the same kind of house. They can't entertain on the same scale because that is a requirement. I think the type of entertaining they do there should be the same type that they do here, not pheasant breasts under glass but creamed chicken on toast.

8. He must avoid the traditional practices of the European in a non-white area.

It's always bothered me that we go out there and try to sell the idea that the United States is a democracy and if prejudices exist, we are making efforts to overcome them. That may go down well to start with, but anybody who looks around will notice that the American is putting his children in segregated schools, joining segregated social clubs; and when he entertains he is overloaded with white guests, maybe with a sprinkling of locals to make it look good. That's one of the things to which I don't have a ready answer.

The importance of personnel selection is underscored by the belief that in any country the information program is largely shaped and determined by the character, talents, and interests of USIA personnel. A PAO's professional background often determines which operations receive strongest emphasis.

> If a member of his staff has a particular interest in music, is talented along musical lines, you can see what direction the extracurricular activities are going to take. If you get a chap who in college has been interested in sport lines, you can see what direction his extracurricular activities will take. You can't expect an athlete to lead a glee club or the other way around. Now that does not mean at all that an individual who has not been an athlete is told to go out and develop softball teams.

> Suppose he's the former president of a small college and he's in Calcutta. He has a staff that supplements and complements him. Because of the kind of man he is, by virtue of his own interest, he is apt to select, out of all the parts he has, the one he is most happy doing, and that is good. The next man that comes along may be an ex-magazine publisher who may gravitate in that direction without changing the whole program. The second point is that because the job is higher than anything that can possibly be done, there is still a lot of flexibility—unless you get an odd ball who wants to work with press only.

This tendency can be seen as either good or bad. On the good side, at a small field post, personnel can be assigned duties that reflect their special talents. On the bad side, a PAO who is an expert in one medium may tend to use that medium at the expense of others intead of being flexible and versatile.

Optimally, personnel, like output, are adapted to the local situation. The PAO who runs a large program should have had management experience in handling people of diverse temperaments in difficult situations and "the ability to keep personality aspects subordinate."

> In a large post you have got to be a real administrator. In a one-man post you don't need any administrative ability—just the ability to stay out of trouble and keep your vouchers right.

Physical attributes may also be important.

> I would use guys on the basis of their physical attributes. I wouldn't send a six-foot giant to a population where the average person was four feet tall, and I wouldn't send a little wizened guy who looked like a Spaniard to work with the Swedes.

> The type of PAO you get is going to be dependent on the type of ambassadors you have. A career ambassador is going to want someone with general know-how rather than someone with specific propaganda skills.

The Public Affairs Officer must be able to get along well with the ambassador; he must also be able to stand up to him. A PAO who surrenders to the Chief of Mission on important matters is weak and incapable. A capable one either brings the Ambassador around or realizes that he is right and convinces the home office of it too.

Field personnel are most often criticized for being insufficiently familiar with the life of the people and having contact only with unrepresentative locals.

What I saw in Rome, London, and Vienna is a tightly knit group that sees mostly other Americans and has local contacts mostly with locals who work for the agency and people they meet on a social basis who are not at all typical of the country at large. This is an impression I have for many, many places. The Americans in Germany have no real contact with the country. They might as well be in Washington. The only difference is that your distribution problems are somewhat simplified, in that gold-plated slum in Bonn. If you're willing to acknowledge that there's an insulation between the American and the people he tries to reach, that the few people he is in contact with are atypical, then its obligatory to teach certain methods that give him a more realistic assessment of the country and its whole power structure.

The people I saw normally down there, if they were not pro-American, they were pro-American in talking to me. I don't think I was aware of it then, but in looking back at it, .the people you associate with are friendly to you and your country's ideals. If not, you wouldn't associate with them; you would find it repulsive to be with them. Your associates overseas have to be people who are pleasant to you; otherwise you wouldn't see them unless it were officially necessary, and even there it's natural for a person to submerge his feelings in talking to you. In Guatemala today I am sure our embassy people are not at the throats daily of the people in the Guatemalan foreign office whom they have to see constantly on business.

A PAO admits that there is truth in these charges as the inevitable result of the time he must devote to the mechanics of running his post:

By the time you've kept up the routine activities of the office, a ten-day or two-week trip makes an awful crimp in your office upkeep. I must confess quite frankly that with minimum staff I have been so absorbed with keeping the operation going that I really haven't given the thought that I should have given to our aims, objectives, and effectiveness. Naturally I have developed certain opinions, but these are the result of absorption rather than contemplation.

While some people charge that PAO's lack sufficient area knowledge, others believe that *too much* knowledge may lead to a danger that the man in the field will go native. In other words, when a country's representatives are sent abroad, a two-way indoctrination takes place. The attitudes of the foreign personnel become subject to the opinions and influence of people among whom they live, just as they have an impact on the attitudes of the native population. As a result, field personnel should not be kept too long in a particular area. Others believe that rotation of personnel is right for diplomatic or consular work but has no place in USIA, which needs area experts.

You have to have more flexibility than the foreign service personnel procedure permits, because you can't make a man of that sort fit into rigid patterns. He doesn't have to demonstrate that he's a damn good man for making out passports and visas and he is not someone you want to switch every two years from one country to the next. You're deliberately picking someone who must be identified with that area. He should become a true specialist in that limited area. He certainly can't be rotated all over hell and gone. This business of expecting a man to be in touch with a whole group of warm Latinos one year and then sending him off to Iceland the next to deal with a different group of personalities—I don't see it.

A man is merely beginning to know the local language, people, and customs by the end of two years, at which time he is rotated. It takes long, slow effort before people—especially sophisticated people—accept the PAO as a personal friend.

> My feeling is that you have got to have the area expert. There is a danger in the individual going native, but that is not an insuperable problem. It can be dealt with in training programs. It can be dealt with in terms of policy controls from the central office. And what you gain in terms of better understanding of problems is infinitely more desirable than what you lose.

USING LOCAL PERSONNEL IN THE FIELD [1]

According to one estimate, "90 percent of our effectiveness overseas depends upon having friendly, intelligent local employees in the centers." Local people are most effective in contacting schools or key individuals, since they know the people, the language, and the customs. They are better able to get cooperation and inspire sympathy. Also, for budget reasons Americans can be allocated only to the most trying situations.

Local employees cannot do everything, however. They cannot see classified directives and are not allowed to make such policy decisions as selecting library materials.

The status of local employees in the public eye may be of critical importance, and their USIS salary scale may partly influence public opinion. Locals cannot be counted on to meet American standards of speed or technical competence. It is often difficult to get them to carry out the wishes of American propagandists. For example, a Filipino artist cannot be told, "I want a comic book that does this and this." He will resent it. The local cannot interpret American thinking or answer questions about the U. S. Americans, not locals, must make personal contacts.

An American has the further advantage of being familiar with library techniques and of being able to plan a "dynamic" program. Americans are considered the only people who can teach English properly. An American creates confidence. When a visitor comes to a library, he wants to speak to an American. Translators need Americans to explain colloquialisms in American books.

PERSONNEL SELECTION—WHOSE PREROGATIVE?

The media operator sometimes questions whether the personnel administrator who has no direct knowledge of media or areas can pick people with the

---

[1] See the discussion of émigré employees in the section on radio in Chapter XII, "Using the Media."

proper qualifications. The area expert feels he should be the one to decide on an applicant's qualifications. The personnel official may perceive this as a hindrance.

> We lean heavily on the professional man for judgment of the person's professional competence. They like to interview people, and even though we have people coming back from foreign service with excellent records they're reluctant to hire them sight unseen. Yet we have to do advanced planning so we try to overcome that reluctance on the part of the media organizations.

A personnel office looks for people who can work well with others. "Obnoxious individualists" are undesirable.

As the critics see it, civil service regulations force the Agency to retain "mediocrities" and inadequately use qualified aliens. The long time required for security clearance is a major obstacle to recruiting. The regulations also prevent the best assignment of personnel.

> The people in this area are drawn from all over the information field. Some creep in because they have worked overseas, some because they have a newspaper background. If we had an institution that could specifically train people, we would be going along farther in the right direction. This is getting to be a profession, and any profession should have good educational facilities to prepare newcomers.

The U. S. should have "schools for propagandists, like the Soviets." No one should be sent to the field for any technical job without at least three months' indoctrination.

Spontaneous references to the quality of personnel occur frequently in discussions of USIA operations. The positive view is that USIA personnel complement each other in media skills, individual talents and personal qualities, and area knowledge. They are "capable, interested, dedicated people" who understand USIA objectives.

The detractors advance these views:

1. USIA is not intellectual enough. "There are just not enough smart people here."

> It will take you ten years to build the organization into something. The tradition of mediocrity is so strong, the inhibitions have been developed to the point of being willpower.

> We suffer from intellectual poverty. In the battle for men's minds, let's not use our heads. This, of course, is the egghead's complaint.

2. "There are too damn many intellectuals." Successful overseas personnel are apt to be pragmatic "operators," not "thinkers," and fail to think in terms of the abstract theoretical principles underlying a propaganda problem.

> We have got a lot of dull people. We are handling pretty dull stuff. I'm pretty heavy-handed myself. . . . There's a tendency, because there are too damn many intellectuals in the program, to think in rational terms. How many people are there like that? That's probably a very strong and influential audience. It's your university professors, your man who likes to dabble in all different sorts of philosophies. He's

flattered by these intellectual approaches, but I do think we tend to do that entirely too much. We are sort of humorless, dry, dull as dishwater.

3. Many operators are untalented or untrained. Insufficient funds for employing talent, moreover, produce output that has "become all of one piece without variation." Low field personnel salaries create difficulty in hiring, and low morale. The agency therefore gets "inexperienced" and "incompetent" people. It has "never had a high grade of administrative talent, because competent people will not go to work for the government." Quality suffers from a lack of good writers and personnel qualified to do accurate, interpretive reporting of domestic news. VOA is "unprofessional." It is run by people who are "not accomplished broadcasters." "No one cares" whether operators are professionally experienced, and no training in techniques is available. Librarians know nothing professionally about music. Teachers in the Bi-national Centers have previously taught a foreign language only in an American college.

4. Skilled propagandists who should be willing to fight "no holds barred" are attracted to jobs in private business.

This is a dirty business. It ought to have dirty people in it, and you don't get those people, because if people are going to be dirty they're going to want to be paid for it. And they're not going to be paid for it in this Agency. It needs a more conscious, more cynical, approach on the part of the practitioners, and if you're sufficiently cynical and have the skills, you can get paid more than you are in government. So if you don't have the skills, you rationalize that you're really pure.

5. Overseas personnel sometimes lack human-relations skills. As a result, influential people have been alienated. "Unintelligent, gum-chewing Americans" are bad representatives overseas.

6. "Information people are charlatans in foreign affairs." They are not sufficiently trained "to know whether Metternich was a man or a dog."

7. Operators don't know enough about communism. This deficiency is partly ascribed to the political atmosphere arising from the McCarthy investigations. A man who has never read a book on communism is "woefully unfitted" for any USIA job.

8. There is great pressure to produce quick results.

We are a group of Americans and one of our peculiarities is undue haste. Even to the extent that we understand what's involved in trying to really buck communism and therefore realize that it's a job that may take a couple of generations, when we come down to the actual disposition of our resources, manpower, money, things that we undertake today or study, we get too much from tactical considerations rather than strategic considerations. There isn't enough time to think. We are primarily in the business of generating ideas and through our programming efforts to translate those ideas into actions. To generate ideas you have got to think. You can't just do it between telephone calls and other interruptions.

9. There is an unprofessional approach to propaganda. "The average USIA person does not realize what a propaganda agency is supposed to be

doing.'' He may believe that area knowledge is the important thing rather than propaganda expertise, per se. Operators may be defensive about their jobs and inherently feel ''that propaganda, as such, is a bad thing.''

10. Operators are absorbed in their own tasks and lose sight of the broad picture. They are victims of operational momentum. In sending mobile units to the hinterlands of Brazil, broadcasting minority languages to the Soviet Union, teaching English, or transmitting news to other countries, operators think of their medium rather than of their propaganda objectives.

You continually run into people who forget that they're no longer working for a press or radio agency or station or a newspaper and that we are a propaganda agency and are trying to do different things.

One of the basic dilemmas of the organization is, is it a news operation or a propaganda operation? If it were propaganda we wouldn't say too much. We would keep harping on a few things. But the inherent feeling in the organization is that propaganda is a bad thing. It tends to produce this kind of defensiveness. There are very few people in the whole organization who see themselves as propagandists. The Press Service people see themselves in the news business in the best tradition of Lee Tracy.[2] The movie people think they're somehow related to Hollywood. The only people who make any pretense of being propagandists are the planning staff.

MORALE

USIA operators frequently complain that their work lacks prestige and dignity. Prestige might offer some compensation for inadequate pay. In wartime, people of ability are willing to work for low salaries. But not in a period like the present. Americans do not have the British concept of a corps of civil servants relatively unaffected by political changes.

I suspect that the entire attitude of working for the government here is different than in England. The prestige of it is higher there. Competent people here go either into a good newspaper like the *Times* or into academic work, whereas there there was the same choice; the nucleus of regional chiefs and others in the BBC, which did seem to be particularly competent, could most of them get better jobs in the British press if they wanted to, and it was partly patriotism and belief in the cause that made them stick where they were. Partly it was morale and esprit de corps.

The Congressional investigations of the Agency have been interpreted as a ''rejection'' by Congress and the public, most concretely manifested by budget cuts. This has produced ''fearful people,'' ''cautious people,'' ''time servers,'' and ''people who want quick results.''

We have no esprit de corps, no morale, no feeling of being looked up to by our own country here, and on top of that our financial situation is precarious and McCarthy makes it worse. A tightening up of guidance that was already over-rigid makes it

---

[2] Star of ''The Front Page.''

still worse—makes people feel they're not trusted, that they're being looked upon as wild horses that have to be kept within rather tight rein, and that's humiliating and drives people out whom we need.

Morale was also lowered by successive changes in the Agency administration, with turnover of top officials, and phases of reorientation and "distrust" on the part of new managements:

> There was no pattern; competent people were dropped along with incompetent. Aside from these people, a lot of our most competent people have resigned out of a sense of frustration, a sense that they could no longer do a good job, and all of them that I know have succeeded in getting other jobs—and for the most part better-paid jobs—in private industry, newspapers, radio. The fact that there were so many changes and unpredictable changes that nobody knew what was going to happen until very recently, produced a general state of uncertainty, demoralization, and timidity. Nobody is quite sure of what is required of them.

Good operators want to feel that they are effective. Yet they may not believe they are successful. "There is no sense of an echoing communication with the audience."

> Every man, if he's worth his salt, wants to be convinced that he can win the war for us. He must feel that what he's doing is worthwhile and to feel that he must feel it's effective.

Discussion is not frank and open, say the critics. There are no debates between levels in the hierarchy. There is discussion, but "you don't fight up or sideways in a bureaucracy, you fight down."

When important documents or memoranda are circulated for comment, there are diminishing returns. It becomes known that Agency top management like certain things; no one wants to stick out his neck and disagree. Criticism at meetings is muffled because "people do not want to detach themselves from the mainstream."

There is never overt disagreement in the Agency, so it is impossible to convince anyone he is wrong.

> My general feeling of what happens with disagreement is that in great part it does not take on an overt characteristic. Disagreement takes on the guise of "agreement, but", and the "but" generally means that you slow it down until nothing happens.

> Things have changed. The place doesn't blaze anymore. There's a tendency to be safe. To be safe is to be generally deadly, dull and uninteresting. . . . What happens in the final run is that you sound un-American. Americans don't sound like our broadcasts. Would Europeans characterize Americans as formal, tired, scared, routine, dignified people? But that's what our scripts sound like.

> It's only going to have this ability to imagine the people at the other end if the people producing it are able and imaginative, and it's unimaginative people that seem to remain here.

Output generally is too ideological, because operators are "afraid."

> Most of our stuff is much too intellectual and ideological. They actually think they're talking to the other diplomats. It was forced into that tone by scared people, people who knew that if they stuck to the official thing that would never be off the line. People who were scared to use their imaginations.

Operators' morale is affected by conflicts with policy makers and controls over output. The writer who produces effective propaganda must be inspired; he must have a sense of freedom.

> One of the problems of keeping our audience is having our programs lively and varied in style and having people who know how to write vivid scripts. One of the tendencies of the bureaucrat is to try to make all the articles and scripts sound and look as though they were written by the same person. The tendency of a bureaucrat is to bleach out the color. And when you get people who are varied and skilled at their trade, you can't do that. What you should do is give the writers, as writers, their head insofar as it doesn't conflict with the basic tone and objectives. Otherwise your program is going to become deadly dull.

> We have a huge apparatus and it looks as though they are all standard replaceable parts, but there are really only a few men who know what the problems are. Routine bureaucratic reactions will never win such a fight. A routine bureaucrat is aware that if you do nothing you're not likely to make any egregious mistakes. This is one of the things I don't think we can fight without a little bravado in the spirit of the man who does these things, who will play his hunches in an emergency.

But there are also those in the Agency who describe its morale favorably. Anyone doing a good professional job should be happy working in USIA. The Agency has a high degree of family spirit and agreement on the concepts of propaganda. As one opinion has it, if people in USIA are not doing a good job, it is their own fault, since the top direction of the Agency is good.

Loyalty to the program exists even among those who feel the Agency is not doing as much good as it might. This implies a faith in the essential morality of USIA's mission—a faith which goes well beyond the criticisms and disappointments which many operators frankly express: "I suppose you think I don't like this Agency. I like it as one might a wayward child."

XV

Evaluating the Program

EVALUATING THE EFFECTIVENESS OF A PROGRAM of the scope and complexity of USIA's calls for systematic research, as well as the informal and intuitive judgments of operators on the job. Success stories are readily cited, but the Agency's research professionals call for study of the program's content, audiences, and media as well as of the basic communications problems it faces. To translate research findings into practice requires a good working relationship with operators. Some say it should be close, others impersonal. There is criticism of the Agency's research, and a lack of agreement on the criteria of USIA's effectiveness. The program's impact is hard to evaluate, especially in relation to all the rest of America's communications to the world. Operators' favorable or pessimistic ratings of USIA's effects reflect the state of their own morale, and vice versa.

USIA'S RESEARCH FUNCTION has been appraised and reorganized a number of times, and its purposes are defined in a number of different ways:

1. As a management aid to the director to help him evaluate the program (or, as a cynic puts it, to reassure the administration that the program is operating effectively).
2. "To help structure the thinking of responsible personnel away from an American frame of reference to foreign frames of reference."
3. To reduce snap judgments and guessing.
4. To provide operators and management with "a better idea" of target audiences.
5. To test and improve existing products; to find out what appeals are successful and how acceptable output is to the audience.
6. To give management and policy makers an accurate picture of actual output to determine whether it conforms to what they thought they were producing.

7. To provide helpful material in selling the program to Congress and the public.

It is commonly accepted in USIA that research and intelligence operations should be closely coordinated. However, there is disagreement as to the exact relation of the research and intelligence functions, and as to the degree to which intelligence is itself a research activity. One shades into the other. As a result, research and intelligence operations are reported to have traditionally vied with each other in hostile fashion. The term "intelligence" is equivocal, encompassing both "cloak and dagger" work and also the more routine pedestrian examination of documents. Intelligence in government is defined as anything in which anyone happens to be interested. "Anything they want to call intelligence they do, and this gives them the right to classify it."

RESEARCH AND OPERATIONS

The research function must have a direct channel to top management and should be closely coordinated with operations. However, research has had varying degrees of acceptance in different parts of the Agency. There is no relationship between an operator's competence and his willingness to accept research.

There is a disposition to continue with any existing propaganda operation on the basis of sheer inertia. Research personnel start with the assumption that they must be willing to take any part of the program and question its value. Good research is always resisted as it looks into well-established activities of an ongoing organization.

> As you began to probe into media you started to get into people's jobs, you started to threaten them, and that's something you shouldn't do unless you recognize in advance there is going to be opposition to it. You can get wonderful reactions to any study you put out that praises an operation. And the same guy that one day was convinced that you were the greatest scientific genius since Steinmetz was sticking pins into you the next day.

The inevitable lot of the researcher is to be caught in the crossfire of conflicting interests between operators and administrators.

> In practice a lot of pressure was always exercised to clear evaluation reports with the operating desks, and this was done because the Director of the Voice so desired it. The desk heads became worried that uncleared reports might reflect on some aspects of their operations.
>
> One criticism came from the Voice Program Department, saying that this evaluation staff was a dangerous group of people who whispered into the ears of headquarters all kinds of untrue information about the effectiveness or lack of it of 58 language services.
>
> The other came from that very headquarters and said, "This is a bunch of venal

characters who sell us a bill of goods about the effectiveness of the Voice of America and don't tell us the truth.'' I say these are the two necessary elements of the atmospheric conditions under which a research staff should live. It should always be in a limbo with respect to the operators; it should believe that facts can be adduced as to the impact of a program, but it should also protect the program and its continuity. The continuous screams against this operation are in a way a slightly sickish expression of what is healthy.

The more influence research has in the organization, the more opposition it meets.

The resistance is correlated with the degree of immediate involvement with the individual being researched. The less a person is immediately involved in it the more he will resist it.

Hence, it is a mistake to launch studies without discussing them with the operators concerned. An evaluation unit should work closely with the operators. The best work of a research unit is done informally. But, objective research requires minimal contact between the evaluators and the people whose work is evaluated. To avoid censorship, external contract research jobs should be done without supervision by the operators. Operators have no right to determine whether or not research should be undertaken.

LAY ANALYSIS OF USIA ACTIVITIES

Operators frequently make informal assessments of program activity in the form of personal observation, interviews, or case histories. They may work on the following premises:

1. Local leaders are good judges of what public reactions to output are likely to be.

   In the case of a classified film, we can show it to selected groups—persons in whom they have confidence, some local government representative, some legal specialist, a leading surgeon, the head of the university, a mayor, a leading editor—persons who have a close touch with the grass roots people in their own community and who can be depended on to give a solid answer, one that would mean something, as well as someone who had proved himself to be in sympathy with us.

2. Local USIA employees are good judges of probable effectiveness of output.
3. Informal observations can be highly informative. An American operator on an overseas assignment can learn a great deal about the customs of a foreign people and "their general attitude toward ordinary Americans" from the attitudes of taxi drivers and hotel clerks. The tastes of the people in a Middle Eastern country can be ascertained from the type of American movies being shown in the poorer quarters of the capital city.

The effectiveness of a film can be gauged by sending employees into nearby cafés afterwards to eavesdrop on the conversations of the audience, or by observing them at the performance.

That's a difficult problem for anyone in the field—they simply have to judge audience reaction as the film is shown. They may have one man there and he's going to be absorbed with the projection equipment. If they have more than one man there, they can observe audience reaction at key points within the films, they can interview a number of people after the film, they can use questionnaires. They can pick out certain key persons, because they track through these towns again and again and they get to know the local leaders, the local characters, and they can make a spot survey—of the mayor, the physician, the principal of the school and say on leaving, "I hope our show was good. Have you heard any comments?" Frankly this is a field where a lot more could be done.

Problems are reported here. A film audience will always make favorable comments within the earshot of a USIS representative; and thus the comments he hears are not necessarily a good basis for evaluation.

In contrast to such observations, research is considered by researchers as a professional function in which amateurs often blunder. Technical media expertise is not necessarily a basis for making professional evaluations of international propaganda. (Operators may disagree. Propaganda can be evaluated only by competent practitioners of propaganda.) A PAO may make wrong predictions because of the sources of opinion on which he depends. He may rely too much on "local experts" who are not really informed. Local USIA employees are not good judges of the effectiveness of output intended for a less educated and less sophisticated local audience.

The pamphlets were intentionally oversimplified, written to a person with a pretty low IQ, and low educational level. The person with a better education was apt to be revolted by the thing. My experience was that I would show some of these things to my own staff before sending them out to get their reactions and some of the more flamboyant chaps of my staff, who are all well-educated people, would say, "You can't send these things out—they're horrible, they'll get people angry and if they find Americans are sending them out they will scream." Then we would always send out a small number to test them out. Some of these same publications that my staff took exception to, we would get letters applauding the thing.

Case histories are no proof of success. The collection of case histories of effectiveness is sharply criticized by research personnel.

You don't save anecdotes, little success stories. For every success story there's a failure story, and unless you collect all of them you don't have a complete picture. As long as you are going to delude yourself with little minor success stories you will never have a research program going.

TYPES OF RESEARCH ACTIVITY

What kinds of research should be conducted?

1. *Audience research.* There is insufficient information on target countries. What kinds of people should be reached—a mass audience or opinion leaders? What type of program content is acceptable in one part of a country or another?

(*Dissent,* from a management position: Questions about the nature of the target audience or the character of output are not strictly research questions.)

Top priority for research should go to studies of national communications habits. These studies should find out what the images of the principal world powers are, and what media (including informal ones), domestic and international, filter down to different kinds of people, even at the village level.

> The effectiveness of persuasion depends on intimate knowledge of the listening audience, clear understanding of one's own objectives, and creative imagination with regard to how to move this particular audience in the direction of these particular objectives.

Thus full information on what the audience "already accepts as the truth" is necessary for program planning. Data are needed on the degree to which USIA themes are accepted or met with skepticism. If such information is available on a trend basis, an approximate evaluation can be made of the effect of the information program, as one of many influences, in producing any changes that occur. Criteria of effectiveness can then

> be applied not only to entire target groups, but also to subdivisions representing different degrees of exposure to VOA output, or to different kinds of VOA programming. In this way, it may be possible, for example, to determine the optimum amount of radio effort to direct to any country, and thus to lead to a determination of the optimum balance between geographical coverage and intensity of effort.

USIA does not know very much about the areas about which it should know most. Communications studies are needed in Asia precisely because mass media are just beginning to develop. "The more important a country is policy-wise, the harder it is to do research." The most important countries are those behind the Iron Curtain and those in underdeveloped areas.

Basic communications studies may not be important in Western Europe, an area familiar to operators, most like the U. S. and most thoroughly researched, and also because the information program is "not too important" there.

2. *Media research.* In distinction to the approach that starts by considering communications patterns in the target countries, research may begin with the media and their output. This approach takes as its main task the job of establishing what audiences are reached by particular media. Present studies of audiences for USIA output in all media are incomplete. Questions like the following remain unanswered: Who buys USIA-sponsored books? Who or how many listen to the Voice behind the Iron Curtain? Is radio a mass medium in the Free World? How many readers of foreign language newspapers in the U. S. are stimulated by their editorials to write to relatives overseas? Does press-service output reach neutralists or people already friendly to the United States?

3. *Basic research in communications and propaganda.* USIA needs to learn more about the political motivations of its audiences. Why do people in the underdeveloped areas, principally in the neutralist bloc, feel as they do?

The Agency should study such basic questions as the problem of credibility and objectivity in news reporting.

4. *Analysis and control of output.* Continuing analysis of program content is sometimes mentioned as a necessary task for research. This rests on the belief that USIA management has insufficient knowledge and control of output. Analysis of program content presents difficulties. There is a disposition on the part of operators to question analyses that are purely qualitative, merely an outsider's opinion, and a feeling that purely statistical analysis of themes and subject matter fails to capture the important niceties of creative expression.

′ Monitoring is necessary to give "a bird's-eye view of output," to judge whether the program is achieving its objectives (or moving to achieve them), to make sure that there is consistency in the themes employed from post to post, and to make certain that all output is kept within the limits of overall objectives and policy rules. Media sometimes contradict each other, because there is no control. Even if a media service follows policy guidance strictly, there is no knowledge of whether the field follows guidance. Controlling output is particularly important in VOA, because its top officials are not familiar with the languages used, and few field posts monitor output in the local language.

Research already conducted for USIA is criticized on a number of grounds:

1. The wrong subjects have been studied. "Research has been conducted on a grab-bag basis." The focus of research has been determined unduly by the areas in which contractors were available to do the work (Europe, Latin America) rather than by the areas of highest priority (Asia).
2. Statistical data has been neglected. "Pedestrian" factual information on media and populations is most needed, but has been neglected because it was not of sufficient excitement or interest to the researchers.
3. Basic research has been neglected.

   There is no propaganda analysis—there is no day-to-day look at what you are countering. There is no one specifically assigned here to follow through on what the Russians are doing.

4. USIA should not sponsor basic research. Studies in basic communications processes are the proper concern of private foundations, not the government.
5. Research (like intelligence) is not sufficiently coordinated with that of other agencies.
6. Security classification raises problems. Much classified material is of little value to operators because it cannot be used in output; classified material from other agencies often contains unevaluated statements.
7. Resources are not fully utilized. A great deal of information about foreign areas and target audiences has not been tapped.
8. Research is essentially quantitative in nature; a creative program involving propaganda and the skills of the propagandist can only be judged in qualitative terms, not in terms of numerical measurements. "Dry statistics" cannot be applied.

9. (By implication): Researchers don't really know their job. They base their conclusions on small and inadequate samples. They try to apply American research techniques to backward areas, where they will not work. Some researchers go overboard in applying their theories. There are some "who felt that people were manipulated psychologically, who felt that if we knew all about Japanese toilet training we could give them a nervous breakdown by shortwave."

10. Research takes too long.

11. Research is not presented properly. "When we get an evaluation report it comes in books, and I don't have time to read all that stuff. What's the use of trying to provide an operator with measurement information that's from 2 to 12 inches in thickness? It comes in by weight."

12. Research reports are not put to use. A research report, once completed, should be discussed to get maximum value from it. "It doesn't get circulated except for an individual operator when the stuff happens to cross his desk. There's a tremendous pyramid of intelligence stuff that we never see."

13. Research is too abstruse, complicated and impractical.

It would be better to have a good ordinary research department, competent people who know something about research, to have a small group of that kind, competent, not necessarily brilliant, with a sense of integrity and character, enough so that they won't do things that they shouldn't do. Then I think you can get most of the things that are needed, one, for the Director to find out some things about his own operation, and second, enough background to get material to present a picture to Congress of what was going on. My guess would be that the kind of research to be presented to Congress has to be simple. From the standpoint of a practical working tool of management, I think there is a great continuing need for just ordinary sound research that would give you some idea of what you should do, whom you should reach, how you should reach them, and what results you are getting.[1]

14. Research is used for promotional purposes, or to justify activity. Operators expect research to prove that their work is effective. Much good research is either ignored or used to prove prejudices. Research that praises an operation will arouse enthusiasm, but it is always possible for a media administrator not to "go along with" a study critical of his activities. Research personnel themselves feel that they have the responsibility of protecting the program in its public relations, particularly at the time of budget hearings. Promotional research may be valuable in getting appropriations.

CRITERIA OF EFFECTIVENESS

How effective is USIA? There is no single answer or common agreement on criteria of what effectiveness is. Without such definitions no efforts can be evaluated.

---

[1] The marvelous naiveté of this last statement makes it worth noting that it was uttered by one of the top officials of the Agency.

My basic criticism comes from seeing these guys develop plans for proceeding in their countries and then reading what they have done and getting an impression of great undirected activity ultimately justified by occasional bread-and-butter letters from high government officials saying, "You're doing a good job." An assessment of what they do can be made only if they first determine what they intend to do, but that imposes a terrific challenge on the guy because it puts him on the spot.

Nor will all-pervasive criteria suffice. For specific targets, specific tasks must be set up as yardsticks.

We have not got any clear-cut impression throughout the world about what we are, who we are, what we are like, and what we stand for. It sometimes seems incredible that there are tens of millions of people in this world who don't know but what we are the war party. There it is. It seems to me that unless you start out with a master blueprint and then cut that up into sections and have considerably more criteria, you will go on hoping that the coincidence of a thousand ideas will inspire confidence.

In the eyes of some critics within the Agency, USIA has a "frightening tendency to confuse activity with accomplishment."

There's a curious egocentric approach which you get. People in an organization knock themselves out in the belief that if they don't do it the world will fall apart and if they do it the world will be saved, that it totally rises and falls with their actions. It's bad because it tends to distort the actual situation. A man comes into a country with a population of 10,000,000 and he's there with a couple of people. He works frantically. He tends to confuse his activity and output with impact, with results. This feeling that "because I am very busy things must be happening" is a very bad thing because it gets everything out of focus.

There is a plus factor to it. It happens mostly to people in the field because they're closer to their conditions and work harder. It happens also to radio people who also have a sense of immediacy, which may be a good thing. This doesn't mean that I advocate the converse of this, because that's even worse. With it comes something I call the Chanticleer Complex. The rooster thinks the sun comes up because he crows. One day he gets up late and discovers to his great horror that the sun has risen anyway even though he hasn't crowed in time. A great many people had that. They had to crow or else the sun wouldn't come up. It epitomizes it—the confusion between activity and actual results.

This generalization finds support in comments made by operators. "To the extent that USIA output is on European national radios, exhibited in the theaters and at exhibitions, there is no question that it is very, very effective."

The program may be evaluated pragmatically in terms of the concrete actions that it influences, such as the surrender of troops after a leaflet barrage or the results of an election. The size of the Communist vote in a country may be taken as an inverse measure of USIA effectiveness. (The outcome of an election does not necessarily indicate the success of a propaganda campaign. The campaign may actually have no effect, or a "boomerang effect.")

Communist failures signalize USIA successes. In Norway, the campaign to show American cooperation with the Norwegians worked so well that some

Communist publications had to stop printing, others had to get subsidies from Russia.

Effectiveness may be demonstrated by successfully distributing output or getting it run in foreign publications.

The cooperation of local authorities may be the criterion. (For example, stimulated by the book translations programs, foreign publishers are being "trained" to ask for more American books to translate.)

Or it can be merely that more donated time or material went into an activity so that USIA's investment was decreased. Operators commonly refer to the size of the audience they reach as the major measure of their effectiveness. If a great many people are reached with a product, it is bound to have some desirable effect.

> I realize that attendance (at a library) does not mean that you have influenced a person, but it seems to me that the old system that merchants used has some validity. It seems to me that over a period of time a given percentage of the people that come in are going to be influenced by something they have read.

The program may reach a large number of people without reaching many in the top-priority target groups. Because it reaches people does not mean that a program is affecting them. A critic of the U. S. might use the USIS library to document his critical views, as a favorable person might use it to document his opinions.

> Numbers don't mean anything. Who is coming in and what are they looking at? If it's only the *Saturday Evening Post* type of a thing, how much progress are we making?

Changes in tne climate of opinion may be measured on a trend basis by research. Where evaluation studies show an increase in information favorable to the U. S., this is perforce a sign of effectiveness.

Liking for output is held to be evidence of effectiveness. Output is effective if the audience remains with it after a long period of time or keeps coming back. Popular reaction to discontinuing a USIA activity is another criterion. "We operators believe the best way to manifest the need for a program is to cut it out, but it is a very dangerous way of showing it."

The protests aroused when a USIS library is closed are often mentioned as proof of its value. However, this is also disputed.

> When we tried to close our library in Venice, there was such a storm of protest from the Italians that in the end they wound up locating the funds by themselves. The area director takes that as evidence of effectiveness. All it proves is that the Venetians want a library. When they found they couldn't have one financed by our money, they dug deep and found the money to get one. That doesn't answer the question of what it does to serve American interests.

The information program's success may be judged by its standing with Congress ("If even Congress likes something, it must be good") or with foreign service personnel.

Informed local reactions are indicators of effectiveness. (This assumption is criticized within the Agency.) The value of a film used in the Philippines is shown by the fact that a local priest said it was worth a thousand sermons. USIA musical activity has received favorable criticism even from Communist critics. Achievement is proved by complimentary letters from high government officials in the target countries. Effectiveness may sometimes also be determined negatively from the "boomerang effect" of bad output.

> All you can do is accept the judgment of people who are generally considered competent. You can say this is good because a French newspaper printed it. That doesn't mean it's good at all. What did the reader go out and do that was in the interest of American foreign policy and how did you find out? You can say, while we have been doing this they had a national election and our side won it. Maybe they would have won it by a bigger margin if we hadn't done it. All we can say is that the field says this is a good thing.

Whether USIA is achieving results may also be judged by Communist reactions: If the Communists object to something USIA is doing, this is prima facie evidence that its ends are being accomplished. Communist press and radio attacks upon VOA prove the effectiveness of VOA broadcasts. If anyone found with USIA materials is ordered killed by the Communists, this is also proof. Under the Arbenz regime in Guatemala, the success of USIA posters was demonstrated by the fact that newsboys were arrested for passing them out.

A modification of the Communist attitude is also a good sign. (For example, two weeks after USIA's full treatment on the President's atomic energy proposal the Soviets reversed their first position on it; this showed that the Agency had effectively stated the American position.)

VOA operators freely refer to their mail as proof of effectiveness. Conservatively stated, audience mail provides proof that "there are listeners and that they care." Most audience mail consists of routine requests for programs. Mail must be answered; this creates good will (especially in Asian countries where replies may be "shown around").

Operators are usually careful in estimating audience size from the number of letters, but they still consider them (for Free World broadcasts) to be a general indication of audience size (and size is taken as evidence of effectiveness).[2] The operator is stimulated in every way to increase the volume of mail by giveaway offers and other devices.

Audience mail is an important resource for research. It offers clues as to what people are thinking. It serves a kind of intelligence function. It provides reception data which may be useful for countries where other data are not available. Inferences may be drawn from it as to the psychological character, or range of interests, of the hard core of listeners.

The dissenting view is that audience mail is not very important as source material for research, particularly not as a statistical indication of audience size.

---

[2] In domestic broadcasting research both of these assumptions were discarded during the 1930's.

The fact that a large number of people write in for program booklets or information is irrelevant to American political objectives. Audience mail statistics may be quoted to challenge legitimate research.

> To believe that the audience mail is any indication of your impact is just silly. It's no different from other fan mail. It's 99 percent positive and the small percent which is critical is mostly from cranks.

PROBLEMS IN EVALUATING EFFECTIVENESS

Many operators quickly point out that there is little evidence of USIA's effectiveness, and it must be judged on faith rather than documentation. "It is rarely possible to show a propaganda victory."

1. Although the operator "believes and hopes" that a great many people come to scoff at his program and stay to cheer, there is no way of proving this.

> It's very hard to evaluate the showings on the basis of comments we got back. As to the general impression of the people who saw the films, it's rather hard to generalize on it. I hope that they came away with a feeling that the films were pro-American or that the effects were pro-American on the people who saw the films.

It is hard to attribute an achievement to USIA activity or to something else, particularly in inaccessible areas. "The usual type of program effectiveness studies are virtually worthless in countries about which USIA lacks the basic facts."

Effectiveness can be evaluated only by surveying target audiences. Apart from the Iron Curtain, in many countries (for example, Indonesia) political difficulties inhibit the operation of field surveys. The only persons who can be interviewed about VOA programs beamed behind the Iron Curtain are refugees. Refugee survey findings "will never be more or less reliable than military intelligence reports in wartime."

2. It is impossible to determine effectiveness, to measure the degree to which one facet of the USIA program succeeds in accomplishing objectives, or to which acts by the U. S. or its allies retard USIA's success.

There is no way to evaluate scientifically the effects of correspondence between Americans and people overseas, the Exchange of Persons Program, or films. Criteria of effectiveness differ. Material that is effective in one area is not in another.

> Everyone expects the research you do to tell them how effective their program is. This is virtually impossible.

> We don't have any way of determining who buys the books.

> No one in USIA has known yet how to evaluate the accomplishments of the publications program.

Thus, the operator often must "construct his own audience to suit his own prejudices," and make assumptions about the effects of his output.

Is the Agency's success to be judged by the cumulative effect of its routine accomplishments or by an occasional special effort? One view is that USIA cannot be judged by the success or failure of specific projects. Its success as a propaganda agency is in having "a broad residual effect."

> It's almost impossible to go down to technical evaluation of the effectiveness of a film. The best evidence we have of effectiveness is that over a period of time something has happened.

The contrasting view is that USIA effectiveness will be proved by having a few striking successes.

> Basically the conception has been that if things flow properly, if they're planned to flow properly, you have a minimum of disruption; therefore you are doing a good job. That's not the basis of good propaganda. It doesn't matter that it's chaotic and that it doesn't flow right if somewhere in it occasionally there are people with a spark and the spark itself emerges.
>
> I think the system as followed is designed to raise the over-all average but reduce the outer limits of striking successes. But you're not interested in the over-all average; it's the striking success that counts. It's not important if you produce 150 reels a year, by and large good, with no bad reels in it. I would produce 149 bad ones if I could produce one film like "TVA" which would make a worldwide impact. I don't think you make striking successes with an average. The basic objective is to move people in some direction, and I don't think you want the average. You want something which is very striking.

USIA AS PART OF THE TOTAL U. S. IMPACT

While to operators, preoccupied with their jobs, the Agency's output may easily appear to be the world's main source of information about the United States, anyone in USIA will acknowledge that information activities cannot be isolated from other American impacts on foreign areas: non-official mass media (films, magazines, books), tourists, businessmen, advertisers, and the armed forces. In some countries, USIA activity is only part of the total information impact of a number of American agencies, including the State Department exchange program and the Ford Foundation.

USIA's part may be seen as important in creating the over-all impression of the U. S., or it may be seen as having only a modifying effect on that impression.

> If I were going to write a book on this, I would have a chapter called "The Grand Illusion"—that we control the image of America. We don't control it; as the greatest power of the world the impact that we have goes far beyond what we, as an agency, do. What we have is not an impact but an effect on the way in which they adjust the lenses through which they see us.

How should USIA fit into the total picture? If its output represents only a small proportion of all information about America there are these possibilities:

1. The information program may be so small that it is totally wasteful. For example, if it is too small to reach the designated targets, it should be scrapped.
2. It should concentrate on broad, long-range activities that go beyond the day-to-day impact of the U. S. through nonofficial channels:

   As long as the voice of the U. S. government is such an infinitesimal fraction of the total impact, wouldn't it be more realistic for us to be acutely conscious of that every hour of the day and perhaps trim our sails greatly? Some people have argued that just because of that fact it doesn't make a hell of a lot of difference whether we play this line or that line and try to elect this particular candidate or try to influence them on this immediate issue. Since we are only a fraction of the total impact, isn't that an argument for concentrating more on the so-called slower long-range activities?

3. USIA has a supplemental or corrective function. Its job is to selectively supplement (or counteract) all the other influences on foreign opinion. It cannot "manipulate" the minds of its audience. The importance of USIA output in the total picture depends on how much access the audience has to commercial and nongovernmental information channels and their integrity and influence. USIA operations in the Free World must be distinguished from those behind the Iron Curtain. There is no point in using a "propagandistic" medium there. Further, in countries such as France or England, where every large newspaper has its own American correspondent, problems of dealing with the press are different than in countries which have no American correspondents, such as Turkey, or where the press is controlled, as in Spain, Yugoslavia, or Portugal.

In less-developed areas, USIA activities may be extremely important. If there are few books and libraries the USIS library becomes a major source of information about the U. S. In some Asian countries, the information center is the only public library.

In advanced countries private channels supply American technical books, periodicals, or films, obviating the need for USIA to offer them. But in areas that do not have these outside private sources of information about America, it is important for USIA to fill the void.

JUDGMENTS OF USIA'S EFFECTIVENESS

Although this study did not systematically attempt to gather opinions about the Agency's effectiveness, many opinions were volunteered spontaneously in the course of the interviews, if only to generalize that knowledge of what VOA says is "a factor in the climate between Communists and anti-Communists in Eastern Europe" or that "on the whole the Agency's impact is greater than is believed. It's much greater than it should be on the basis of its resources and its output."

Success is frequently linked to specific incidents.

As the result of pressure from a USIS Cultural Officer and his British counterpart, English replaced French as the second language of the schools in one country.

Elsewhere, American books have replaced Russian books in the bookshops.

In a Middle Eastern country, negotiation of a new treaty of commerce and friendship with the U. S. was facilitated by personal contacts arising from a film showing for the Minister of Commerce and Industry.

Children's books produced locally are now done in several colors to follow the American pattern popularized by the library.

Denying that USIA is successful, others say its work is naive, that many projects neither do good nor serve as the means to an end, and devoted key employees do not do their country "a particle of good."

> Between you and me and the lamp post, you know very well that if this whole Voice of America were closed down tomorrow it would make not the slightest bit of difference, not the slightest. . . . The only reason VOA has not done more damage to United States foreign policy is the bad quality of our engineers.

Critics may cite the fact that the volume of USIA activity in the Cold War is much less than that of the Communists or their feeling that the big propaganda problem remains unsolved. In spite of everything, there still is a great deal of misunderstanding about the U. S. and its position in world affairs.

> When we say capitalism here we are talking about a system which as it is today is virtually unknown anywhere else in the world. But after 12 years of government propaganda the people abroad still don't know that.

Summing up these pessimistic views leads to one of several conclusions:

1. USIA performs a minor insurance function. It is better than nothing.
2. The Agency should be overhauled. "A campaign of truth should win some battles or change its top command."
3. "The whole Agency should be abolished because I think what we are doing is so infinitesimal that it makes no difference at all."

Conclusions

THIS STUDY began with the supposition that, as the Agency's operating assumptions were identified, it would be possible to embark on a research program to explore the principal questions on which opinions and practices were in conflict or uncertain, and to weigh the validity of assumptions which were generally accepted but which lacked conclusive support in existing research or theory in social science. (This means that some assumptions which are a matter of consensus within the Agency might also require re-examination.)

It has been a persistent finding throughout this study that the purely general premises and principles which guide the Agency's thinking and activity cannot be separated from problems of organization, personnel, and internal communication, or from extraneous political factors. A report which evaded such matters and confined itself to the most narrow possible definition of the term "assumption" would be far from realistic or usable.

The study was undertaken with the aim of raising and defining problems, since this is the first step toward solving them. It is easier to pose questions than to suggest answers. The problems cited in this report cover so wide a range and are so diverse in character that it would be beyond the scope of any individual to recommend solutions to all of them. This was understood at the time the study was planned.

This is an unfinished report, both in that it deals only with the outlines of intensely complex problems, and also because it deals with a constantly changing situation as it existed at a single point in time which has already passed. Among the questions posed here, it is precisely the perennial and important ones which seem old and familiar.

Many of the controversies within the Information Agency stem from basic and long-standing differences in outlook which are not likely to be resolved easily as a result of executive or policy decisions. In part they reflect the profound moral issues of ends and means that face democracy in its struggle

226

with a ruthless enemy. These issues are likely to remain alive regardless of the future course of events, and regardless of the philosophy of the incumbent Agency administration, although the position of minority and majority might shift. Top leadership can largely determine the direction of the program and the nature of its concrete activities, but it cannot eliminate disagreement, nor can it easily change the individual operator's attitude toward his work problems.

The research suggested by this report cannot be expected to solve USIA's major conflicts, but it may contribute to easing them.

A first step might be for the Office of Policy and the media to consider the findings of this study as a basis for stating and defining positions which may now be ambiguous.

Questions are raised here about many issues on which the Agency's policy has been clearly defined. Differences of opinion and practice in such matters are not automatically eliminated by the preparation of official directives. An organization like USIA requires the highest degree of dedication on the part of its working operators. This in turn demands a genuine sense of participation in finding solutions to the major problems they face in their jobs. It might therefore seem advisable for Agency management to examine the major points on which this report shows its own views to be challenged within the organization.

1. Some policy or management positions may be based on incomplete research or intelligence, or may be unsuitable or unwarranted for other reasons. If there is any likelihood that this is the case, there is room for reconsideration and fresh study. The very fact that such a review takes place should do much to overcome any feeling that the original decision was arbitrary or unreasonable.

2. Management positions, however sound, may not be accepted because the evidence and reasoning which supports them has not been made fully clear to the operators. Here there is evidently a need for better communication.

Many of the differences in judgment described in this report can be resolved through an accumulation of research evidence based on many studies undertaken in different countries with varying cultures, social structures, and political climates. As far as possible, these problems should be kept in mind in designing area, opinion, or media studies, and the data from these studies should be periodically reassessed in the light of these problems. In a number of cases, the questions discussed suggest specific research projects.

It is not necessary for the Agency to commission fresh studies to look into all the problems raised. What is required (if only as a preliminary move) is a pooling of existing knowledge and its application to Agency problems.

In keeping with the Schramm Committee's recommendations, a series of memoranda should now be prepared, summarizing existing research findings relevant to the major problems raised.

It was the belief of the Schramm Committee, in recommending that this study be made, that the academic research which would yield most fruitful results in answering the questions which faced the Agency would be from such fields as ''attention, perception, motivation, learning, attitude formation and change, the nature of meaning, group interaction, group and mass behavior, and intercultural communication." Actually this study, once begun, quickly focused on other questions. Academic communications research is concerned with a different range of problems than those faced by the working propagandist. It is concerned with a higher level of abstraction. It does not encompass fields of social science which have important bearing on the practical, day-to-day operations of the Information Agency. A high proportion of the problems raised in this report impinge upon history, political sociology, social geography, cultural anthropology, the study of social movements, social organization, and comparative government. This goes considerably beyond a commonly held conception of research.

There is apparently no widespread recognition in USIA that research entails more than the collection of data, that it requires reflective thinking guided by the existing body of theory on the subject studied.

Similarly, there is a lack of general awareness that many important findings in social science cannot be expressed in statistical terms. This is revealed in the tendency to question the value of research interpretations made from intensive study of a limited number of cases (especially in a field of inquiry where cases are obtained only with great difficulty and at great expense, as in interviewing satellite defectors).

The study indicates the need for more information on many of the fundamentals in USIA operations: on what is being said, whom the message is reaching, and with what effect.

The question of what is being said is reflected in the different assessments and descriptions of output which are made within the organization, and in the sense of remoteness from the final product, which in many instances exists among media operators. This appears to call for the creation of a special unit with the function of monitoring and analyzing USIA final output on an over-all, worldwide basis.

The questions of "what you should do, whom you should reach, how you should reach them, and what results you are getting" are, as one Agency executive described them, "simple" questions, which appear to call only for "ordinary sound research." Actually, they represent extremely difficult research problems which call upon the full battery of techniques, simple and complex, within the repertoire of the researchers. There are certainly no quick and easy methods of coming up with answers to questions as basic as these. Those who exercise the research function within USIA face a real problem in making operators and management aware of the difficulties that make sound research costly and lengthy to execute.

It may be asked whether USIA has drawn to the fullest extent on the professional judgment and experience of foreign area specialists, and on the ideological and tactical knowledge of defectors from the world Communist movement.

Many of the Agency's dilemmas might be clarified through a series of conferences or discussion-meetings at which social scientists and area and media experts from outside the Agency could pool information and ideas, particularly on those major questions which are not easily answered by short-range empirical research. Conference arrangements should allow for some continuity of personnel and leadership, and for extended sessions, so that the participants can either arrive at a consensus of judgment, or a clear definition of the differences in judgment.

In many instances, the Agency has its own specialists and experts in the fields from which outsiders might be called in. It would be a mistake to regard the outside consultant as a final authority on what the Agency is doing, but he can serve a highly useful function, if his ideas can interplay with those of the operators directly concerned.

A great potential strength of a democratic information program is that it can draw upon the resources of free and unrestricted social research. Here the Soviets are handicapped, since social science is incompatible with Marxist dogma.

It is all the more urgent that USIA make the most of its advantage in this sphere, because it faces a range of important questions which remain unanswered, and which cannot be answered without more knowledge.

QUESTIONS FOR RESEARCH

Differences of opinion or practice exist within USIA on the following points. In many instances, an official position has already been stated, but that position faces questioning or opposition. This list of unresolved questions represents an agenda for the Agency's research program.

1. Is friendship for the U.S. on the part of a target audience translated into political action?

2. Does familiarity with the U.S. lead to friendship?

3. Does knowledge of the English language lead to a better understanding of the U. S.?

4. Can propaganda successfully change opinions and attitudes if it is carried out at a purely verbal level, without actions to support it?

5. Is the character and content of the information program shaped primarily by target requirements or by media potentialities?

6. To what extent does USIA through its various media actually reach a mass or elite audience in different parts of the world?

7. If USIA is to be selective in its choice of targets, should it direct its attention to the political (ruling) or the opinion-forming elites?

8. Can the political elite and the opinion-forming elite generally be considered the same group for purposes of the information program, or not? Should USIA direct attention to the political "outs?"

9. Should USIA seek mass audiences in democratic countries?

10. What influence does public opinion have on political decisions in authoritarian or colonial countries? What should USIA's target be in such countries?

11. Are the true leaders of public opinion persons who have special status or functions (like editors or clergymen) or are they perhaps influential individuals buried in the mass?

12. Are sophisticated, educated, audiences essentially the same everywhere in the world?

13. Can important targets be effectively influenced through intermediaries (like their children and wives)?

14. Is USIA reaching the same people the Communists do, or a different group?

15. Do USIA media by their nature single out certain types of audiences (socially, educationally, politically)?

16. How much sophistication and prior knowledge should be assumed on the part of the audience for each USIA medium?

17. Do the various media in most places tend to reach the same people, or does each medium reach a different audience?

18. Should the weight of the program be addressed to those already disposed to be friendly, to the neutralists, or to those hostile to the American position?

19. Should Communists be a target of USIA activity? If the "hardcore" Communists should be ignored, how should they be defined?

20. Are neutralists a major target for USIA? Is neutralism a "lack of position"—a refusal to take sides; or is it a positive "third" position?

21. Should USIA be directing output to persons already favorable to the U.S.?

22. To what extent can or should the program be the same in content and emphasis throughout the world, without adaptation to the audience?

23. Is the English language an effective medium of communication to intellectuals and to the opinion leaders of most countries?

24. Should USIA publications in impoverished areas be "slick" or rough and indigenous-looking, if they are USIA-attributed?

25. Are people governed primarily by self-interest in their thinking on political subjects and in their reactions to propaganda?

26. How much interest do people overseas have in the activities of their dignitaries, officials and other nationals visiting the U. S.?

27. Should USIA output be geared to the events and interests of direct importance to the foreign audience, or to events and problems of domestic importance in the U. S.? How much interest do people overseas have in purely American subjects which have no relation to their immediate interests? Are they interested in the details of American domestic news?

28. Should one minimize or call attention to real differences of interest or values between the U. S. and the target countries?

29. At what point does distortion or slanting in news lead to a loss of credibility?

30. How should USIA handle news and comment on controversy among or within other countries or on American actions adversely affecting other countries? Should such items be ignored, played down, explained away or given complete but noninterpretive coverage?

31. Should unfavorable news (or descriptions of unpleasant features in American life) be reported in output, or should they be ignored?

32. When information harmful to America is reported, must it always be mitigated by favorable information or explanations in the same context, or is it better to avoid any appearance of justification?

33. Should USIA portray the American standard of living and American military strength as they really are, or should they be underplayed?

34. Is American cultural achievement substantial enough to provide an effective propaganda weapon in advanced and sophisticated countries, or does USIA's program in the arts have only the defensive purpose of offsetting unfavorable stereotypes of American culture?

35. Do the moral and spiritual values of American life make a suitable and effective subject for USIA in making people more favorable to America?

36. Are USIA's objectives furthered by publicizing American overseas aid? If so, how can aid be publicized without offense?

37. Are the statements and activities of American leaders a suitable and effective subject for USIA output?

38. Does an attack on communism require a specific news event as a point of departure, or can it be made in more general terms?

39. Should communism be attacked in output to areas where many people do not know what it is?

40. Should anti-Communist output be "hard-hitting" or "subtle"—to Free World, satellite and Soviet audiences?

41. Is the main source of Communist strength ideological or organizational? Can communism be fought effectively if it is viewed as a criminal conspiracy?

42. Is Communist propaganda effective (or is it Communist organizational and military activities which have won success)?

43. Does Communist propaganda aim at a mass or selective audience?

44. Should Communist charges against the U. S. be answered? If so, should the charges be stated, or not, when a rebuttal is made? Should they be stated in their most persuasive or least persuasive form? Should Communists be quoted against themselves?

45. Should the program accurately reflect all aspects of life in America, or should it selectively emphasize the favorable aspects?

46. Should material critical of the U. S. be included in output if it is not being disseminated by other (unofficial or foreign) media? Should material critical of the U. S. be included in output if it is being disseminated by other media?

47. Should USIA dramatize the differences between the Communist and Free World sides by painting a "black-and-white" picture, or should it show "differing shades of gray?"

48. Does the use of "soft" or unauthenticated news stories damage the credibility of USIA fast media?

49. Should USIA accurately represent the division of American public opinion (as represented by editorial comment) on purely domestic issues—and over foreign policy—or should it select and weight its reports of press opinion to the administration's position?

50. Does the foreign audience distinguish between official commentary and press or other unofficial commentary reported over USIA fast news media?

51. Is American press commentary reported by USIA considered by foreign editors or audiences to be accurately representative of American press opinion?

52. Should the output of the fast media be official and impersonal as far as possible, or should it utilize individual personalities (columnists or commentators) who are made to seem unofficial and private in their views?

53. To what extent does a personal touch add to the acceptance and credibility of press columns or VOA commentaries?

54. Is it better for USIA always to maintain its official role, or should it offer a variety of opinions or interpretations (apart from quotations of press comment)?

55. To what extent does an emotional tone make output more effective and convincing—to the Free World, to the satellites, to the Soviets? To what extent do subtlety and abstractions, humor and satire, add to the effectiveness of output?

56. How many major themes can be efficiently developed by USIA at a given time?

57. How much repetition is permissible in output before it becomes boring (and perhaps has a "boomerang effect")?

58. Does output (like films or printed matter) lose any of its value if it is made available free of charge?

59. In dealing with key target audiences, is credibility increased when a familiar communicator and conventional communications channels are used, or is this not necessarily so?

60. How much attention do foreign audiences pay to the attribution of films or publications?

61. Does American attribution reduce the credibility of output—on American and political subjects? Is local attribution better?

62. Is it better to have a fictitious attribution, or no attribution at all?

63. Do foreign audiences generally distinguish between official and nonofficial American sponsorship of information activities? What, if any, are the advantages of nonofficial American attribution?

64. Can enough of USIA's principal targets be reached by personal contact to have any substantial effect?

65. Does interpersonal contact tend to reach only people who do not need to be convinced of the American position?

66. To what extent are field activities shaped by the talents and interests of field personnel? Does the program gain or suffer as a result?

67. How much media output should be designed for across-the-board use? Should the content of output be adapted for each area or country?

68. Should all requests from the field be met by the media if possible? If not, what should determine which ones should be met?

69. Is it necessary and desirable to use one medium as "bait" to attract audiences for other parts of the program?

70. When news, entertainment, or service is provided as "bait" to attract an audience for activity of program value, does the audience "swallow the bait without touching the hook?"

71. Do the mass media in themselves change attitudes? Or do they stimulate personal contacts with Americans?

72. Does the main value of the information center lie in the materials it contains or in the personal contacts it provides with Americans?

73. Is it better to maintain an information center on a basis of reduced service (or even locally sponsored operation) when the budget is cut, or should activities be discontinued when they cannot be carried out on a standard professional basis?

74. Should information centers contain books by non-American authors? Should they contain books on the target countries?

75. Should libraries contain representative publications or "the cream?"

76. Is there value in getting the maximum possible circulation of American (commercially produced) books, magazines, and films overseas?

77. Should fiction be selected for information centers on the basis of literary merit or of historical or sociological description of America—or should it be included simply as bait to attract an audience? Is there a gain or loss for the program in excluding from the libraries bestselling novels, strongly critical of some phase of American life (where the security status of the author is not a factor)?

78. Are the Bi-national Centers thought of as officially sponsored by the U. S., or not?

79. Should IBS be oriented to the Free World or to the Communist world? Or should there be increased emphasis on Free World output?

80. How suitable is IBS's Central Services output for use by the Soviet orbit desks?

81. What is the value and function of local packaged radio programming?

82. Does pure entertainment have any place in broadcasts—to the Free World, to the satellites, to the Soviets?

83. Does music have a legitimate place in shortwave broadcasting?

84. Do giveaway offers by VOA help build its audience?

85. Does the radio audience distinguish between VOA news and commentary?

86. Is there any value in VOA broadcasts to the Free World?

87. Should VOA maintain token operations in all languages to provide for any possible contingencies?

88. Do listeners to VOA in the satellites—and in the Soviet Union—listen under conditions of extreme fear and secrecy or "relatively openly?"

89. What kinds of people listen to VOA in the satellites—in the U.S.S.R.?

90. What are the attitudes of listeners in the satellites—in the U.S.S.R.— toward their Communist regimes?

91. Are program purposes served by having USIA talk to the Communists and their audience behind the Iron Curtain?

92. Do the peoples of the satellites want liberation at the risk of war? How much hope of liberation should be held out to them?

93. Should the focus of attention in broadcasts to the satellites and the Soviet Union be on the news and problems of their area, on world news generally, or on America?

94. Should IPS's Wireless File output be designed to appeal to the opinion leaders (who may receive it in mimeographed form), the newspaper editor, or the average newspaper reader?

95. Should the Wireless File be planned to be reproduced directly by the foreign press, or be used as background material by foreign editors?

96. Does the overseas audience compare USIA news reporting with that of the commercial press services?

97. Does USIA lose credibility by failing to report unfavorable news items?

98. Are audiences in any one part of the world interested in news dealing with other parts of the world?

99. Are motion pictures more effective when they are made in the target countries than when made in America?

100. Should all IMS films, if possible, conform to American technical production standards?

101. Can a single film create an impression on the attitudes of the audience?

102. Are area or media skills more important as qualifications for USIA personnel?

103. Is knowledge of the local language a necessary skill for an operator dealing with a country?

104. Should USIS field personnel be maintained in their posts (with the danger

that they may go "native"), or should they be rotated in accordance with Foreign Service practice?

105. What part does USIA play in creating the total impact of the U.S. overseas?

106. How well is America thought of in various parts of the Free World?

107. Is the over-all effect of Hollywood films, in creating foreign impressions of the U. S., good, bad, or indifferent?

108. Does radio-audience mail provide a basis for research on the VOA audience?

109. To what extent can operations be evaluated by persons untrained in research techniques?

110. By what criteria should the effectiveness of USIA operations be measured?

111. Should USIA effectiveness be judged in terms of the over-all average, or in terms of the "striking successes?"

112. Can the effectiveness of USIA operations be judged on the basis of individual case histories of successful operations?

113. What *is* the over-all effectiveness of USIA?

QUESTIONS FOR POLICY REVIEW

The study points to differences of opinion on a number of questions of strategy or policy on which research cannot be directly helpful. These require either that an Agency position be adopted or that an existing position be clarified and communicated to operators.

1. Should USIA be concerned primarily with changing people's attitudes or with producing direct political action?

2. Is friendship with the U.S. in itself an objective?

3. Is increasing familiarity with the U. S. an objective or a means to an end?

4. Is the support of worldwide democracy a USIA objective?

5. Should USIA support democracy in authoritarian but anti-Communist (or non-Communist) countries if this threatens the stability of the regime? Should USIA interfere directly and openly in the domestic politics of other countries?

6. Should broadcasts to authoritarian non-Communist (or non-Soviet orbit) countries be outspoken in support of democracy at the risk of reprisals to USIS activities on the spot?

7. Where output may face censorship in one or more countries of an area, is it better to "water it down" to avoid the censorship or to leave it at full strength for the other countries covered?

8. Is it suitable for USIA as a government agency to sponsor American art, music, and other cultural activities abroad?

9. Should USIA make any attempt to influence foreign distribution of Hollywood films which may support undesirable impressions of the United States?

10. In areas of the world which are are not power-centers (or in low-priority countries), is the objective of the program to win active support and participation on the American side of the world struggle, or is the objective the defensive one of preventing any Communist gains or diversionary maneuvers?

11. Is Soviet expansionism or communism the main adversary?

12. Is it an objective of USIA to work for the overthrow of communism behind the Iron Curtain?

13. Should the emphasis in USIA output be on the positive themes of projecting America or the negative themes of fighting communism?

14. Should objectives be expressed in long-run or short-run terms?

15. Is the Agency a voice of national (foreign) policy, or should (and does) it actually help shape national (foreign) policy?

16. Should policy directives be stated only in broad general terms, or should they also give instructions on specific instances in which broad policy is applied? How much leeway should the operator have in interpreting policy guidance?

17. Should independent programming decisions (which go beyond merely implementing or carrying out orders) be made at all levels in the Agency, or should they be made almost entirely at the top level, and by IOP?

18. Should the broad lines of programming for each country be worked out in the field or in Washington? Are field personnel in a better position to make major programming decisions? To what extent should the field be autonomous in directing its activities?

19. Should USIA be talking to the largest possible number of people, or to selective audiences?

20. Should an available target audience be ignored even if it does not have high program priority? Should media which by their nature tend to reach, or are suitable for reaching, mass audiences (motion pictures) be limited to small target groups; or should the relatively small additional expense of reaching wider audiences be allotted them?

21. What choice should be made between areas of maximum program opportunity and areas of the greatest political urgency?

22. Should the same agency handle both overt and covert propaganda?

23. Is truth necessary in USIA output for its own sake on moral grounds, or for pragmatic reasons? Or is it permissible to deviate from the truth where this seems altogether expedient? (For example, if a calculated distortion serves a larger truth, and is not likely to be detected?)

Appendix

CATEGORIES FOR THE ANALYSIS OF ASSUMPTIONS

In the description of "How the Study Was Made" it is pointed out that nearly 10,000 "assumptions" gleaned from the interviews were placed on cards, which in turn were coded and classified. The categories used in this analysis were continually expanded and revised.

The major categories used in the final stages of the coding process are outlined in the following pages. This outline does not include the hundreds of subcategories which were developed under the major headings. Certain categories, especially those related to the communications process, yielded few assumptions, and were dropped as the analysis proceeded.

Assumptions listed under a number of categories were classified by specific media, or by geographic areas. Assumptions which fell into several related categories were coded under all the relevant headings, although an attempt was made to avoid unnecessary duplication of subject matter in writing the report itself.

I. Objectives
   A. Of the United States government, generally?
   B. Of the Information Agency, generally?
   C. Of the Information Agency, through a particular medium?
   D. Of the Information Agency, directed at a particular target?

II. Character of the U. S. and of its Opponents
   A. How does the Agency's view of America affect the information program?
   B. What are the traits of the Communists
      1. As opponents? What is the nature of Communist propaganda?
      2. As targets?

III. Targets

    A. Is selection of specific targets necessary or desirable?

    B. If so, what criteria should be employed in selecting them, and in determining their order of priority?

        1. For the program, generally?

        2. For a particular medium?

        3. In a particular area?

    C. Are our targets final, or intermediary?

    D. What are the characteristics and vulnerabilities of the targets?

        1. Considered by nationality and cultural groupings?

        2. Considered by cross-national groupings (i.e., the intellectual elite, journalists, labor union officials, etc.)?

        3. Considered by political attitudes?

IV. Media Capabilities and Limitations

    A. What is, and should be, the internal organization of each media service?

        1. How can political objectives and "autonomous" media objectives be reconciled?

    B. What kinds of audiences does a medium ordinarily reach in a given area or country?

    C. Media Content.

        1. What kinds of information can each medium most efficiently convey, and why?

        2. What types of emotional tone can each medium most adequately express, and why?

    D. Media Combinations.

        1. What is the proper division of functions among the media?

        2. When is a medium the "final" form of communication; when is it "bait" for another medium?

        3. How should the different media be coordinated?

    E. Social Aspects of Communication.

        1. How much credibility does each medium carry to each particular target audience, and why?

        2. What concepts as to the psychological processes of attitude change should be considered in selecting or using media?

    F. Mass Communications and Attitude Change.

        1. Can change be induced by acts without communication, or by communication without acts?

        2. Can mass communications change attitudes, apart from any interpersonal contact?

    G. Interpersonal Contacts.

        1. What type of contacts can be and should be solicited?

        2. How can these contacts best be carried out?

   3. How can mass media be utilized in relation to these contacts?
   4. What is the effect of interpersonal contacts with Americans abroad who are not connected with the information program?
 H. Institutional Contacts.
   1. How can indigenous media best be utilized to carry USIA messages?
   2. How can indigenous organizations best be utilized to distribute USIA output?
   3. How can maximum cooperation be secured from foreign governments?
 I. Relations with Commercial American Media.
   1. What is the effect of the commercial media (Hollywood, popular literature, the wire services) on foreign attitudes toward the U. S.?
   2. What is (and should be) the relation between USIA and the commercial media?

V. Organizational Problems
 A. Policy.
   1. What is and should be the Information Agency's relation to national policy?
   2. How is policy guidance transmitted to media operators, and how should it be?
 B. Relations Between Washington and the Field. What is and should be the relationship of the central office to field operations?
 C. Personnel. What are the ideal qualifications and actual traits of Agency personnel in terms of skills, training, personality, and motivation?
 D. What is the relation of USIA to outside organizations?
   1. To the State Department?
   2. To other executive agencies?
   3. To Congress, in terms of appropriations, influence on objectives, and influence on output, tone, and content?
   4. To private American enterprise?

VI. Content
 A. Criteria for Selecting Content.
   1. What criteria determine the selection of themes for USIA output?
   2. What is the value for the information program worldwide, and for particular targets, of the various themes or subjects now stressed (such as, anti-communism, culture, religion, atomic energy, foreign aid, the American standard of living, military strength, and statements by American officials)?
 B. Handling of Themes.
   1. How should these themes be treated for maximum effect?
   2. To what extent should there be concentration on a few themes?

C. Adapting the Message to the Audience.
   1. To be accepted, must an idea be congruent with the existing values, needs, motives, and suspicions of the audience as individuals, as members of a group, with its own norms, values, and intellectual level?
   2. Suggestibility and attitude change. Is a suggestion more readily accepted if it reinforces an existing attitude than if it fills a vacuum of opinion or information? Are attitudes always harder to change if they are held with greater intensity? Is it easier to transform attitudes or modify them?
   3. How far need we go in adapting ourselves to the audience? To what extent should one avoid offending the sensibilities of target audiences and of local governments? To what extent should we speak to the points that are of interest or importance to the audience? To what extent should output be related to the audience's self-interest? To what extent is it necessary to promote the self-esteem of the audience?
   4. To what extent should local media techniques be adopted (in production, format, symbolism, etc.)?
D. Truth and Credibility.
   1. Is adherence to truth an end in itself, or a consideration in achieving credibility?
   2. What are the limitations of truth in possible direct harm to the achievement of program objectives? Does it lend itself to misinterpretation?
   3. When do you disseminate material critical of yourself?
   4. What can be done to unpleasant truth, in terms of ignoring it, editing it, explaining it?
   5. What other ways are there to achieve credibility?
   6. Attribution. Is credibility greater where conventional and customary channels of communication are used? Does familiarity increase credibility? Does friendliness toward the communicator increase credibility? How and when does authoritativeness increase credibility? What form of attribution is most appropriate for a given medium—local, U. S. official, or U. S. private? Can or should USIA distribute output with no attribution at all, or with fictitious attribution?
E. Answering the Opposition.
   1. When do you initiate controversy?
   2. When do you join controversy?

VII. Techniques

A. Tone.
   1. What place does emotion have in our output?
   2. What is the function, if any, of hard-hitting invective?

3. When, and with whom, should we be subtle; when direct?
4. When, and with whom, is it possible to use abstractions or generalizations? When must one be specific?
5. When, and with whom, should we be intimate; when impersonal and objective?
6. How much satire and humor can be injected into USIA output for particular audiences?

B. Technical Handling of the Media.

1. For a given medium, should the language be English or local?
2. What technical standards of production must be maintained?
3. How should illustration be used to complement print output?
4. How can symbols be used to add impact to themes?
5. Where in a message should the main point be made?
6. How much repetition is desirable in output?

VIII. Research and Evaluation

A. What is the relation of research to intelligence, evaluation, policy, actual operations?
B. What are the criteria of effectiveness?
C. What is the evidence of effectiveness of USIA in relation to total American output, in relation to program objectives?

Books about USIA

EDWARD W. BARRETT, *Truth Is Our Weapon*. New York: Funk and Wagnall's, 1953. *A former director of the Voice of America and assistant secretary of state contrasts America's propaganda philosophy with that of the Soviet Union.*

EUGENE W. CASTLE, *Billions, Blunders and Baloney; The Fantastic Story of How Uncle Sam Is Squandering Your Money Overseas*. New York: Devin-Adair Co., Inc., 1955. *A polemic: the title tells all.*

WILSON P. DIZARD, *The Strategy of Truth: The Story of the U. S. Information Service*. Washington: Public Affairs Press, 1961. *A description of the operations of USIA (not just the Information Centers) by a long-time overseas employee who believes in and defends its policies and methods.*

MURRAY DYER, *The Weapon on the Wall; Rethinking Psychological Warfare*. Baltimore: Johns Hopkins Press, 1959. *A study prepared for the U. S. Army's Operations Research Office on the general problems of "psychological warfare" through both military and civilian agencies.*

ROBERT E. ELDER, *The Information Machine; The United States Information Agency and American Foreign Policy*. Syracuse: Syracuse University Press, 1968. *An authoritative scholarly exposition of USIA's structure and operating procedures by a distinguished political scientist.*

ARTHUR GOODFRIEND, *The Twisted Image*. New York: St. Martin's Press, 1963. *A USIS man in India offers a charming personal narrative of his experiences and problems as a working propagandist.*

GEORGE N. GORDON, IRVING FALK, and WILLIAM HODAPP, *The Idea Invaders*. New York: Hastings House, 1963. *A general discussion of propaganda, focusing on the (then) current problems confronting the United States.*

JOHN W. HENDERSON, *The United States Information Agency*. New York: Frederick A. Praeger, 1969. *A rather dry history and description of USIA structure by a retired foreign service officer who served the Agency overseas.*

ROBERT T. HOLT and ROBERT M. VAN DE VELDE, *Strategic Psychological Operations and American Foreign Policy*. Chicago: University of Chicago Press, 1960. *A historical review from a political science perspective.*

International Information, Education, and Cultural Relations: Recommendations for the Future. Washington, D. C.: Center for Strategic and International Studies, Georgetown University, 1975. *Report of a panel, chaired by Frank Stanton, which recommends separation of VOA from the Information Agency.*

WALTER JOYCE, *The Propaganda Gap*. New York: Harper & Row, 1963. *A kind of personal commentary on propaganda policy in the Kennedy-Murrow years, with appraisals of various outside reports and reviews of the subject.*

HAROLD D. LASSWELL, RALPH D. CASEY, and BRUCE LANNES SMITH, eds., *Propaganda and Promotional Activities; An Annotated Bibliography*. Chicago: University of Chicago Press, 1969. *The indispensable bibliography on the subject, prepared for the Social Science Research Council.*

MARTIN MERSON, *The Private Diary of a Public Servant*. New York: Macmillan, 1955. *A memoir of the McCarthy period by a man who served briefly as a high USIA official.*

ARTHUR E. MEYERHOFF, *The Strategy of Persuasion; The Use of Advertising Skills in Fighting the Cold War*. New York: Coward-McCann, 1965. *An advertising man's pungent critique of USIA operations.*

RONALD I. RUBIN, *The Objectives of the U. S. Information Agency, Controversies and Analysis* New York: Frederick A. Praeger, 1966. *An examination of reports, Congressional hearing transcripts, and other documents that illuminate the controversies over USIA's purposes.*

THOMAS C. SORENSEN, *The Word War: The Story of American Propaganda*. New York: Harper & Row, 1968. *A former deputy to Edward R. Murrow describes USIA's history and operations from a personal vantage point.*

OREN STEPHENS, *Facts to a Candid World*. Stanford: Stanford University Press, 1955. *A generalized discussion of the problems involved in international propaganda and public opinion at the time of this study, with special emphasis on the American effort.*

CHARLES A. H. THOMSON, *Overseas Information Service of the United States Government*. Washington: The Brookings Institution, 1948. *An influential historical study of America's propaganda efforts, especially in World War II and immediately thereafter.*

JOHN B. WHITTON, ed., *Propaganda and the Cold War*. Washington: Public Affairs Press, 1963. *A series of papers by both theorists and practitioners of U. S. propaganda presented at a 1962 symposium at Princeton University.*

Index